Moral Panics in the Contemporary World

Moral Panics in the Contemporary World

Edited by

Chas Critcher, Jason Hughes,
Julian Petley and Amanda Rohloff

BLOOMSBURY
NEW YORK · LONDON · NEW DELHI · SYDNEY

Bloomsbury Academic
An imprint of Bloomsbury Publishing Plc

1385 Broadway	50 Bedford Square
New York	London
NY 10018	WC1B 3DP
USA	UK

www.bloomsbury.com

First published 2013

Library of Congress Cataloging-in-Publication Data
Moral panics in the contemporary world / edited by Chas Critcher,
Jason Hughes, Julian Petley and Amanda Rohloff.
p. cm.
Includes bibliographical references and index.
ISBN 978–1-62356–893–1 (hardcover : alk. paper) 1. Moral panics. 2. Mass media –
Moral and ethical aspects. 3. Mass media and public opinion. 4. Mass media and
crime. I. Critcher, C., editor of compilation. II. Hughes, Jason, editor of compilation.
III. Petley, Julian, editor of compilation. IV. Rohloff, Amanda, editor of compilation.
HM811.M68 2013
302.23 – dc23
2013000252

ISBN: HB: 978-1-6235-6893-1
e-PDF: 978-1-6235-6893-1
e-Pub: 978-1-6235-6405-6

Typeset by Newgen Imaging Systems Pvt Ltd, Chennai, India
Printed and bound in the United States of America

In memory of Amanda Rohloff (1982–2012)
Academic, colleague, friend

Contents

List of Illustrations

Figures

Tables

Acknowledgements

This book began with the three-day international conference, 'Moral Panics in the Contemporary World', which was held in December 2010 at Brunel University, London. At the conference, we asked delegates to build on recent criticisms, debates and developments within moral panic studies, to explore and evaluate how the moral panic concept has developed and continues to do so, and how relevant it is to the analysis and understanding of current fears, risks, social problems and controversies. The central aim of the conference was to further the development of moral panic research via theoretical analyses, methodological discussions and empirical studies.

Some of the best papers from the conference are published here (others were published in a special issue of *Crime, Media, Culture*). We thank the contributors to this volume, along with all the other presenters and delegates at the conference whose input to papers and discussions provided invaluable contributions to aid in the development of ideas, both within and beyond this book.

At Brunel University, we would like to thank the Research Support and Development Office, the School of Social Sciences, the School of Arts, and the Graduate School for their financial support. Without their assistance, we would have never held the conference from which this book developed.

Special thanks to every member of the organizing team of the conference for their hard work.

The original conference, this collection of papers and the field of moral panic studies in general benefited hugely from the boundless enthusiasm, intellectual acumen and organizational ability of Amanda Rohloff, who died suddenly from what appears to be an epileptic seizure in December 2012. Mandy was an exceptionally gifted academic, and something of a rising star in sociological circles. She passed her PhD viva (with flying colours) just months before her death, and had already embarked on what was sure to be a stellar academic career. Even before the completion of her PhD, Mandy had managed to develop an impressive publications record, including papers in major sociological journals. She took a leading role in developing a series of conferences, workshops and scholarly meetings, including the one upon which this edited collection is based. Mandy also took the lead in establishing an international network for moral panic studies, the website devoted to this network, a working paper series and a special reserve collection on moral panics at the Brunel University library. Mandy had an enormous impact upon university life at Brunel, and was widely known within the scholarly community more generally. She is sorely missed by family, friends and colleagues alike.

List of Contributors

Yasin Aktay long a Professor of Sociology at Selcuck University in Konya, Turkey, is now a Senior Professor of Sociology at the Yildirim Beyazit University in Ankara, Turkey. Dr Aktay has published and presented widely in several areas including the Sociology of Religion, the Muslim World and the West, and the Sociology of Deviance, including, especially, the social processes giving rise to Islamophobia. Dr Aktay is a frequent commentator and discussant, in print as well as television, on aspects of sociological and popular interest. He is also the director of the Institute of Strategic Thinking (Stratejik Düsünce Enstitüsü) based in Ankara, Turkey. The Strategic Thinking Institute is an independent think tank that provides a major network for scholars worldwide.

Jeremy Collins is Senior Lecturer in Media Studies at London Metropolitan University. His research interests include the sociology of news production, news management, media representations of science, risk communication and journalism and media ethics. He has published book chapters and journal articles on topics including food scares, general election news management techniques, public perceptions of mobile phone risks, moral panics about drugs and news media constructions of 'media effects'.

Chas Critcher is Visiting Professor in Media and Communications at Swansea University and Emeritus Professor of Communications at Sheffield Hallam University. He originally co-authored *Policing the Crisis* (Macmillan, 1979), a study of social reaction to mugging. A second edition will appear in 2013. His most recent publications include *Moral Panics and the Media* (Open University Press, 2003), an edited collection *Critical Readings in Moral Panics and the Media* (Open University Press, 2006) and a series of subsequent journal articles. His current research interests focus on exploring the relevance to moral panic analysis of the concept of moral regulation.

Jason Hughes is Professor of Sociology at the University of Leicester. His research interests span a range of concerns but include: the sociology of consumption; the sociology of the body and health; emotions, work and identity; figurational sociology and sociological theory; moral panics and regulation. His first book, *Learning to Smoke* (University of Chicago Press, 2003) was winner of the 2006 Norbert Elias prize. More recently he has completed, together with Eric Dunning, a major study of the work of Norbert Elias entitled *Norbert Elias and Modern Sociology: Knowledge, Interdependence, Power, Process* (Bloomsbury, 2013). He has also published a number of edited books, including *Visual Methods* (Sage, 2012) and *Internet Research Methods* (Sage, 2012); and co-edited books, including *Documents of Life* (Sage, 2013) and *Communities of Practice: Critical Perspectives* (Routledge, 2007).

Jørgen Kirksæther is a games researcher and journalist. He is currently a games expert for the national broadcaster NRK, and has a weekly radio spot on NRK P1. He has worked extensively with Norwegian and European policy and awareness development and analysis, within Norwegian and Nordic government institutions and through several EC Framework Programme projects. His primary research interests are game history, game politics and censorship.

Aurélie Lacassagne is an Associate Professor of Political Science and vice dean of the Social Sciences and Humanities Faculties at Laurentian University (Canada). Her research centres mainly on identity politics and popular cultural studies from a figurational perspective. She has co-edited two books entitled *Belarus, l'état de l'exception* and *Investigating Shrek: Power, Identity, and Ideology*. She is a collaborator on two major research initiatives on the inclusion of visible minorities and immigrants in small and medium-size cities in Canada.

Paul Lashmar is a lecturer in journalism at the School of Arts at Brunel University. His research interests include investigative journalism, reporting terror, crime reporting, media bias, UK media coverage of the EU and the philosophy of journalism. He is interested in synthesizing practitioner experience with academic theory. Paul has been an investigative journalist in television and print. He has worked on the staff of *the Observer*, Granada Television's *World in Action* current affairs series and the *Independent* newspaper. He was awarded 'Reporter of the Year' in the 1986 UK Press Awards. Paul has broken many major domestic and international stories. He has also produced television programmes for a number of strands including BBC's *Timewatch* and Channel Four's *Dispatches*. His book include *Britain's Secret Propaganda War* with James

Oliver (Sutton, 1998) and *Spyflights of the Cold War* (Sutton, 1996). He has also published in paperback and in a wide range of translations. Paul is an adviser to the Centre for Investigative Journalism. His full CV can be found at www.paul. lashmar.com

Elias le Grand is Associate Lecturer at the Department of Sociology, Stockholm University. He was previously Postdoctoral Research Fellow at the Swedish School of Textiles and Kyoto University. His research has focused on class identity, consumer culture and youth, particularly the formation of white working-class identities in present-day Britain.

Marcello Maneri is Associate Professor of Sociology at the University of Milano-Bicocca. His research focuses on the media, power, racism and criminalization. He recently published 'Media Discourse on Immigration. Control Practices and the Language We Live By', in S. Palidda (ed.) *Racial Criminalisation of Migrants in the 21st Century* (Ashgate, 2011) and 'Peacetime War Discourse: The Political Economy of Bellicose Metaphors', in A. Dal Lago and S. Palidda (eds), *Conflict, Security and the Reshaping of Society* (Routledge, 2010).

Sarah E. H. Moore is a Senior Lecturer at the Centre for Criminology and Sociology, Royal Holloway. Much of her research concerns the cultural and social construction of threats to women's health and safety. Previous research has looked at the feminization of breast cancer, the origin of health awareness campaigns and the media depiction of sexual assault. She is the author of *Ribbon Culture: Charity, Compassion, and Public Awareness* (2008/10), which was awarded the British Sociological Association's Philip Abrams Memorial Prize for best first sole-authored book in Sociology. She has published in a range of international journals, including the *British Journal of Criminology; Crime, Media, Culture; Feminist Media Studies* and *Health, Risk, and Society*.

Jon Oplinger has graduate degrees in sociology and anthropology from Kent State University, United States. He is a Professor of Sociology at the University of Maine at Farmington where he teaches courses in sociology and anthropology. His interests include paleo-anthropology, archaeology, comparative sociology and, especially, the sociology of deviance. He has published in the area of mid-Western archaeology, military sociology, comparative sociology and the manufacture of deviance. More recently his research activities have included a survey of the acceptance of the Islamic Community in the United States, with Dr Ertan Ozensel of Solcuk University, Konya, Turkey. Lately, he has ventured into children's literature with a blatantly ethnographic tale about a mill town in Maine entitled *The Wicked Small People of Whiskey Bridge.*

Julian Petley is Professor of Screen Media in the School of Arts at Brunel University, co-chair of the Campaign for Press and Broadcasting Freedom, and a member of the advisory board of Index on Censorship. His most recent books include *Film and Video Censorship in Modern Britain* (Edinburgh University Press, 2011), *Censorship: A Beginner's Guide* (Oneworld, 2009) and (with Philip French) *Censoring the Moving Image* (Seagull Books/Index on Censorship, 2008). He first wrote about 'video nasties' in 1984, in the journal *Screen*.

Amanda Rohloff was Postdoctoral Research Fellow in Sociology at Brunel University. Her research interests included consumption and addiction; climate change; moral panic and regulation; sociology of health and illness; and figurational sociology. Having completed her PhD on the development of climate change (synthesizing Elias and moral panic), she later worked on projects in the areas of alcohol studies, epilepsy and end of life care. Her previous publications included articles in *Sociology, Current Sociology, New Zealand Sociology* and *Crime, Media, Culture*; and book chapters in *Moral Panics and the Politics of Anxiety* (Routledge, 2011) and *The Ashgate Research Companion to Moral Panics* (Ashgate, 2013). At the time of her death she was working on two articles based on her alcohol research, while also writing her first book, *Climate Change, Moral Panics, and Civilization* (Routledge, 2014).

Elisabeth Staksrud is Associate Professor and Head of Studies at the Department of Media and Communication at the University of Oslo and a Research Fellow at the Berkman Center for Internet and Society, Harvard University, researching online risk, regulation and rights. She is part of the management group of the EU Kids Online project, and has a long international track record in practical policy, regulation and dissemination work in the field of internet safety for children.

Richard Talbot received his doctorate from the University of New Hampshire. He is an Associate Professor of Criminal Justice and Sociology at Anna Maria College, Paxton, MA. His research interests include race and ethnic relations, military sociology, crime and inequality. Talbot is also interested in the manufacture of deviance, an area in which he has published in a previous collaboration with Oplinger and Aktay. He has recently submitted an article on social stratification and military casualties which statistically explores the ethnic proportionality of American deaths in Southeast Asia through time (from 1965 to 1973). He is presently involved in a project examining the impact of data modules on learning outcomes in Introductory Sociology classes.

Morena Tartari lives and works in Italy. In 2012 she completed her PhD in sociology with a dissertation about moral panic and paedophilia at the University of Padova. Her research interests concern crime and deviance, media and collective reactions as moral panic. She specializes in qualitative research methods. Before her formal education in sociology, she received a degree in psychology, trained as a psychotherapist and she worked as an expert witness on child abuse.

Henry Yeomans is a Lecturer in Criminology and Criminal Justice Studies at the University of Leeds. His research to date has focused on how historical developments in public attitudes and legal regulation have shaped the manner in which we continue to understand and regulate alcohol in England and Wales. He completed his PhD at the University of Plymouth in 2011 and has published in several academic journals and edited collections. Henry was also awarded the SAGE Prize for Innovation and/or Excellence 2012. He continues to employ historical approaches to social science and is currently researching moderation, minimum pricing for alcohol and precautionary governance.

Moral Panics in the Contemporary World: Enduring Controversies and Future Directions

Amanda Rohloff, Jason Hughes, Julian Petley and Chas Critcher

This book seeks to explore the enduring significance of the concept of moral panic. It does so reviewing conceptual and empirical extensions to this analytical frame via a range of contemporary examples. In this introduction we commence with a consideration of the development of the concept, including a brief review of some of the key debates that have surrounded its usage and application. We then move on to some of the defining issues and challenges that arguably must be addressed in order for moral panic research to retain its analytical utility in relation to a rapidly changing social and cultural landscape. At the end of this broader exposition of the concept, we shall introduce the chapters of the volume, and consider how each seeks to take forward some of the core debates within the field.

The first notable use of the term 'moral panic' can be traced back to the 1964 publication of Marshall McLuhan's *Understanding Media* (McLuhan [1964] 2007: 89).[1] The term was taken up and developed into a fully fledged concept principally by Stan Cohen and Jock Young in the research they undertook for their PhDs in the late 1960s, later to underpin a series of publications in the 1970s. Young's (1971b) chapter entitled 'The Role of Police as Amplifiers of Deviancy, Negotiators of Reality and Translators of Fantasy'; his (1971a) book *The Drugtakers*; and Cohen's (1972) *Folk Devils and Moral Panics* stand out as landmark publications in the development of the concept.

The period during which these seminal studies were undertaken was a time of rapid social change, growing bohemianism, and a burgeoning climate of challenge to the opinions of 'parents, politicians, journalists, opinion leaders, magistrates', and others in positions of power (Young 2011: 246). This broader questioning of authority was reflected in a number of what were then becoming increasingly influential approaches to sociology. From the United States, particularly in the work of scholars such as Howard Becker, Edwin Lemert, Kai Erikson and others, came the influence of symbolic interactionism, and the related developments of the social reaction perspective and labelling theory. In the United Kingdom, core facets of these approaches were reworked by a new generation of researchers in criminology and sociology, some of whom combined and synthesized these with critical/conflict-based frameworks based centrally around various manifestations of Marxism – approaches which later came to be known as the 'new criminology' and 'new left realism' (in turn, offshoots of 'critical criminology').

This new wave of criminology spurred the creation of the National Deviancy Conference – a series of symposia commencing at the University of York in 1968 and recurring throughout the 1970s. The conference series proved to be highly influential, leading to the development of several further key publications. These included *Images of Deviance* (Cohen 1971); *Politics and Deviance: Papers from the National Deviancy Conference* (Taylor and Taylor 1973); *Contemporary Social Problems in Britain* (Bailey and Young 1973); *Capitalism and the Rule of Law: From Deviancy Theory to Marxism* (Fine et al. 1979); and *Permissiveness and Control* (National Deviancy Conference 1980). The progenitors of this new criminology shared to varying degrees several core understandings of the relations between the media, the state, moral entrepreneurs, agents of social control, the general public, and those labelled 'deviant'. The influence of labelling theory in particular appears to have been pivotal. For example, a focus upon the mobilization of moral discourses; the significance of moral entrepreneurs and the 'moral majority'; and a consideration of the nexus between morality, media representations and social power, all figure prominently in this early work. More particularly, the engagement with how social reactions are constitutive of social categories which, in turn, feed back to that which is categorized – a process that Merton famously called the 'self-fulfilling prophecy' – is an older analytical motif that found new modalities of expression under the guise of moral panic analysis. Similarly, it is arguable that Becker's ([1963] 1991) examination of the emergence and impact of the Marijuana Tax Act as a defining moral campaign is in many ways an early forerunner of a 'classic' moral panic analysis.

Defining concerns

The concept of moral panic, and the new deviancy theory more generally, involved a focus on particular types and examples of deviance (and social reactions to these) that came to be regarded as paradigmatic exemplars. These concerns, again, reflected the wider social changes that were occurring at the time – a broader generational critique of 'the Establishment': 'The conflict between the Establishment and the new youth culture seemed to be gathering pace, the reactions quite disproportional to the offences and the number of police and of newspaper columns exhibiting something of a panic about the morality of "today's youth"' (Young 2011: 246).

To this extent, moral panic analysis inherited from symbolic interactionism and labelling theory an in-built critique of positivist criminology, shifting the focus from the 'causes' of deviance to reactions to and representations of it. As Young describes it, the combination of labelling and sub-cultural theory 'gave meaning to deviancy, in contrast to positivism which took meaning away'. Thus the approach regarded 'the reaction against crime and deviance as a cultural product, not simply a technical problem of social control and the deviant act itself as a cultural product, an attempt by groups of actors to solve the social problems which confronted them' (Young 2011: 247). Such a notion is nowhere better illustrated than in the 'deviancy amplification spiral', where media reporting, and the reactions of moral entrepreneurs and agents of social control, collectively serve to distort and otherwise amplify the perceived deviance which is the object of their outrage – exacerbating the social problem they were in part defining and in this sense producing and reproducing the very behaviour about which they were so exercised in the first place.

Reflecting on the origins of the concept of moral panic, Young (2011: 247) observes:

> For me the saga of the trial [of two of the Rolling Stones, on drugs charges, in 1967] and the everyday experience of the prejudice engendered by long hair and exotic clothes, by the paranoia of the impending raid and the knowledge of police planting of drugs, fabrication of evidence and other malpractices set off a train of thought that gave vitality to the idea of the moral panic as a moral conflict between authority and subculture which was of a cultural nature and could not be reduced to humanitarian interventions on the level of protecting the weak and vulnerable or simple punitive moves to deter the wicked.

Here we clearly see the emergence, at least in the case of Young, of a more or less consciously defined political agenda to expose the malpractices of authority, and, in so doing, to liberate the victims of Establishment prejudices (in this case, anyone who looks like a stereotypical 'hippie' or 'druggie'); an agenda that undergirds much of his moral panic analysis, as well as the analyses of those it has influenced.

By contrast, Cohen's focus has characteristically centred not just on exposing the ideological underpinnings of social reactions to deviance, and of competing social spheres of perception – the differences between those of, say, mods and rockers, the police, bystanders, reporters and so forth – but also on identifying how reactions are deflected onto objects that are not, so to speak, the 'real' problem. Drawing upon his more recent work on the sociology of denial, Cohen explains how this concern in his work relates explicitly to a fundamental commitment to human rights, suggesting that in determining whether there is an over-reaction or an under-reaction to a given phenomenon: 'Only with a prior commitment to "external" goals such as social justice, human rights or equality can we evaluate any one moral panic or judge it as more specious than another' (Cohen 2002: xxviii). Thus, for Cohen, the central purpose of the moral panic concept is to expose inappropriate social reactions in the sense of being disproportionate, tendentious and displaced (see Cohen 2002: xxxi). As Garland (2008: 15) has expressed it, 'Moral panic targets are not randomly selected: they are cultural scapegoats whose deviant conduct appals onlookers so powerfully precisely because it relates to personal fears and unconscious wishes . . . The achievement of the best moral panic analyses is to render these involvements and anxieties conscious and intelligible and to show how they contributed to the outcry in question'.

In the 1960s and 1970s researchers such as Cohen and Young (among a rapidly increasing number of others) were 'often culturally closer to deviants than to their controllers', and as such 'saw criminal law as a misplaced form of repression, at least as it applied to the soft deviance of drug taking and sub-cultural style' (Garland 2008: 19). Moral panic research began, then, with a focus on particular types of reactions to particular types of actions – those activities, groups and behaviours which the Establishment found objectionable and tried its best to suppress, but with which the researchers conversely personally identified (e.g. youth subcultures and marijuana smoking). These kinds of deviance were generally relatively at a low level, more typically being examples of 'delinquency' than archetypal criminal behaviour as such. Moral panic research thus tended to take place in the wider context of moral reaction against an increase in what established opinion referred to disapprovingly as 'permissiveness' (Thompson 2011: viii).[2] Conversely, the idea that there could be a moral panic regarding a phenomenon about which a researcher was personally concerned – a 'good' moral panic, to use Cohen's later (2002) term – was, until very recently, largely neglected.

Why moral?

The concept of moral panic was, therefore, very much a product of its time. Just as a 'moral majority' was understood to be reacting to an increasingly 'permissive' society, so too researchers were reacting to these particular reactors. As Garland (2008) observes, it was not until Stuart Hall and colleagues applied the concept to a serious crime – street robbery, re-termed 'mugging' – that it came to be more intensely critiqued. While the disproportionality of moral outrage and condemnation could be relatively easily demonstrated in relation to the kinds of cases and examples that were the mainstay of the first moral panic studies, later applications such as this raised more fundamental questions regarding the applicability and utility of the concept. In this connection, Waddington (1986: 258) argued:

> Without some clear criteria of proportionality, the description of publicly expressed concern, anxiety or alarm as a 'moral panic' is no more than a value judgment. It simply says that the person using the term does not believe that the particular problem is sufficiently serious to warrant these expressions of concern or actions designed to remedy the problem . . . it is a polemical rather than an analytical concept. It seems virtually inconceivable that concern about racial attacks, rape, or police misconduct would be described as a 'moral panic'. This is because the term has derogatory connotations: it implies that official media concern is *merely* a 'moral panic' without substance or justification. If official reaction to crime and deviance is to be analysed adequately perhaps it is time to abandon such value-laden terminology.

Waddington's now much-cited arguments stimulated considerable debate, though many of the points he raised remain moot. At the very least, since Waddington first wrote these words, the concept has been empirically extended to an ever-widening range of examples. Indeed, there are now numerous moral panic analyses of reactions to incidences of rape, child abuse, paedophilia and a range of other 'sex panics'. That said, Waddington's more general argument nonetheless serves to raise some pertinent concerns; it draws attention to the unspoken and to a degree assumed politico-intellectual stance that has been effectively 'baked into' moral panic research – a stance which even Cohen himself has now attempted to review via his discussion of 'good' moral panics.[3]

It is significant that Cohen sought to correct, or at the very least expose to scrutiny, a normative tendency inherent in moral panic analysis through recourse to the term 'good' – a term which itself is highly value-laden, and shot-through with 'moral' connotations. Cohen no doubt did so quite self-consciously in order to highlight head-on, so to speak, the fundamental, yet largely unexamined, question once posed by Becker (1967), namely: 'Whose side are we on?' (Cohen 2011). As we have already suggested, the terms 'moral' and 'panic' are not simply concept descriptors, they are also a kind of short-hand for a partly unspoken cultural politics of moral panic analysis. The assumed politico-intellectual position of early moral panic research was, admittedly to over-simplify, one in which 'we' researchers were seeking to highlight the inappropriateness of 'their' morally outraged reactions to the activities and behaviours of 'our' generation. The term 'moral' was thus employed not so much to invoke a philosophically discrete 'moral' category, but as a by-word for a pervasive conservative 'moral' outrage mobilized in relation to particular social causes. It was thus, in certain respects, a pejorative term as much as a technical one: a short-hand for unenlightened, reactionary viewpoints which, under the banner of morality, were promoted as an insidious smokescreen for dominant ideological interests. In this way, 'we' might deem a generalized social reaction of a kind that 'we' consider to be politically or ideologically reprehensible to be a 'moral panic', while another equally acute social reaction to a particular problem – and here climate change might serve as a guiding example[4] – 'we' might regard as an 'appropriate response', or perhaps even a response which is insufficiently urgent in that 'they' are not panicking enough (e.g. see Cohen 2011; Rohloff 2011a; Ungar 2011). Indeed, Cohen's idea that there might be 'good' moral panics involves the notion that researchers might in fact *encourage* 'moral panics about mass atrocities and political suffering' by facilitating the conditions under which successful moral panics of the past have flourished – 'exaggeration, sensitization, symbolization, prediction, etc.' – in order to overcome passivity, indifference and 'strategies of denial' which prevent a full recognition of 'human cruelty and suffering' (2002: xxxiii). However, this raises the question as to whether moral entrepreneurs involved in (what Cohen and others might call) 'bad' moral panics in the 1960s and 1970s viewed their own moral campaigns as 'good' campaigns to direct attention towards those social problems which they felt were not receiving sufficient attention. The key point, then, is that notions of 'good' and 'bad' vary according to political standpoint in that there was, and remains, a sharp demarcation between 'their' idea of 'good' – that of influential moral entrepreneurs – and 'ours', the assumed stance of moral panic researchers. As such, while Cohen's introduction of the term 'good' moral panic may help researchers move beyond a simplified understanding of panics as being merely negative developments, at the same time it serves to reinforce a normative stance towards moral panic studies, whereby certain issues are considered to be worthy of concern while others are not.

More recently, a number of researchers have sought to jettison altogether the underlying cultural politics of moral panic theory as part of a shift involving the re-working of moral panic analysis into sociological approaches to moral regulation (Hunt 1999, 2003, 2011; Hier 2008, 2011; Critcher 2008, 2009) and, following Elias ([1939] 2012), civilizing processes (e.g. Rohloff and Wright 2010; Rohloff 2011a). As Hunt (2011) observes, the sociology of moral panics and the sociology of moral regulation have followed, until recently, different trajectories of development, some aspects of which, he suggests, present serious obstacles to any simple or straightforward integration of these analytical traditions. Nonetheless, it is through a focus on moral regulation that we might explore how it is that certain social issues become transmuted into moral issues – how a particular group might be able to shift from saying 'we don't like that' or 'we disapprove of that', to saying 'that's bad', 'that's wrong' or 'they're evil', usually leading to 'it/they should be stopped'. It is through this process of moral transmutation that a particular stance on an issue comes to be increasingly firmly established as purely a moral one: by posing questions about risks only as moral questions, all arguments other than those that are moralistic become effectively closed off (Hunt 2003). Moralization makes statements less easily contestable, with the ultimate result that the interests and opinions of particular groups can eventually become transformed into apparently immutable facts, unassailable positions and incontestable standpoints. In the case of moral panics, then, processes of moralization that might otherwise be inherently contestable become rapidly crystallized into explicit moral causes that are effectively employed to preclude and obstruct all legitimate forms of contestation (for an example of this in relation to discourses about welfare see Lundström [2011]).

Moralization processes range from short-term, episodic and intentional campaigns through to rather longer-term 'blind' processes that may be largely unintended, arising from the interlacing of the plans, actions and intentions of many individuals, many competing social groups and factions, which together comprise a 'web of interdependencies' (Elias [1939] 2012) spanning many generations. Thus, for example, in the work of Norbert Elias, long-term changes within explicitly 'moral' treatises – etiquette and manners; prevailing social proscriptions and mores; standards of 'courtesy', 'civility' and 'civilization'; and so forth – are considered in relation to the development of monopolies over violence and taxation, and other aspects of state formation (Elias [1939] 2012). Implied in much moral panic analysis is something akin to a state, a concentration of power, the proxies for which are connoted by such terms as the 'moral majority' or competing class interests. The nexus of class and morality is crucial. A common underlying theme is the deployment of morality to obfuscate dominant ideological interests; to act as a veil over the workings of power. In the sociology of moralization, however, such concerns – the fundamental relationships between power, morality and moralizing discourses – are not simply assumed: rather, they are typically conceived in terms of dynamisms that must be understood in the context of, indeed perhaps as integral components of, much broader, longer-term developments.

Hunt (2011: 57) has suggested that in many of the definitional disputes over moral panics, a key criterion employed is that of 'volatility': that is, that moral panics by definition 'involve sensational, inflammatory, and spectacular discourse, and that they are eruptive, short-lived, and quick to subside'. Such a definitional restriction serves to exclude considerably 'longer-running episodes such as those stimulated by paedophiles, pornography, and sex-violence in the media' (Hunt 2011: 57). Moreover, a focus only on the 'eruptive phases' of such episodes ignores their much longer-term character and the context of their development, and obstructs a consideration of their potential inter-relationships (e.g. the inter-relationship between a long-term moralization of alcohol use and enduring concerns about youth that have been combined in certain recent campaigns about binge drinking). However, in many ways, these arguments have long been anticipated by early moral panic researchers. As we shall shortly discuss, Cohen was well aware of the recurrent and in some ways cyclical character of moral panics. He intended his early study of mods and rockers to serve as a model of processes which were considerably longer-term than those involved in the specifics of the case he examined. Indeed, he suggested that the case highlighted archetypical patterns of social reaction and moral panic which, he proposed, would likely endure into the foreseeable future.

Hunt (2011) is also critical of the definitional exclusion of medical problems by the likes of Ungar (and, in part, Cohen) on the grounds that issues such as AIDS and smoking (Ungar 2001), and BSE (Cohen 2002), present a class of concern that is not intrinsically 'moral'. However, Hunt suggests, moral and medical frames are by no means mutually exclusive. Indeed, the relationship between moral and medical designations of deviance has long been the central concern of sociological work on medicalization. To take the subtitle of Conrad and Schneider's now seminal ([1980] 1985) text as a case in point: a major impetus in the reclassification of social concerns has involved a shift from 'badness to sickness'. Just as ideological interests may be masked and solidified by moralization, elsewhere it is possible to observe how moral concerns are translated into medical ones and in doing so gain a rhetorical scientific authority and legitimacy that may not be possible through recourse solely to discourses of morality. For example, the extension of medical jurisdiction over certain sexual crimes is most pronounced in the coining of the term 'sexually violent predators', a newly invented category which has been mobilized in US law as a legitimization for, and mechanism of, social control – to keep those convicted confined indefinitely, even after they have served their sentence. Here, medical language is combined with legal language to effectuate a result that moralization alone could possibly not achieve. Conversely, efforts to medicalize such issues as sexuality and alcoholism were in part attempted in order to remove the stigma associated with these forms of perceived deviance, and to diminish the moral burden of individual responsibility. However, the degree to which these attempts were successful varies. A certain degree of stigma remains attached to mental illness, even in those social and cultural contexts where mental health is more openly discussed. Similarly, for example, while giving someone the identity of an 'addict' in some ways absolves them of the responsibility for deviant actions, it simultaneously pathologizes a behaviour as a class of 'disease'. The net consequence remains broadly similar – the question persists: 'What is wrong with you?' Medical and moral modes of classification involve different forms of authority, allow different degrees of discursive purchase, different alloys of legitimation, in different times and places. For instance, in some contexts, religion might take precedence over medicine. It is therefore important to consider modes of classification and categorization beyond simply that of moralization, and to explore how these in turn are related to the competing interests and power chances of different social groups. Moreover, 'morality' comprises a shifting and contested discursive terrain. Sociologically speaking, it makes better sense to talk of 'moralization processes' than 'morality' or 'moral' as such, since many facets of human behaviour that were once profoundly moralized may now be less so and vice versa: shifting attitudes towards sexual conduct in Western societies present a particular case in point (see, for example, the work of Wouters on informalization [1977, 1984, 2004, 2007]).

The question still remains of why 'morality' and the term 'moral' have taken centre stage in moral panic analysis, and whether, indeed, they should remain there. In certain respects, 'moral' is a more neutral category than certain others: it can easily be linked to a range of different problems and approaches which variously centre on the importance of, say, religion, class, status, and so forth. As we have seen, since the earliest studies, a number of researchers have developed sociological analyses of 'sex panics' (panics about sex), 'media panics' (panics about media) and so on, and in so doing have further problematized the definitional scope of moral panic analysis. Again, the extent to which 'sex' and 'media' panics represent a genuinely different class of social reaction, a different 'order' of social phenomena (e.g. because there are no clearly identifiable/ marginalized folk devils), or whether they are simply moral panics with a focus on 'sex' or 'the media', remains open to debate. Thus, while a focus on the 'moral' has allowed the concept to be applied to an ever-widening range of topics, and combined with a diverse array of sociological orientations, it has equally led to numerous definitional debates concerning what can and cannot be said accurately to constitute a bona fide 'moral panic'. We shall shortly return to this tendency below.

Why panic?

The emphasis upon panic in the work of Cohen appears to have stemmed from an engagement with disaster studies, collective delusions and urban myths (2002: xxvii). Common to these frameworks is an interest in disproportionate reactions to often imaginary events. The theme of disproportionality is thus a defining one for Cohen and for the field of moral panic studies more generally. The term 'panic' neatly evokes a sense of a knee-jerk response that is not carefully measured or balanced, and is prone to exaggeration and distortion. However, 'panic' also carries with it certain other connotations which are rather more problematic and, arguably, have underpinned some of the core controversies surrounding the concept. As Cohen acknowledges, the term 'panic' has also imbued the concept with connotations of irrationality and loss of control, conveying the sense of 'a frenzied crowd or mob: atavistic, driven by contagion and delirium, susceptible to control by demagogues, and in turn, controlling others by "mob rule"' (2002: xxvii). 'Panic', like 'moral', is often employed as a pejorative term; used individually to refer to those who lack restraint, need to exercise self-control, or who otherwise need to get a grip. This notion in particular has underpinned the appropriation of the concept by conservative newspapers and commentators to designate and decry what they perceive as over-sensitivity towards particular social concerns and the whipping up of concern about something which in their view is a non-issue, as exemplified in the much-used phrase 'political correctness gone mad'. Nonetheless, for early moral panic researchers the term was useful for effectively directing a component of the discourse of the 'moral majority' back towards itself. To put it provocatively, these early researchers were telling those in control that they in fact needed to exercise more self-control and, in effect, to become more 'civilized'. In so doing, these researchers were, rhetorically speaking, reversing the discursively implicit notion that the 'moral majority' were defending 'civilization' against a 'feral', 'uncivilized' youth.

Panics are often viewed as counter-productive. For example, the lack of careful judgement that sometimes accompanies a spontaneous social reaction can lead to a series of unintended consequences that might have been averted by a more cautious and measured response. A good example of this would be the media-fuelled panic over dangerous dogs. This came about because a few attacks by dogs such as pit bull terriers were greatly amplified by sections of the press, and the ensuing panic prompted the government to pass the Dangerous Dogs Act 1991, whose inadequate drafting and over-zealous enforcement led to various harmless family pets being threatened with extermination by the courts (e.g. see Hollingshead 2005). Panics are alleged to obscure real social problems by concentrating on side-issues, often distorting and exaggerating them in the process. For example, the murder of two-year-old James Bulger in Liverpool in 1993 by two other children was blamed by sections of the press on the alleged effects of watching 'video nasties'. There was not the slightest evidence of this, but the remarkable furore which this story generated served, whether intentionally or not, to obscure the social conditions under which the murder took place, including the institutional failings which prevented the realization that the two boys responsible for the killing were growing up in such a way as to pose a considerable threat to others (for a fuller discussion of this aspect of the Bulger story, see Petley 2001).

Another rather more conspiratorial notion of 'panic', however, involves the idea that a response has been strategically manipulated, amplified or refocused, so as to draw attention away from contentious issues that present a threat to the moral order. Thus, for example, in the wake of the summer riots of 2011 in the United Kingdom, there was a conscious move by the government of the day to promote a de-politicized reading of events in an attempt to steer popular opinion towards the view that the riots comprised little more than the wild, greed-fuelled, unprincipled 'disorder' symptomatic of a 'broken society', rather than, say, 'uprisings' or 'popular protests' against the austerity cuts that were at that time beginning to come into full effect. At a speech in Oxfordshire on 15 August, a week or so after the riots had begun, Prime Minister David Cameron was explicit: 'These riots were not about government cuts: they were directed at high street stores, not parliament. And these riots were not about poverty: that insults the millions of people who, whatever the hardship would never dream of making others suffer like this. No this was about behaviour . . . people showing indifference to right and wrong . . . people with a twisted moral code . . . people with a complete absence of self-restraint'. The intention in Cameron's statement to reframe the riots as indicative of moral decline, not social unrest, hardly needs to be pointed out. The moral orchestration of the response was later solidified around a familiar folk devil – the 'uncivilized rabble' who reside at the margins of society. This can be seen, for example, in Home Secretary Kenneth Clark's later statement that the 'hardcore of rioters came from a feral underclass, cut off from the mainstream in everything but its materialism' (quoted in *the Guardian*, 6 September 2011). While a few sections of the liberal media, including *the Guardian*, strongly criticized Clark's statements, the right-wing press played an active part in promoting this interpretation – as straightforward underclass criminality – quite some time before Cameron's and Clark's public statements. For instance, from a very early stage *the Daily Mail* made it clear to its readership that 'to blame the cuts is immoral and cynical. This is criminality – pure and simple – by yobs who have nothing but contempt for decent, law-abiding people' (8 August 2011).[5]

A further key attribute of the term 'panic' is that it is a descriptor of a particular kind of emotional response. However, the constitution of the emotions involved in these processes has largely been neglected. As we have seen, Cohen originally employed the term metaphorically to illustrate how responses to social problems might resemble reactions to natural disasters (2002: xxvii). However, other than the conceptualization of panics as 'irrational', there has been little in the way of research to explore the actual emotions involved. The emotions at play in, say, a reaction to 'Islamic terrorism' may include a great deal more than just panic. An Islamophobic reaction literally involves the notion that fear is the defining experiential emotion.[6] But many other emotions – to the extent that these terms point towards distinct affective states – may be involved too: pride, anger, hatred, embarrassment, humiliation, excitement, voyeuristic passion, self-love, shame, guilt, to name but a few. Such emotions are by no means restricted solely to the example of Islamophobic social reactions; they arguably feature in many other 'panics'. Both Cohen and Young have alluded to this in looking at how various actors involved in panics enjoy the spectacle (excitement) and/or experience feelings of *ressentiment* towards those who are seen to be rule breakers (Young 2009). That little research has been undertaken on the full panoply of emotions involved in a moral panic is perhaps not surprising, particularly given that the sociology of emotions remains a relatively young area of research. Nonetheless, more recently, Kevin Walby and Dale Spencer (2011: 104) have begun to contribute to this area, arguing that moral panic research should explore emotions 'by empirically investigating what emotions do, how emotions align certain communities against others, and how emotions move people towards certain (sometimes violent) actions against others whose actions pose alleged harms'.[7] Thus, again, the term 'panic' warrants further investigation, particularly in relation to affective dimensions of moral panic, and the more general relationship to social psychological work, especially in the areas of social representation and social identity theory (Pearce and Charman 2011).

Policing the concept: Orthodoxy, extension or revision?

Recent debates in moral panic studies have revealed tensions over the scope of the concept. A number of researchers (e.g. Hier 2008; Rohloff 2011a) argue that it has not been extended far enough, while others (e.g. Critcher 2003; Goode and Ben-Yehuda ([1994] 2009) have suggested that these extensions have gone too far, and that the concept is thus in danger of losing its original political (and analytical) focus. A range of increasingly elaborate and nuanced definitional criteria have been introduced to demarcate the concept. Critcher (2003) advocates something akin to an ideal type model of moral panics as a means of addressing this concern. The key advantage of such an analytical device is that it permits the retention of certain core facets of moral panic analysis, helps to guard against the over-extension of the concept and prevents it from becoming 'a catch-all term which encapsulates everything and nothing about the inter-relationship between the media, social problems, social policy and public opinion in the contemporary world' (Hughes et al. 2011: 214). Critcher suggests that, when combined with ideas about moral regulation, moral panic analysis can aspire to be what Merton described as a middle-range theory: a set of concepts used primarily 'to guide empirical inquiry . . . close enough to observed data to be incorporated in propositions that permit empirical testing.

Middle-range theories deal with delimited aspects of social phenomena, as is indicated by their labels' (Merton 1967, cited in Critcher 2009: 32). As a theory of the middle-range, then, it follows that a degree of delimitation is necessary, perhaps inevitable, in order to sustain the concept's precision.

Nonetheless, there remains the core issue of the *degree* to which the concept of moral panic is autonomous or independent from the empirical cases it encompasses. In the context of a rapidly changing social and cultural landscape, if it proves too problematic to adapt the moral panic analytical frame beyond certain limits, to extend its empirical reach to keep pace with social and cultural changes, the concept may risk obsolescence. To this end, Rohloff (2012) has suggested, following Blumer (1954), that we might employ moral panic as a kind of 'sensitizing concept' which avoids the definitive taxonomic formalism of, for example, Goode and Ben-Yehuda's delimitation of the concept, and permits it to be adapted and developed in relation to specific empirical applications. Indeed, the idea of a sensitizing concept implies a far more even relationship between the concept and empirical data; it by no means obviates the need for analytical focus – essentially, orientations towards 'where to look' and 'what to look for' – but this focus can be developed and continuously redeveloped, drawn and redrawn in relation to empirical studies, rather than being uncritically imposed, and in certain instances, superimposed onto the cases considered. Indeed, even the paradigmatic cases or guiding exemplars around which the concept was originally developed – Young's drug takers, Cohen's Mods and Rockers – are not static; the players involved have changed over time. For example, youth culture, the media, the control culture, the organization of policy and the general public – and indeed, the inter-relationships between these – are all in important respects radically different from how they were in the 1960s. Indeed, in the preface to even the first edition of his *Folk Devils and Moral Panics* (written, in 1971), Cohen was prompted to ask: 'Who on earth is still worried about the Mods and Rockers? Who – some might ask – *were* the Mods and Rockers' (2002: xlv). Significantly, Cohen (2002: xlv) continues thus:

> I too would have preferred this book to have appeared when the phenomenon it describes was still a contemporary one, but . . . I carried on writing in the belief that this study has implications beyond its immediate subject matter. For the most part I have resisted the temptation to make such implications explicit or up to date; I will have failed if they are not transparent enough for the reader to make himself. The processes by which moral panics and folk devils are generated do not date.

In other words, the details may change, but the core dynamics, the generative processes, the constitutive forces remain the same. But it is this last point in particular that, as the chapters in this volume serve to demonstrate, remains perhaps the most moot.

Faced with the thorny problems surrounding the enduring utilization and application of moral panic analysis, researchers might pursue a number (or combination) of different strategic alternatives: (1) adopt the position that anything that does not fit the orthodox moral panic model, in its most elementary form, is ipso facto not a moral panic (while also elaborating on the criteria by which such judgements might be made); (2) seek to extend, amend or otherwise rework the concept through empirical-theoretical dialogue with new kinds of examples drawn from the changing sociocultural universe; (3) draw upon alternative conceptual architectures either to revise, resituate, or perhaps even partly or completely abandon the concept as part of a more general reframing of moral panics, moralization, public anxieties and generalized social reactions. Below we review some of these different approaches as they have been employed in the chapters that comprise this volume. We explore some of the core debates surrounding these extensions and revisions, and the potential problems they present for the future direction of moral panic research.

Theoretical and empirical extensions

Several of the chapters in this collection question the scope of the moral panic concept. In her chapter on the 'cautionary tale', Sarah Moore argues that the term moral panic has been too loosely applied to rather too broad a range of examples, which has had the effect of weakening 'the overall explanatory power of the moral panic paradigm'. Accordingly, she concludes, we need to employ an array of paradigms, a greater diversity of concepts to make sense of a variety of different social reactions. Moore's own approach is to employ the analytical device of the cautionary tale to accompany that of the moral panic, sitting alongside it rather than replacing it. Distinct from moral panic, the cautionary tale is used to analyse media examples that focus on 'marginalizing female victims' (and potential victims') behaviour'. Yet while she argues that they are distinct, Moore conceives of both concepts as being forms of moral regulation. Also, with the aim of limiting the scope of the moral panic idea, Marcello Maneri, in an effort to locate moral panics in his chapter examining two case studies of alleged rapes, situates moral panic within different kinds of media hype, proposing that while all moral panics are media hypes, not all media hypes are moral panics. Conversely, Jon Oplinger, Richard Talbot and Yasin Aktay, in their chapter on the Dirty War in Argentina (which involved the abduction, torture and murder of up to 30,000 people by the state military regime between 1976 and 1983), argue for the scope of moral panic research to be expanded, open to exploring how other instances of state-sponsored terrorism, and indeed instances of genocide, may have been assisted by elite-manufactured moral panics. It is worth noting, however, that this latter example may be rather less contentious to those wishing to police the concept, for it is unlikely to threaten the political project of moral panic research. Finally, Paul Lashmar in his chapter exploring the perspectives of journalists in moral panics, in a similar vein to Moore argues that for moral panic to remain a useful concept, it needs to be situated within a wider empirical conceptual framework. He suggests we develop a schema or continuum of moral concern which would allow for justified moral indignation to be factored in – something which accords strongly with Cohen's notion of 'good' moral panics.

Following Hier (2002, 2008) and Critcher (2009), several authors in this volume discuss the relationship between moral panic, risk and moral regulation. Sarah Moore, in her account of cautionary tales, argues that both the cautionary tale and moral panic are distinct forms of moral regulation: that is to say, that not all volatile episodes of moral regulation are moral panics. In addressing Ungar's risk society critique of moral panics, Moore argues that cautionary tales impel people to limit the risks posed to them, consistent with the reflexivity and future-orientation of the risk society but, in contrast with Ungar's arguments, cautionary tales place greater emphasis on individual responsibility. Drawing on Hunt, Moore interprets risk discourse as a moralizing discourse, and as such, the cautionary tale is, in turn, a variant of moralizing discourse. A similar fusion of risk society and moral panics perspectives is advocated by Morena Tartari in her chapter on moral panic, paedophilia and satanic ritual abuse. Tartari maintains that the risk society thesis helps explain how social issues are constructed both locally and nationally, whereby risk pervades the framing of social concerns, demands for remedial action and the suspicion of experts. At the same time, Tartari proposes, analyses of risk can be fruitfully combined with – perhaps set within – established moral panic models, notably Goode and Ben Yehuda's emphasis on the strategic role of interest groups in mounting moral panics. In this way, Tartari employs classic moral panic analysis to elucidate how threats to children so easily provoke social reaction, and risk analysis to illustrate the subsequent framing, construction and development of such reactions in local and national media.

Another extension involves placing moral regulation in considerably longer-term perspective than that typically employed in risk analyses or established moral panic research. In his chapter on theorizing alcohol in public discourse, Henry Yeomans looks at how British concerns about drinking have developed throughout history, and assesses whether moral panic and/or moral regulation are useful concepts for exploring concerns about drinking in both the past and the present (see also Critcher 2011). Yeomans conceptualizes moral panics as extreme forms of moral regulation, arguing that the temperance movement was more characteristic of moral regulation, but was punctuated with 'high points in concern'. He suggests that moral panics are examples of such points, but that these must be understood as occurring within more 'long term processes of problematization and regulation'. Likewise, Aurélie Lacassagne, in a similar manner to Rohloff (2008, 2011b) and Rohloff and Wright (2010), argues in her chapter on the reaction to the Burqa in France, that certain elements of the Eliasian approach can be employed to 'thicken' the concept of moral panic with regard to longer-term processes of moralization. In particular, she advocates utilizing Elias's concepts of 'established-outsider relations' (a model of inter-group conflicts and tensions), and conceptualizing moral panics as 'decivilizing processes' – erosions of 'sociogenetic' monopolies over violence and taxation – that occur in tandem with 'civilizing processes' (historically emergent centripetal processes of state formation involving, at the 'psychogenetic' level, a social constraint towards self-restraint), thus connecting short-term moral panics to very long-term social processes.

Indeed, there are at least two ways in which moral panics might be fruitfully connected with longer-term processes. First, through considering the media in long-term perspective we might look beyond, for example, recent tabloid newspapers to, say, pamphlets of the seventeenth century, or to social media of today, as a means of exploring the continuities and discontinuities between shifting modalities of mediated communication. Through engaging processually and developmentally with aspects of the kinds of social phenomena that have long been the mainstay of moral panic research, it may be possible to avoid the 'expiry date' of the paradigmatic cases. Second, adopting a long-term perspective avoids a 'retreat to the present' (Elias [1983] 1987), and helps to direct attention away from a preoccupation with specific social actors of the here and now. Thus, for example, as Lacassagne shows, the recent controversy about the Burqa in France can be better understood as an aspect of a much broader figuration of Christian–Muslim tensions – a set of long-term social processes in which

Muslims have been historically positioned as outsiders, particularly via relations between the Europeans and the 'Turks' since the Crusades. This long-standing discourse, she argues, endures today under a number of guises. It can be seen, for example, in textbooks aimed at schoolchildren, which continue to emphasize a divide between the 'civilized European' and the 'barbarian Turk'. In relation to alcohol, Yeomans illustrates how sudden events – for example, the outbreak of the First World War; the development of 24-hour licensing in 2005 – combine with long-standing discourses (particularly older understandings about alcohol dating from the times of the temperance movement) to produce a moral panic about drinking: 'an intense, heightened drive for moral regulation over a short period of time'. Seeking to form a bridge between short-term processes of moral panic and longer-term processes of moral regulation, Yeomans argues that the concept of 'moral inheritance' can be used in conjunction with the concepts of moral panic and moral regulation to 'understand how certain chronological points relate to each other'. He contends that a methodology for moral panic research needs to encompass 'the historical, discursive and processual as well as [the] episodic'. Similarly, Elias le Grand, in his chapter about the creation of 'chavs' as folk devils, considers how long-standing stereotypes of the lower classes inform the moral panic about chavs. This negative construction, le Grand argues, is connected to two long-established folk devils: young, violent, working-class males, and single, welfare-dependent, young working-class mothers. Likewise, Julian Petley argues that the moral panic over 'video nasties' needs to be understood in the context of centuries-old fears on the part of the British establishment about the allegedly corrupting effects of popular entertainments of one kind or another.

Enduring controversies

Beyond some of the analytical and conceptual extensions of the moral panic concept touched upon above, the chapters in this volume also contribute variously to a number of enduring controversies that surround moral panic analysis. We now turn to consider some of these long-standing issues and debates with a consideration of how these have been addressed by the contributors to this volume.

Banishing the folk devil?

One of the core disagreements in moral panic studies is whether or not a particular case needs to have a folk devil for a moral panic to occur; this debate is played out in several of the chapters included in this volume. In developing her concept of the cautionary tale, Moore notes how media coverage of drug-facilitated sexual assault (DFSA) appeared to follow the contours of a classic moral panic, but that there was no clearly discernible folk devil. For Moore, a moral panic must include a recognizable folk devil; it is on these grounds that she here employs her alternative classification of the cautionary tale. Similarly, Maneri argues that 'in the absence of folk devils . . . the moral panic concept loses its specificity', and he proposes that while one of the cases he considered in his comparative analysis was a clear-cut moral panic, the other was simply a panic (not a moral panic proper) because it did not include a folk devil. For Maneri, the folk devil is a crucial designation – marking a division between 'us' and 'them' which is a decisive ingredient of a moral panic. Likewise, in le Grand's example, chavs are constructed as folk devils which are used as an 'other' in contradistinction to whom many middle-class people and 'respectable' working-class people would want to distinguish themselves. By contrast, Jeremy Collins, in his chapter exploring moral panics in relation to governmentality and risk, argues that moral panics do not necessarily need a folk devil; his empirical example of media coverage of mephedrone use does not include one – the focus is instead on the dangers of the drug, rather than on the dangers of a particular type of person. Here we might observe a notable shift away from concerns over the users of dangerous drugs (as was extensively documented by Young), towards concerns over dangerous drugs in and of themselves. Collins's example presents the possibility of objects and substances coming to 'embody' that which might previously have been personified by a folk devil, as in the case of 'video nasties' in the United Kingdom in the 1980s and 1990s which are the subject of Petley's chapter.

Fighting back?

Another common debate centres around the extent to which folk devils and others have access to the resources necessary to disseminate alternative accounts and counter-perspectives to those of the 'moral majority'. A key question is that of whether the concept of moral panic is relevant and whether only certain sections of the media are contributing to the panic. A related question is what happens when stigmatized groups, or those speaking on their behalf, fight back? Their capacity and ability to do so may, of course, vary considerably. In their chapter on the reaction to the video game *Rule of Rose*, Elisabeth Staksrud and Jørgen Kirksæther note how, following inaccurate and distorted press reporting of the game in the United Kingdom, the Video Standards Council (which represents the interests of video distributors and sellers in the United Kingdom) accused newspapers of exaggerating, and even inventing some aspects of, the stories which they published. However, even such official recognition and criticism of media distortion did not prevent the distributor of the game from withdrawing it from distribution in the European market. Nor, as Petley points out, were any voices in defence of 'video nasties', or critical of the campaign against them, able to make themselves heard in most of the national press at the time of the panic.

With a focus particularly on the Italian media, Maneri argues that despite there being a growing number of media outlets, different media – especially news media – tend to copy one another's stories. This, he suggests, serves only to generate even greater consensual representation than was apparent in the 1960s, when there were far fewer media outlets. Moreover, Maneri argues, despite the proliferation of social media, blogs and micro media, where alternative arguments can be voiced, such sources and outlets cannot compete with the dominant mainstream media in which, in the Italian case, dissenting viewpoints were all but entirely excluded. By way of a more pronounced example, Oplinger et al. provide an account of how alternative media accounts were stifled during a moral panic in the Dirty War: most of the media complied with the military-issued 'Principles and procedures to be followed by the mass communication media', and those who did not were either made to comply or were killed. For the media, and for anyone else, any criticism of the military was punishable by imprisonment. Alternative voices were thus effectively silenced. On the other hand, in democratic states it is undoubtedly easier, if by no means always easy, to criticize dominant representations of demonized groups or individuals. For example, le Grand observes that, even within the mainstream media, the moral panic about chavs was contested: certain newspapers fanned the panic (*Times*, *Daily Telegraph*, *Daily Mail*), while others were severely critical of it (*The Guardian*), and journalists within the same paper sometimes disagreed with one another. Again, social media sources, notably YouTube, provided a platform for other critical voices. In a further critique, the chav identity was celebrated and valorized as a positive identity in several books and in a Sky 1 documentary by Julie Burchill. The examples presented in this volume thus serve to demonstrate the need to explore the extent to which, the social conditions under which, and in what manner competing voices are heard, drowned out or silenced; how some come to establish a relative monopoly and others remain in relative obscurity on the margins.

nuanced. For example, anti-terrorism legislation has served both to fuel private suspicion about 'foreign others', as well to expand forms of direct control through, in particular, a raft of new policing and anti-terrorism powers. Similarly, new laws against even the possession of certain kinds of images of children run in tandem, and not simply in sequence, with heightened anxieties about the photographing of children. The fundamental inter-relationship between social constraint and self-restraint; government and governance; state-control and self-control; the diffusion and internalization of social power through the micro politics of bodily regimens, discursive practices, identification processes, self-perceptions, dispositions, personal values, principles and orientations, classifications, and so forth are, of course, major concerns in much of the literature on moralization, particularly that which draws on the work of writers such as Michel Foucault and Norbert Elias. Such forms of regulation are arguably as significant as, and perhaps even more pervasive than, formal and explicit shifts in government policy; yet conventional definitions of moral panic seemingly preclude or underplay them. As Elias in particular has extensively documented, a rule – in the form of a proscription, a standard, an ideal, or otherwise – is all the more pervasive when it no longer needs to be stated, when it becomes 'second nature': when it does not require even the threat of enforcement through external sanction (see Elias [1939] 2012). This is not to discount the crucial role of successive forms of explicit and sanctionable social proscriptions against particular behaviours, groups, forms of association and so forth (whether or not these become successfully enshrined in legislature or statutes) in the development of social control and the expansion of state power, but to highlight the dynamic interplay between the development of legislative frameworks and forms of control that effectively come to be embedded in the psyches of particular groups in particular historical periods. This debate is substantively illustrated by Staksrud and Kirksæther in their consideration of how it was the media (not legal) responses that effectively regulated the distribution of the game *Rule of Rose*. In a similar manner, le Grand explores how certain shopping malls and pubs in the United Kingdom effectively invented their own 'rules of discrimination' against those regarded as chavs, banning people who were deemed to be wearing 'chav' clothing from entering their establishments.[9] In the case of the Burqa in France, Lacassagne found police were fining women for wearing the Burqa even before a law against the practice came into effect. Finally, Collins identifies two forms of regulation in the moral panic about mephedrone: first a neo-liberal form of governance, where users are provided with information in order to take the drug in a safe way; another, more dominant moral panic discourse, however, contributed to criminalizing the drug and its users.

All in all, the chapters in this volume attest to the enduring significance of moral panic, both as an analytical focus and as a research orientation. Whether pursuing an 'orthodox', 'extension' or 'revision' pathway, the challenge for future researchers is to refine and renew the approach and its attendant controversies. That way moral panic research can sustain its utility to apprehending, confronting, and perhaps even changing, core facets of the contemporary world.

Notes

1 While Cohen (2002: xxxv) claims that he and Young came across the term through reading McLuhan, it is quite possible that others used the phrase before McLuhan, albeit not in the way in which Cohen subsequently developed it.

2 An important exception in this respect is research on child abuse. From an early stage in the development of moral panic research, child abuse was a major concern. The issue was not in any simple or direct sense related to 'permissiveness', and did not involve the researchers 'taking sides'. Indeed, no researchers supported child abuse; rather, they wanted it to be defined and constructed accurately. This is an often neglected example of early moral panic research (e.g. Parton 1979) that deserves careful attention.

3 An example of a moral panic that might be approved of by both a liberal intelligentsia and the 'moral majority' is sex trafficking. It is not yet proven that the incidence of sex trafficking is anything like as widespread as claims makers would have us believe: the jury, so to speak, remains out. However, the example is illustrative of the difficulties and dangers attendant upon seeking to mobilize moral panics to highlight 'genuine' social concerns. For instance, a moral panic about sex trafficking might easily be hijacked by a xenophobic moral response to East European pimps. Accordingly, the plight of subjugated migrant women, and indeed, the pressing social issues pertaining to the migrant sex trade more generally, could easily become eclipsed by the spectre of 'bad foreign men' – the predominant folk devil of our time. In the case of moral panics, exposure and distortion often go hand in hand, and as such, moral panic researchers might be on safer ground if they endorsed the proportionate moral regulation of 'real' social problems *without* their distortion. Such an ambition could, for example, accord with the political goals of anti-rape campaigners (for a useful illustration of this point, see Davies [2009]).

4 As we shall see, there is considerable disagreement over whether campaigns surrounding climate change might be usefully classified as forms of 'moral panic'.

For instance, to extend the arguments of his (2010) paper somewhat, Critcher maintains that it is very largely unhelpful to place climate change in the same category as such social concerns as, say, paedophiles or asylum seekers – irrespective of personal beliefs about the topic. To do so risks, once again, over-extending the concept, and loosening its analytical 'grip'. Conversely, Rohloff (2011a) has critically explored how the empirical case of climate change might be used to highlight some of the problems with 'classical' moral panic analysis and the related definitional disputes that have arisen in recent years.

5 It is noteworthy that remarkably similar rhetoric was used by the Thatcher government in response to inner city riots some 30 years earlier in 1981. Subsequently, the Scarman inquiry raised serious questions about the culpability of police racism for provoking the riots, undermining the claim that they were simply outcomes of opportunistic criminality. This is perhaps why Cameron resisted all calls for an inquiry into the 2011 riots.

6 Once more, the extent to which 'islamophobia' constitutes a *moral* panic is open to question. The term itself is hotly contested, mobilized by competing groups with strikingly different interpretations. To the extent that the term may mean 'an irrational fear of Islam' – and again, there is no firm agreement on this interpretation – one might view an increasing 'moralization' of Islam: as 'bad', 'wrong', 'evil', particularly in relation to its received associations with terrorism (for a fuller discussion of the concept see Petley and Richardson [2011: 3–14]).

7 One criticism of Walby and Spencer is that the way they write about emotions devolves them from people, conceptualizing emotions as separate things that act on their own.

8 Once more, there is no widespread acceptance that the case of passive smoking qualifies as a moral panic. For example, Critcher (personal correspondence) has argued that since there was a scientific evidential basis for passive smoking, the development was neither 'moral' in origin (though, of course, it later came to take on moral dimensions through subsequent attributions and reframing), nor necessarily a 'panic' since the growing welter of evidence supported the need for a considerable shift in health policy. That said, other writers have proposed that the evidence in support of the case for curbing exposure to secondary smoke was in fact more a product of stylistic creation than scientific discovery. Jackson (1994), for example, has argued that the notion of 'passive smoking' was developed through the 'production' rather than the 'revelation' of facts based upon a stylized reading of bio-chemical markers. Jackson explores how a social pressure to shift perceptions of smoking from a private self-inflicted 'vice' which affected only smokers themselves to a source of 'harm to others' in part fuelled the ostensible 'discovery' of scientific evidence (a claim, in turn, partly disputed by others; see Hughes [2003]).

9 Le Grand's example serves to highlight how a moral preoccupation with chavs serves, once again, to obscure an arguably much more significant issue concerning the privatization, surveillance and disciplining of public spaces (see in particular Minton 2012).

Bibliography

Bailey, R. and Young, J. (eds) (1973), *Contemporary Social Problems in Britain*, Westmead: Saxon House.

Becker, H. S. ([1963] 1991), *Outsiders: Studies in the Sociology of Deviance*, New York: Free Press.

— (1967), 'Whose Side Are We On?', *Social Problems*, 14: 239–47.

Blumer, H. (1954), 'What Is Wrong with Social Theory?', *American Sociological Review*, 19(1): 3–10.

Cohen, S. (ed.) (1971), *Images of Deviance*, Harmondsworth, Middlesex: Penguin.

— (1972), *Folk Devils and Moral Panics*, St Albans: Paladin.

— ([1972] 2002), *Folk Devils and Moral Panics: The Creation of the Mods and Rockers*, 3rd edn, London: Routledge.

— (2011), 'Whose Side Were We On? The Undeclared Politics of Moral Panic Theory', *Crime, Media, Culture*, 7(3): 237–43.

Conrad, P. and Schneider, J. W. ([1980] 1985), *Deviance and Medicalization: From Badness to Sickness*, Columbus, OH: Merrill.

Critcher, C. (2003), *Moral Panics and the Media*, Maidenhead, Buckingham: Open University Press.

— (2008), 'Moral Panic Analysis: Past, Present and Future', *Sociology Compass*, 2(4): 1127–44.

— (2009), 'Widening the Focus: Moral Panics as Moral Regulation', *British Journal of Criminology*, 49(1): 17–34.

— (2011), 'Double Measures: The Moral Regulation of Alcohol Consumption, Past and Present', in P. Bramham and S. Wagg (eds), *The New Politics of Leisure and Pleasure*, Basingstoke: Palgrave Macmillan, 32–44.

Davies, N. (2009), 'How Misinformation Flooded the Sex Trafficking Story', published online, www.nickdavies.net/2009/10/19/how-misinformation-flooded-the-sex-trafficking-story/ [accessed 28 October 2012].

Elias, N. ([1939] 2012), *On the Process of Civilisation (The Collected Works of Norbert Elias, Vol. 3)*, Dublin: University College Dublin Press [previously published as *The Civilizing Process*].

— ([1983] 1987), 'The Retreat of Sociologists into the Present', *Theory, Culture & Society*, 4(2): 223–47.

Fine, B., Kinsey, R., Lea, J., Picciotto, S. and Young, J. (eds) (1979), *Capitalism and the Rule of Law: From Deviancy Theory to Marxism*, London: Hutchinson.

Garland, D. (2008), 'On the Concept of Moral Panic', *Crime Media Culture,* 4(1): 9–30.

Goode, E. and Ben-Yehuda, N. ([1994] 2009), *Moral Panics: The Social Construction of Deviance*, 2nd edn, Oxford: Wiley-Blackwell.

Hall, S., Critcher, C., Jefferson, T., Clarke, J. and Roberts, B. (1978), *Policing the Crisis: Mugging, the State, and Law and Order*, London: Macmillan.

Hier, S. P. (2002), 'Conceptualizing Moral Panic Through a Moral Economy of Harm', *Critical Sociology*, 28(3): 311–34.

— (2008), 'Thinking Beyond Moral Panic: Risk, Responsibility, and the Politics of Moralization', *Theoretical Criminology,* 12(2): 173–90.

— (2011), 'Tightening the Focus: Moral Panic, Moral Regulation and Liberal Government', *British Journal of Sociology*, 62(3): 523–41.

Hollingshead, I. (2005), 'Whatever Happened to Dangerous Dogs?' *Guardian*, 5 November, www.guardian.co.uk/uk/2005/nov/05/animalwelfare.world [accessed 22 August 2012].

Hughes, J. (2003), *Learning to Smoke: Tobacco Use in the West*, Chicago: University of Chicago Press.

Hughes, J., Rohloff, A., David, M. and Petley, J. (2011), 'Foreword: Moral Panics in the Contemporary World', *Crime Media Culture,* 7(3): 211–14.

Hunt, A. (1999), *Governing Morals: A Social History of Moral Regulation*, Cambridge: Cambridge University Press.

— (2003), 'Risk and Moralization in Everyday Life', in R. V. Ericson and A. Doyle (eds), *Risk and Morality,* Toronto: University of Toronto Press, 165–92.

— (2011), 'Fractious Rivals? Moral Panics and Moral Regulation', in S. P. Hier (ed.), *Moral Panic and the Politics of Anxiety,* London: Routledge, 53–70.

Jackson, P. (1994), 'Passive Smoking and Ill-Health: Practice and Process in the Production of Medical Knowledge', *Sociology of Health and Illness,* 16(2): 423–47.

Lundström, R. (2011), 'Between the Exceptional and the Ordinary: A Model for the Comparative Analysis of Moral Panics and Moral Regulation', *Crime Media Culture*, 7(3): 313–32.

McLuhan, M. ([1964] 2007), *Understanding Media: The Extensions of Man*, London: Routledge.

Minton, A. (2012), *Ground Control: Fear and Happiness in the Twenty-First-Century City*, 2nd edn, London: Penguin.

National Deviancy Conference (ed.) (1980), *Permissiveness and Control: The Fate of the Sixties Legislation*, London: Macmillan.

Parton, N. (1979), 'The Natural History of Child Abuse: A Study in Social Problem Definition', *British Journal of Social Work*, 11(4): 391–415.

Pearce, J. and Charman, E. (2011), 'A Social Psychological Approach to Understanding Moral Panic', *Crime Media Culture*, 7(3): 293–312.

Petley, J. (2001), 'Us and Them', in M. Barker and J. Petley (eds), *Ill Effects: The Media/ Violence Debate,* 2nd edn, London: Routledge.

Petley, J. and Richardson, R. (eds) (2011), *Pointing the Finger: Islam and Muslims in the British Media,* Oxford: Oneworld.

Rohloff, A. (2008), 'Moral Panics as Decivilising Processes: Towards an Eliasian Approach', *New Zealand Sociology,* 23(1): 66–76.

— (2011a), 'Extending the Concept of Moral Panic: Elias, Climate Change and Civilization', *Sociology,* 45(4): 634–49.

— (2011b), 'Shifting the Focus? Moral Panics as Civilizing and Decivilizing Processes', in S. P. Hier (ed.), *Moral Panic and the Politics of Anxiety,* London: Routledge, 71–85.

— (2012), *Climate Change, Moral Panic, and Civilization: On the Development of Global Warming as a Social Problem,* unpublished PhD thesis, Brunel University, London.

Rohloff, A. and Wright, S. (2010), 'Moral Panic and Social Theory: Beyond the Heuristic', *Current Sociology,* 58(3): 403–19.

Taylor, I. and Taylor, L. (eds) (1973), *Politics and Deviance,* Middlesex: Penguin.

Thompson, K. (2011), 'Foreword', in S. P. Hier (ed.), *Moral Panic and the Politics of Anxiety,* London: Routledge, vii–xi.

Ungar, S. (2001), 'Moral Panic Versus the Risk Society: The Implications of the Changing Sites of Social Anxiety', *British Journal of Sociology,* 52(2): 271–91.

— (2011), 'The Artful Creation of Global Moral Panic: Climatic Folk Devils, Environmental Evangelicals, and the Coming Catastrophe', in S. P. Hier (ed.), *Moral Panic and the Politics of Anxiety,* London: Routledge, 190–207.

Waddington, P. A. J. (1986), 'Mugging as a Moral Panic: A Question of Proportion', *British Journal of Sociology,* 37(2): 245–59.

Walby, K. and Spencer, D. (2011), 'How Emotions Matter to Moral Panics', in S. P. Hier (ed.), *Moral Panic and the Politics of Anxiety,* London: Routledge, 104–17.

Wouters, C. (1977), 'Informalisation and the Civilising Process', in P. R. Gleichmann, J. Goudsblom and H. Korte (eds), *Human Figurations: Essays for Norbert Elias,* Amsterdam: Amsterdam Sociologisch Tijdschrift, 437–55.

— (1986), 'Formalization and Informalization: Changing Tension Balances in Civilizing Processes', *Theory, Culture & Society,* 3(2): 1–18.

— (2004), *Sex and Manners: Female Emancipation in the West 1890–2000,* London: Sage.

— (2007), *Informalization: Manners and Emotions Since 1890,* London: Sage.

Young, J. (1971a), *The Drugtakers: The Social Meaning of Drug Use,* London: Paladin.

— (1971b), 'The Role of the Police as Amplifiers of Deviancy, Negotiators of Reality and Translators of Fantasy: Some Consequences of our Present System of Drug Control as Seen in Notting Hill', in S. Cohen (ed.), *Images of Deviance,* Middlesex: Penguin, 27–61.

— (2009), 'Moral Panic: Its Origins in Resistance, Ressentiment and the Translation of Fantasy into Reality', *British Journal of Criminology,* 49(1), 4–16.

— (2011), 'Moral Panics and the Transgressive Other', *Crime Media Culture,* 7(3), 245–58.

Part One

Rethinking Moral Panics

2

The Cautionary Tale: A New Paradigm for Studying Media Coverage of Crime

Sarah E. H. Moore

As McRobbie and Thornton (1995: 560) note, there is a tendency, in both media and scholarly accounts, 'to label all kinds of media event as moral panic'. A story is often given this tag simply because it has provoked a degree of public concern or received sustained media attention. Even in the classroom it has become very difficult to bring due attention to the conceptual clarity and theoretical meaning of the term. This chapter seeks to respond to these problems by outlining a new concept for studying media coverage of crime – the cautionary tale – and suggests that, in many instances, this category more fittingly captures the nature of crime reporting. It also argues that the current debate about the relationship between moral panic and moral regulation studies might be fruitfully developed through consideration of this new paradigm.

The chapter is organized in such a way that several examples are analysed, including media coverage of drug-facilitated sexual assault (DFSA), rape perpetrated by taxicab drivers and the 'dope girls' of the 1920s. As will become evident, the cautionary tale is particularly useful in analysing media stories that are centrally concerned with marginalizing female victims' (and potential victims') behaviour in relation to a given crime. Indeed, one thing that is rarely noted about moral panic theory is that, in relation to crime reporting at least, it is primarily useful in understanding the depiction and treatment of specifically *male* deviance. While commentators often point out that young people and those from ethnic minorities frequently become the repository of public anxiety – the 'folk devil' – in moral panics, the same observation concerning maleness is very rarely made. Yet when we look at moral panic research on crime reporting, whether it is the early work of Cohen ([1972] 2002) and Hall et al. (1978) or more recent studies on child molesters and murderers (Jenkins 2004), the juvenile crimes of 'Hoodies', hooligans, 'boy racers' and gangsta rappers (Hay 1995; Springhall 1998; Welch et al. 2002), the terrorist acts of Islamic Fundamentalists (Rothe and Muzzatti 2004), and 'knife crime' (Squires 2009; Squires and Goldsmith 2010), it is predominantly the male deviant who takes centre stage.[1]

That 'folk devils' are more frequently male than female is no coincidence, of course: maleness, as with youth and belonging to an ethnic minority, is frequently associated with criminality and deviance in our culture, and moral panic research is directed towards understanding the process of criminalization (both formal and cultural) that occurs during periods of socio-cultural tension. It is, therefore, understandable that moral panic research would concentrate on the depiction of certain social groups in the media. What is unfortunate is that the dominance of the moral panic paradigm has led to an extraordinary research focus on the mainstream media's systematic marginalization of certain forms of male deviance and, at the same time, a relative neglect of the media's demonization of female victims. While many researchers have, of course, drawn attention to the media's mystification of sexual violence against women, the lack of any equivalent and thoroughgoing conceptual framework to the moral panic paradigm means that the media's *systematic marginalization* of female victim behaviour is something that is rarely seen as a core lever in crime reporting. To put it a little differently, if the mainstream media's depiction of crime is very frequently taken to be partial and sensationalist, the concept of moral panic is often invoked (inside and outside of the academy) as a shorthand way of saying as much; in contrast, the imputation of deviance to female victims is simply not seen in the same way, as one of the central tendencies of crime reporting. Recognizing the prevalence of cautionary tales in the media goes some way toward addressing this oversight.

Before we move on to discuss the characteristics and function of the cautionary tale I want to make clear that this chapter is not suggesting that we need a *replacement* for the moral panic concept, but rather that we treat this as just one possible paradigm for those interested in studying the media's distortion of issues related to crime and justice. In recent years, all sorts of questions have been raised concerning the relevance of moral panic as a concept. Newspapers no longer exert a monolithic influence on public opinion (if they ever did), 'folk devils' have their own niche media and can 'fight back' (McRobbie and Thornton 1995), newspapers self-consciously employ a 'moral panic register' in reporting (Arnold Hunt 1997): perhaps such developments mean that moral panic, as a concept, no longer offers much purchase on the problems of media misrepresentation and demonization. Indeed, looked at from one, increasingly popular, point of view – and we analyse this argument below – the cautionary tale is evidence of a turn towards a rhetoric of risk in news coverage and away from more traditional moral panic reporting. This chapter rejects the idea that moral panic is a redundant concept, and aims instead to urge greater attention to the diversity and nuance in media coverage of crime, whether it conforms to a moral panic or cautionary tale (or, for that matter, crime legend or signal crime). With this must come the admission that the term moral panic cannot incorporate all aspects of news reporting – or all that might strike academics as interesting about news reporting – and that the analytic stretch performed in certain studies to fit the case study to the concept weakens the overall explanatory power of the moral panic paradigm.

We must, I want to suggest, cast our nets wider when seeking out ways of describing media coverage of crime. This does not mean that there are not important shared characteristics between, say, the cautionary tale and the moral panic. Indeed, the last part of this chapter suggests that we see the moral panic and the cautionary tale as working towards a similar goal: both, I argue below, are directed towards achieving moral regulation. Drawing upon literature from moral regulation theorists such as Hier (2002) and Alan Hunt (2003) and the structural-functionalist writing of Mary Douglas (1986), I argue that, while cautionary tales and moral panics might operate quite differently in terms of their normative concerns and the way in which they sketch out for us the parameters of appropriate behaviour, both are directed principally towards moral regulation. In this sense this chapter intends to engage with current debates concerning the future or place of moral panic studies.

Looking for a moral panic and finding a cautionary tale

In 2006 I became involved in a project that sought to understand English university students' concerns about drug-facilitated sexual assault (DFSA). The study aimed to survey student attitudes and ascertain the strength and origin of this group's fears and worries concerning the threat of drink-spiking and subsequent sexual victimization (for a summary of our core findings, see Burgess et al. 2009). The initial round of research showed a very marked level of concern about DFSA, far greater than the likelihood of victimization: respondents judged both the risk and their worry about DFSA to be greater than that for burglary, mugging and being a victim of road crime. We also found that the media was a key source of information (mainly mis-information) for our sample. And so, as an adjunct to the main study, I carried out a content analysis of US and UK newspapers. A central aim in carrying out the analysis was to ascertain whether media coverage of DFSA constituted a moral panic. Indeed, various scholars had referred, in passing, to coverage of DFSA in this way (see, Bourke 2007; Goode and Ben-Yehuda [1994] 2009). In my own analysis everything seemed to initially point in this direction. In the British media, concern had been initiated by the Roofie Foundation, a charity institution aimed at raising awareness about DFSA: their early press releases and readiness to court media attention seemed to indicate their role as moral entrepreneurs in the panic. News coverage had been voluminous and volatile enough to warrant the tag moral panic, with a dramatic increase in reporting in 1998. There had been an almost immediate response from social authorities with Scotland Yard launching an enquiry in 1999 and the re-classification of Rohypnol (a drug associated with DFSA) in the same year – so there had been an evident effort made on the part of the 'control culture' to treat DFSA more punitively. The media coverage was also certainly disproportionate to the 'actual' threat: DFSA had clearly not reached 'epidemic' proportions, as the early newspaper articles in *the Daily Mirror* had suggested. As for public concern about the threat, the results of our survey had established that student worry about DFSA was widespread and deep-seated.

Nonetheless there was one very important criterion that the media coverage of DFSA lacked for it to be judged a moral panic: there was no discernable, fully fleshed-out 'folk devil', no person, condition or episode (as Cohen's original formulation had it) that was being put forward as the repository of public concern. The drink-spiker remained always in the shadows in media reports – indeed, his anonymity and unknowability were core aspects of his characterization. At the same time, a close inspection of media coverage revealed that the female victim, and potential victim of crime, was given centre stage. As I mention elsewhere (Moore 2009), it is noteworthy that while there were only 925 mentions of the terms 'offender', 'culprit', 'perpetrator' or 'suspect' in newspaper reports between 1998 and 2008, there were more than twice as many (2,584) of the single word 'victim'. More than this, there were frequent mentions of the need for would-be-victims to watch their drinks, be on their guard and generally become more aware of the problem of DFSA. In short, it was not male deviant behaviour that was being marginalized here, but rather female behaviour associated (erroneously, often) with an increased risk of victimization. I used the term 'cautionary tale' to capture this dimension of media coverage (Moore 2009). In brief, these are media stories in which the victim's (or potential victim's) behaviour is a focal point for coverage; the threat is represented as being both internal and external to the self (as much to do with one's poor judgement as an insidious criminal); coverage is likely to be slow-burning and across media (appearing, in various guises, in email hoaxes, soap opera storylines, glossy women's magazines and newspapers); and there is an emphasis, in media coverage, on the future or potential crime.

Cautionary tale is a concept that might help us better understand and describe media coverage of crime; indeed, some media stories that have been labelled as instances of moral panic might be better conceptualized as cautionary tales. It is possible, for example, that certain strands of media reporting on child abuse – so frequently grouped together as cases of moral panics – are in fact cautionary tales. We might find, on closer examination, that the coverage of the Madeleine McCann case conformed to the criteria of a cautionary tale. Certainly, it was the mother's behaviour that was frequently marginalized in reports, newspaper articles issued a range of warnings concerning possible future crimes, while email hoaxes about holiday kidnappings of children proliferated. The media coverage on 'identity theft', too, may well fit the cautionary tale paradigm: certainly this is a crime that has been the subject of various email hoaxes, films, as well as newspaper articles. We also get, importantly, rhetoric of precaution directed at future victims: we are frequently enjoined, by newspaper reports, to shred our mail, hide our PIN when using an ATM and take extra care when using the internet.

It is, however, media coverage of sexual violence that most consistently conforms to the criteria of the cautionary tale. Sexual violence is, of course, one of the most popular subjects for crime news reporting. As Reiner et al. (2003) have demonstrated, while property crime has become less newsworthy in the post–Second World War period, violence, and particularly sexual violence, has become increasingly so. Table 2.1 shows the number of headlines over a two-year period in *the Daily Mail* and *the Sun* that featured specific crime categories to demonstrate the different levels of reporting on different types of crime.

Cases of murder, as Reiner et al. (2003) also found, are particularly likely to make headline news, even though it is an extraordinarily rare occurrence. Rape, too, is subject to a very high level of reporting relative to terrorism and theft: like murder it is a staple of crime news reporting. When we look more closely at the substance of these articles on rape we find something very interesting indeed. I took a random sub-sample of 120 articles to look at the core themes in reporting,

Table 2.1 The number of headlines in *the Daily Mail/ the Mail on Sunday* and *the Sun* containing specific search terms from 7 December 2008 to 7 December 2010

Search term	Daily Mail/ Mail on Sunday	Sun	Total
Burglary/Burglar/Theft	36	298	334
Terrorism/Terrorist	75	216	291
Murder/Murderer	247	1,575	1,822
Rape/Rapist	144	1,026	1,170

Note: Parameters were set such that search terms appeared 'in the headline', duplicate versions of stories were discarded and newswires excluded.
Source: Lexis Nexis.

and the results were really quite instructive. For one thing, while a significant proportion of reports concern matters of legal reform and policing, individual cases of those who have been convicted or acquitted, a very significant number (14% or 12%) are about women apparently 'crying wolf'.

Beyond this, and to be closer to the purposes of this chapter, what we see is a range of articles about specific (media-created) sub-categories of assault. We have articles about rapes committed by taxi drivers, holiday rapes, campus rapes, alcohol-induced rapes, stories about women being lured by con-men, footballers and men grooming them on internet 'dating sites', rapes at music festivals, police officers committing rape, women being lured to and then assaulted at posh hotels or mansions. To be clear, and as we see below, in each case these are stories that are centrally about the risks of, for example, taking a taxi on one's own or attending a music festival. In total, over a fifth (26) of the articles about rape – one of the most frequently reported crimes in the two newspapers for the period – tells us stories about incautious women who have been tricked, who should know better, who have been too trusting, and have paid the cost. The familiar rhetoric of precaution that we commonly find in cautionary tales is evident in many of the articles. Take, for example, the first line of an article on an incident of 'campus rape': 'Women students have been warned to lock windows and doors at their halls of residence after two freshers were raped in their first week at university' (*Daily Mail*, 7 October 2009: 12). Later in the article female students are advised to collect and wear personal alarms, walk together, place lockable bolts on windows and keep to well-lit public routes. The offenders, in contrast, are mentioned only halfway through this lengthy article.

We could also look at the articles on rapes committed by taxi drivers. Of the 1,170 newspaper articles in *Daily Mail* and *Sun* that are about rape during the two-year period, 27 of them (2.3%) concern assaults carried out by taxi drivers. Interestingly, a number of the reports (5) concern assaults that have occurred in taxis while women were on a holiday; in this sense, stories of 'taxi rape' overlap with tales of 'holiday rape'. When we look closely at the tone and structure of reports, we find that there is a clear emphasis on female victim behaviour and, strangely, considering the nature of the assaults, a limited concern with the perpetrator. One article, entitled 'Ditch that IT Bag and Heels, Girls, and Dust Off the Rape Alarm', links the revealing clothes promoted by bands like Girls Aloud with the crimes of taxicab rapists (Jones, 29 March 2009: Femail supplement). Other articles warn about the importance of checking a taxi driver's credentials, the loneliness of taxi ranks, not taking a taxi on one's own and refusing any drink from the driver. As with DFSA, the articles are centrally aimed at providing a lesson in how to avoid victimization; it is quite clearly female victim behaviour, rather than that of the taxi driver, that is marginalized. We see this expressed most clearly in the poster produced by the charity Cabwise, a service set up by Transport of London to warn women of the dangers posed by taxi drivers (see Figure 2.1).

The media coverage of 'taxi rape' encapsulates certain core themes in reporting on 'holiday rape', 'festival rape', 'campus rape' and the other media-created sub-categories of sexual assault mentioned above: no one can be trusted, even people in positions of authority (policemen and taxi drivers); being away from home on one's own (at a festival, at university, on holiday) is intrinsically dangerous; and, above all else, it is a lack of responsibility on the part of victims (as opposed to male deviance) that needs castigating.

Accounting for cautionary tales

How are we to explain the existence of cautionary tales in the media? One possible explanation lies in the changing institutional pressures on newspapers. In *Flat Earth News* (2008), Nick Davies shows that commercial pressures on newspapers have led to an increased reliance on material from the Press Agency. As a consequence, press releases from crime prevention charities are increasingly likely to form the basis of news reports. They also, of course, tend to employ a warning tone and advertise future crime problems.

However, while the reliance on press releases might help explain the existence of such articles it does not explain the *salience* of the cautionary tale. One

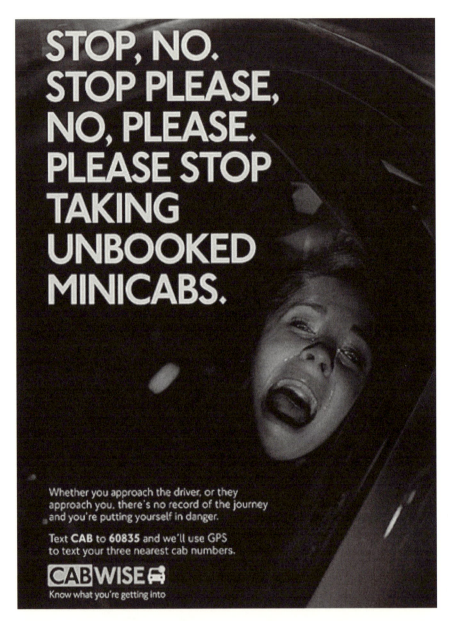

Figure 2.1 Poster produced by cabwise warning of the dangers of 'taxi rape'
Source: 'Get Home Safely', *Cosmopolitan*, http://www.cosmopolitan.co.uk/_mobile/lifestyle/get-home-safely-96801?ignoreCache=1 (accessed 17 December 2009).

argument that has become particularly influential in explaining changes in media coverage of crime concerns the rise of a risk discourse in reporting, and this might provide a framework for understanding the cautionary tale. Ungar (2001) suggests that, in attending to the media's role in stirring up anxiety, reporting on risk has become more important than more traditional moral panic reporting in the past few decades. Ungar argues that the risks of 'reflexive modernization' – ecological disaster, nuclear fallout, and threats connected to medical intervention and discovery – have become more salient for the public in late modern societies, opening up 'new sites of social anxiety' (2001: 271). Unpredictable and uncontrollable, the threats tied up with the 'risk society' are subject to a distinctive form of reporting, Ungar argues, one in which blame is diffused, the concepts of folk devil and social control are less salient, and coverage is extended, rather than volatile. While Ungar's interest rests squarely on reporting on accidents, it is possible to see coverage of cautionary tales from a risk society perspective, and as reflecting what he sees as the new landscape of public fear. One thing that is particularly striking in the cautionary tale is its reliance on a precautionary rhetoric and the insistence that though risks cannot be eliminated, they can be limited through preventative behaviour (not taking a taxi on one's own, watching one's drink and so on). The cautionary tale requires precisely the sort of reflexivity, future-orientation and commitment to mitigation that we would expect in a risk society.

It also requires a strong sense of personal responsibility for risk, and this is something that Ungar does not touch upon, focused, as he is, on the big technological accidents to which late modernity gives rise, as opposed to the everyday experience of risk. For other risk theorists, however, the emphasis on one's personal duty to guard against the more mundane risks of health and safety – what those involved in Criminology and the Sociology of Health commonly refer to as 'responsibilization' – is a core feature of the risk society. Alan Hunt (2003) is among the most articulate in discussing this, arguing that risk has become a moralizing discourse, that is, a rhetorical means of allocating blame and urging self-constraint. In this respect, the *discourse* of risk might be new and distinctive, but, in terms of its function, it participates in rather more enduring social processes. As Hunt puts it, 'in the nineteenth century "the moral" was a distinctive genre; things were considered as "wrong" or "immoral". Increasingly, morality has come to function through proxies, not in its own voice, but in and through other discursive forms, the two most important and closely related being the discourse of "harm" and "risk"' (Hunt 2003: 166).

We might recognize the language of risk and precaution as being distinctive to contemporary society, but, as a mechanism for demarcating appropriate and inappropriate behaviour, it is simply a proxy for, or contemporary manifestation of, morality. I want to argue here that we should resist seeing the cautionary tale simply as a corollary of the risk society, but should recognize its role as a moralizing discourse. With this in mind, it is interesting to note that there are recognizable cautionary tales in early twentieth-century news reporting, and long before the onset of a full risk society. If we look at the British media coverage of 'dope girls' in the 1920s, for example, we find striking similarities to the coverage of DFSA in terms of the tenor of reporting and the behaviour which excites disapproval. 'Dope girls' were young, otherwise respectable women who were being drawn into a world of drug-taking by so-called dope fiends. Both Marek Kohn (2001) and Virginia Berridge (1999) have written about a particular strand of media reporting that emphasized the wantonness of 'dope girls'; they were represented as characteristically impressionable young women who, giddy from their newfound independence during the war, were venturing into the West End unchaperoned to sample the high life – with disastrous consequences. Articles have, as Kohn points out, a didactic quality (Kohn 2001: 5); they warn of the danger of being on one's own and unguarded hedonism, both of which apparently make one a willing victim of the new drug underworld. It is easy to see the lesson here: articles are explicit in their condemnation of a new 'unconstrainable class' (Kohn 2001: 5) of women, and their lack of regard for the traditional norms of feminine decorum that make venturing into a public space, unchaperoned and at night an indiscretion. When we look at cautionary tales in general, this seems to be a common theme. The sites of crime in cautionary tales are nightclubs, bars and holiday destinations, as well as the places that aid our conduit between these places, such as taxis and city streets. There is a particular interest in situations that involve young women being away from home for the first time, whether at university or a music festival. There is, in short, an ongoing concern in cautionary tales with women's autonomous movement and decision making, their embracing of a licentious lifestyle – of drunkenness, sex, staying-out-all-hours – and their willingness to do it all unaccompanied.

It is possible to suggest from this that cautionary tales, like moral panics, are prompted by specific social-cultural conditions or tensions. More specifically, cautionary tales are likely to arise during periods in which a society is particularly concerned about the nature and extent of female emancipation, when the 'moral barricades' need to be manned, as Cohen has it ([1972] 2002: 9). It is no coincidence that the cautionary tale about dope girls was concurrent with British women enjoying new political rights (chiefly, of course, the vote) and increased involvement in work. Nor is it surprising that cautionary tales would proliferate in a post-1970s era, one in which gender relations have undergone profound shifts (both structural and cultural). In both instances – the post–First World War era and the post-1970s era – women have achieved greater freedom in terms of work, education and leisure that has often eventuated in their greater presence in universities, workplaces and nightclubs. Cautionary tales warn, among other things, about the risks of this freedom extending too far, becoming too complete and being enjoyed too freely. The emphasis on precaution that we find in cautionary tales is partly directed toward this, but the rhetoric employed urges something further; a constant self-monitoring. The cautionary tale instructs us in the dangers of failing to 'watch yourself' – to, quite literally, see yourself through someone else's eyes, whether that is an opportunistic drink-spiker who espies an unguarded drink, a taxi driver who spots an immodestly-dressed woman, or a dope fiend who sees a young woman trawling the streets with the insouciance of a prostitute. The implication is clear: a lack of self-reflexivity and a refusal or failure to recognize the dangers that unhindered autonomy brings equate to an abnegation of personal responsibility (or, put differently, an openness to victimization). Matters of responsibility, reflexivity and alertness to threats might be conveyed through a language of risk, but what is really interesting here is how the former operate as a means of moral regulation. It is to this idea that we now turn.

Moral panics and cautionary tales as forms of moral regulation

I want to propose that we see cautionary tales, like moral panics, as a distinctive form of moral regulation. As I discuss further below, this is by no means to collapse the boundaries between any of these concepts – this chapter is, after all, directed towards highlighting the need for greater conceptual clarity – but rather to show up what we might gain, in terms of theoretical understanding, by exploring the role of cautionary tales in moral regulation. It is also worth noting, from the outset, that the notion that moral panics constitute a form of moral regulation is a relatively contentious point. As Hier (2002) explains, moral regulation theorists (Alan Hunt included) are generally resistant to the idea. This is partly because while moral regulation projects urge 'long term processes of normalization' (Hier 2002: 328), moral panics are characteristically volatile and occur when moral regulation has apparently failed. They signal a *sudden rupture* in the social order. Simon Watney ([1987] 1997: 41–2), in his classic study of the British media's treatment of AIDS, notices something similar about moral panics, arguing that this form of media coverage simply shows up the 'current front-line' in an ideological struggle, and fails to capture the long-term and culturally diffused elements of that struggle.

Nonetheless, for Hier (2002: 326), the insistence upon the distinctiveness of moral panics and moral regulation projects masks the fact that, essentially, both 'involve one set of persons seeking to act on the conduct of others', and both are drawing out for us parameters of rightful behaviour. Certainly, by strictly indicating what constitutes wrongful behaviour moral panics produce moral demarcation lines that instruct us on what it means to belong to the moral majority; ultimately, 'thou shalt not' is just as much of an indication of how to act normatively as 'though shalt'. Beyond this, there is, of course, a very strong emphasis in moral panics on what 'right-minded' people should think about an incident or group; expressing in common[unison] these common sentiments of outrage helps reaffirm our commitment to society. As Erikson (1966: 4), in his classic study of witchcraft, puts it, 'the deviant individual violates rules of conduct which the rest of the community holds in high respect; when these people come together to express their outrage over the offense and to bear witness against the offender, they develop a tighter bond of solidarity than existed earlier'.

In this sense, and as Kappeler and Kappeler (2004: 178) have it, 'crime problems become calls to moral action'. The concept of moral panic helps illuminate this moral register. There are, however, other distinct forms of media coverage that operate as moralizing discourses, among them the cautionary tale. In fact, this form of media coverage more obviously conforms to the moral regulation framework as articulated by Hier, because cautionary tales are most certainly part of 'long-term processes of normalization'. The rhetoric surrounding the crimes of DFSA and 'taxi driver assault', for example, reflects a culturally embedded set of ideas concerning female culpability for sexual violence. That cautionary tales are slow-burning, operate across media and are affirmative of social norms suggest that it is appropriate to see this form of media coverage in terms of moral regulation. In fact, if we imagine moral regulation as a spectrum of projects or discursive practices, it might be productive to see the cautionary tale and moral panic as operating at alternative ends of the continuum. This is evident if we look at the manner in which each apportions blame and responsibility, key features of any moralizing discourse. As Mary Douglas (1986) demonstrates, the social process of blaming is central to the maintenance of moral solidarity and regulation. In her writing about risk she identifies two central processes of blaming: outsider blaming and victim blaming (1986: 59). The former enhances loyalty to mainstream society by creating or affirming a 'them and us' division. The latter urges the internalization of social controls. Both, Douglas argues, reinforce our ideas about what it means to be a responsible member of a given society. Each operates quite differently, but participates in the achievement of the same goal: group solidarity and moral cohesion. If Douglas is right, and these are the two core processes of blame employed to rhetorically forge social bonds, it is interesting to note that moral panics and cautionary tales map very neatly onto these conceptual distinctions. In moral panics outsider blaming is used to enhance loyalty to mainstream social norms by urging us to recognize that Hoodies, Mods and Rockers, or owners of dangerous dogs are 'nothing like us'. Cautionary tales make use of victim blaming and this facilitates moral regulation in a different fashion, by urging us to accept certain behaviour as necessary and rightful ('watch your drink', 'shred your mail', 'do not trust strangers'). By not adhering to such strictures, one risks not only victimization, but also partial responsibility for falling prey to a criminal.

While the moral panic and cautionary tale might be conceptually distinct from one another, in both cases, moral regulation serves as a useful overarching framework for understanding more fully the role of each as a moralizing discourse. In this respect, though it has a different point of departure, my argument is relatively similar to that put forward recently by Critcher (2009). Critcher is a firm advocate of the idea that the field of moral panic studies needs to engage with wider theoretical debates within Sociology and Criminology, namely the risk society thesis and work on moral regulation, and his recent article seeks to work out the place of the moral panic concept within the latter field. It is also in part a response to the work of Sean Hier, who he sees as collapsing the distinction between moral panics and moral regulation projects, with the effect of extending the meaning of the former so that it encompasses 'potentially any topic' (Critcher 2009: 24). In embracing the idea that moral panics are a form of moral regulation there is certainly a risk that we stretch still further the meaning of the former and neglect the variety of mechanisms employed in pursuit of the latter. I would suggest that such problems are exacerbated by our failure to embrace a wider range of concepts for understanding media coverage of crime. This is discussed further below.

In recommending how we might avoid collapsing the distinction between moral panics and moral regulation projects, Critcher suggests that we see moral regulation in terms of three core dimensions: the 'degree of perceived threat to basic values' (or 'moral order'); 'the extent to which there is identified a viable solution' (or 'social control'); and the degree to which 'moral regulation of others is represented as requiring ethical formation of the self' (or 'governmentality') (2009: 25–6). Each of these dimensions is then conceptualized in terms of different levels of social problem construction (high, intermediate/ambiguous and low levels, in Critcher's parlance). In terms of moral order, for example, there are occasions when problems are 'successfully constructed as threats' (those operating at this 'high' level are moral panics), other occasions when a problem is perceived by some but not all to be a genuine and significant threat (the example Critcher uses is internet pornography), and still other occasions when a problem is subject to a moral discourse but is not ordinarily perceived to be a threat to moral order (such as STDs) (Critcher 2009: 26–7). In terms of social control Critcher again outlines three different levels: situations where laws can be passed to regulate behaviour, where laws are seen to be problematic and/or ineffective and where laws are completely inappropriate. Again, moral panics operate at the first, or highest, level here. Finally, Critcher outlines three different levels in terms of the dimension of governmentality: self-regulation; regulation that balances self-regulation and control of others (such as in the case of sexual violent content); and regulation that is directed at others (this is the level at which moral panics operate).

In short, in terms of Critcher's schema, moral panics are agreed-upon threats to the moral order, involve legislative and official action and call for the regulation of deviant others' behaviour. A significant number of the issues that are described as moral panics, Critcher points out, simply do not operate on these levels. Take something like obesity, which is an issue that we might rightly see in terms of moral regulation but not, according to Critcher's schema, as a moral panic (for one thing, key to its construction is the notion that it is a problem requiring self-regulation, as opposed to the regulation of others).

I very much welcome Critcher's insistence upon conceptual clarity here. What would help further, I think, is opening up the discussion so that we not only acknowledge but also properly conceptualize other forms of media coverage that operate as forms of moral regulation. Fully attending to alternative paradigms for studying media coverage of crime – and, in turn, considering their relationship to the moral regulation framework – would have the effect of tightening up conceptual distinctions (not only between moral panic and cautionary tale, but also between moral panic and moral regulation). This does not mean schematizing for the sake of it. It might be gratifying to find that the cautionary tale 'fits' Critcher's model[2] (this, after all, suggests the commensurability of this and the moral regulation concept), but gaining a fuller understanding of the moralizing discourses we find in media coverage of crime should surely be our overarching goal.

Notes

1 There are, of course, notable moral panics where the 'folk devil' is female – Goode and Ben-Yehuda ([1994] 2009), for example, write about the moral panic concerning witchcraft in Medieval Europe, and several researchers have detailed the recent moral panic concerning female gangs and violence (so-called ladettes). What is interesting, though, is that such cases involve traditionally masculine traits being imputed to the females in question: the 'folk devil' is 'women acting like men', in other words. Perhaps, then, the cultural preoccupation with the male deviant is more accurately described as a preoccupation with the connections between traditional masculinity and deviance.

2 It is very rarely seen as a threat to the moral order, operates at the intermediate level in terms of social control and requires self-regulation.

Bibliography

Berridge, V. (1999), *Opium and the People: Opiate Use and Drug Control Policy in Nineteenth and Early Twentieth Century England*, London: Free Association Books.

Bourke, J. (2007), *Rape: A History from 1860 to the Present*, London: Virago.

Burgess, A., Donovan, P. and Moore, S. E. H. (2009), 'Embodying Uncertainty? Understanding Heightened Risk Perception of Drink "Spiking"', *British Journal of Criminology*, 49(6): 848–62.

Cohen, S. ([1972] 2002), *Folk Devils and Moral Panics: The Creation of the Mods and Rockers*, 3rd edn, London: Routledge.

Critcher, C. (2009), 'Widening the Focus: Moral Panics as Moral Regulation', *British Journal of Criminology*, 49(1): 17–34.

Daily Mail (2009), 'Rape Alert at University after Two Freshers Are Attacked on Same Day in Same Halls of Residence', 7 October, 12.

Davies, N. (2008), *Flat Earth News: An Award Winning Reporter Exposes Falsehood, Distortion, and Propaganda in the Global Media*, London: Chatto and Windus.

Douglas, M. ([1985] 1986), *Risk Acceptability According to the Social Sciences*, London: Routledge.

Erikson, K. T. (1966), *Wayward Puritans: A Study in the Sociology of Deviance*, Basingstoke: Macmillan.

Goode, E. and Ben-Yehuda, N. ([1994] 2009), *Moral Panics: The Social Construction of Deviance*, 2nd edn, Oxford: Wiley-Blackwell.

Hall, S., Critcher, C., Jefferson, T., Clarke, J. and Roberts, B. (1978), *Policing the Crisis: Mugging, the State, and Law and Order*, Basingstoke: Palgrave Macmillan.

Hay, C. (1995), 'Mobilization through Interpellation: James Bulger, Juvenile Crime and the Construction of a Moral Panic', *Social & Legal Studies*, 4(2): 197–223.

Hier, S. P. (2002), 'Conceptualizing Moral Panic through a Moral Economy of Harm', *Critical Sociology*, 28(3): 311–34.

Hunt, Alan (2003), 'Risk and Moralization in Everyday Life', in R. V. Ericson and A. Doyle (eds), *Risk and Morality*, Toronto: University of Toronto Press, 165–92.

Hunt, Arnold (1997), '"Moral Panic" and Moral Language in the Media', *British Journal of Sociology*, 48(4): 629–48.

Jenkins, P. (2004), *Moral Panic: Changing Concepts of the Child Molester in Modern America*, Connecticut: Yale University Press.

Jones, L. (2009), 'Ditch That It Bag and Heels, Girls, and Dust Off the Rape Alarm', *Daily Mail*, 29 March, Femail supplement.

Kappeler, V. E. and Kappeler, A. E. (2004), 'Speaking of Evil and Terrorism: The Political and Ideological Construction of a Moral Panic', in M. Deflem (ed.), *Terrorism and Counter Terrorism: Criminological Perspectives*, Oxford: Elselvier, 75–97.

Kohn, M. (2001), *Dope Girls: The Birth of the British Drug Underground*, London: Granta.

McRobbie, A. and Thornton, S. L. (1995), 'Rethinking "Moral Panic" for Multi-Mediated Social Worlds', *British Journal of Sociology*, 46(4): 559–74.

Moore, S. E. H. (2009), 'Cautionary Tales: Drug-Facilitated Sexual Assault in the British Media', *Crime, Media, Culture*, 5(3): 305–20.

Reiner, R., Livingstone, S. and Allen, J. (2003), 'From Law and Order to Lynch Mobs: Crime News Since the Second World War', in P. Mason (ed.), *Criminal Visions: Media Representation of Crime and Justice*, Willan: Cullompton, 13–32.

Rothe, D. and Muzzatti, S. L. (2004), 'Enemies Everywhere: Terrorism, Moral Panic, and US Civil Society', *Critical Criminology*, 12: 327–50.

Springhall, J. (1998), *Youth, Popular Culture and Moral Panics: Penny Gaffs to Gangsta Rap, 1830–1996*, London: St Martin's Press.

Squires, P. (2009), 'The Knife Crime "Epidemic" and British Politics', *British Politics*, 4(1): 127–57.

Squires, P. and Goldsmith, C. (2010), 'Bullets, Blades and Mean Streets: Youth Violence and Criminal Justice Failure', in C. Barter and D. Berridge (eds), *Children Behaving Badly? Peer Violence between Children and Young People*, Oxford: Wiley, 199–215.

Ungar, S. (2001), 'Moral Panic versus the Risk Society: The Implications of the
Changing Sites of Social Anxiety', *British Journal of Sociology*, 52(2): 271–91.

Watney, S. ([1987] 1997), *Policing Desire: Pornography, AIDS and the Media*, 3rd edn,
Minnesota: University of Minnesota Press.

Welch, M., Price, E. A. and Yankey, N. (2002), 'Moral Panic over Youth Violence:
Wilding and the Manufacture of Menace in the Media', *Youth & Society*, 34(1): 3–30.

3

The Journalist, Folk Devil

Paul Lashmar

Moral panics and the media

The media are central to Stanley Cohen's conception of moral panic. In *Folk Devils and Moral Panics* he says of the moral panic that 'its nature is presented in a stylized and stereotypical fashion by the mass media'. He states that 'much of this study will be devoted to understanding the role of the mass media in creating moral panics and folk devils' (1972: 17).

Most subsequent debate, at least in the UK, has maintained this centrality of the media. In *Policing the Crisis*, Stuart Hall and his co-authors see the media as being at the heart of creating a moral panic over 'mugging' (Hall et al. 1978). And one of the authors of this work, Chas Critcher, who has in the early years of the twenty-first century attempted to place moral panic theory in a much tighter conceptual framework in order to maintain its relevance, again stresses the importance of media (2003, 2006). Critcher argues that 'modern moral panics are unthinkable without the media, though medieval witch trials managed without them' (2003: 131). He notes that this emphasis on the role of the media is one of the factors which differentiates British approaches to moral panics from US ones, such as the 'attributional' school of moral panic theory lead by Erich Goode and Nachman Ben-Yehuda ([1994] 2009), or the approach taken by the social constructionists. These, he argues, tend to treat the media as mere channels through which passes information about deviance or labels that others have assigned, with little recognition that the media themselves transform information and play a key role in the ways in which individuals or groups are represented as deviant (Critcher 2003: 28–9).

However, by contrast, the approach taken in Canada by Richard Ericson, Patricia Baranek and Janet Chan fully acknowledges that the media have a dynamic role to play in the creation and sustenance of moral panics and is, therefore, closer in this respect to that taken by Hall et al. and Cohen. Thus, for example, they argue that 'news organizations are active in constituting what are social problems and what should be done about them' (1987: 70). And all are concerned, albeit in different ways, with how, precisely, the media do this.

Hall et al. argue that a key way in which the media direct the debate is by giving voice to the primary definers of moral panic; this primary definition then sets the limit for all subsequent discussions of the topic by framing the 'problem' in a particular way. As they put it, 'This initial framework then provides criteria by which all subsequent contributions are labelled as "relevant" to the debate, or "irrelevant" – beside the point. Contributions which stray from this framework are exposed to the charge that they are "not addressing the problem"' (1978: 59). In short, Hall et al. suggest that the media support and publicize the 'dominant ideas' of the powerful with whom they are in a hegemonic relationship while ignoring those without power and who may take a very different point of view. In this framework, the media exclude or even demonize anyone who threatens to upset the status quo. Furthermore, Hall et al. point out that the media can themselves act as primary definers and create stories and issues; they are not merely passive reporters of stories created elsewhere.

To count as a 'classic' moral panic the media's reporting of the issue in question has to be in some way disproportionate. It also has to be motivated by moral concerns and aimed at bringing about some form of change in the law. In this vision of things, the media are seen as moral entrepreneurs who, often in collusion with other moral entrepreneurs, put public pressure on politicians to act; bombarded with the message that Something Must be Done, politicians push through hasty and ill-thought-out legislation. The Dangerous Dogs Act 1997 is often used by moral panic theorists as an example of this process at its worst.

Moral panic theory belongs to that body of sociological and criminological thought which, as John Muncie points out, is less concerned with asking behavioural questions such as 'What causes an individual to commit a deviant act?' than with posing 'definitional and structural questions – why does an act become defined as deviant? deviant to whom? deviant from what?' (1987: 44). However, he also makes the point that the concept of moral panic is an elastic one and 'lacks any precise theoretical grounding'. This, he argues, is in part 'due to its origins lying in a loosely defined labelling perspective rather than a fully blown theory of social structure'. Consequently it can, in his view, 'harbour several diverse theoretical positions and thus opens itself to internal contradiction and criticism from all theoretical sides' (1987: 45). And more recently, even a theorist as sympathetic to the moral panic concept as Critcher has argued that there is a danger that 'moral panics distort our capacity for understanding, even when they appear to recognise a genuine problem' (2003: 117). In recent times, these problems have included phenomena as diverse as happy slapping, helicopter parents, single parents, file sharing, hoodies, boy racers, immigration, binge drinking, gender issues, drug abuse and paedophilia.

The folk devils fight back

As a long-time journalism practitioner, as well as an academic, the question which most interests me about moral panics is this: what does the moral panic concept bring to explaining the way in which the news media work?

As noted above, the moral panic concept has been a much-used tool for identifying and analysing particular social phenomena. That it is still debated after 40 years demonstrates its potential productivity and usefulness. However, it is by no means an all-purpose explanatory tool, and its value as a concept has been frequently challenged, with some critics even suggesting that it is anachronistic and is largely redundant. For example, Angela McRobbie and Sarah Thornton suggested in 1995 that circumstances had changed since the concept had emerged in the 1970s: 'The delicate balance of relations which the moral panic sociologists saw existing between media, agents of social control, folk devils and moral guardians, has given way to a much more complicated and fragmented set of connections. Each of the categories described by moral panics theorists has undergone a process of fissure in the intervening years' (1995: 567). In particular, they suggested that the rise of radical pressure groups of one kind or another have reduced the influence of the traditional moral guardians on the mainstream media and thence on politicians, and that commercial media interests have used the discourse of moral panic simply to attract youthful consumers, thereby devaluing its explanatory potential.

Similarly, Critcher (2006) has observed that Mary de Young's (2004) analysis of the 1980s day-care panic in the United States produced similar reservations. In the United States during the early 1980s, hundreds of day-care providers were accused of sexually abusing their young charges in 'satanic' rituals that included blood drinking, cannibalism and human sacrifice. These allegations of 'ritual' abuse of children then spread quickly outwards to Canada, Europe and Australasia, in spite of rigorous international investigations which found no evidence to corroborate the allegations and warned that a moral panic was exposing day-care providers and other social workers to unnecessary public attention and attracting quite unjustified opprobrium.

But while de Young used the notion of moral panic to conceptualize the 'ritual' abuse scare she also felt that the original concept needed amending and updating. In particular, as Critcher has pointed out, she argued that it needed to be recognized that 'each of Cohen's stages is contestable. All the way from the initial definition and labelling through to measures resorted to, opposition may prove effective' (2006: 253). In Cohen's vision, folk devils tend to be passive victims. De Young's analysis demonstrated that folk devils have developed the capacity to fight back. Thus she details how the day-care providers who were cast as folk devils by what de Young calls 'the child savers' organized and used publicity to counter their persecution.

A deflating phrase

While academics continue to debate the value of the moral panic concept, the term has slipped into the public lexicon and now enjoys a considerable popularity in public discourse. In this respect, de Young argues that Cohen's concept has been 'facilely appropriated by media pundits, social commentators, and the public at large, and its casual use has divested it of much of its sociological relevance. And that is really a shame. It is a robust term, and the theory that surrounds and supports it, although a tad faded and frayed, still has a great deal of explanatory and analytical power' (2004: 4).

Two groups particularly predisposed to using the phrase 'moral panic' are journalists and media students. A search of Lexis Nexis reveals a gradual increase in the use of the phrase in UK national newspapers from the late 1990s onwards, although the prime users are commentators, not news journalists. I can only offer a subjective view of the frequency of its use by students but I have encountered it frequently in both dissertations and essays. Neither of these two groups usually attempts to reference the evolving moral panic framework that gives legitimacy to the use of the phrase. This can be troubling with student academic work, but what is more surprising is that certain academics also use the phrase in published work without reference to any theoretical framework.

In short, the phrase moral panic has all too often become a form of coded shorthand to criticize the media as well as, on occasion, other primary definers. The question then arises: is this intellectual laziness, or the actions of individuals with a political or ideological agenda? In many cases in which someone labels a particular episode a moral panic I feel compelled to ask: Does the writer have a particular ideological position on the subject of the story in question? In this respect, it is worth noting that there has also developed a certain resistance to the concept outside academia. So, for example, on 21 December 1993, in the aftermath of the murder of two-year-old James Bulger, an editorial in *the Independent on Sunday* (hardly a paper associated with the creation of moral panics), argued that 'moral panic is one of those deflating phrases used by sociologists and other allegedly impartial students of human behaviour to condescend to excitements amongst the general populace'. Similarly, a blog on the *Spectator* website which mentioned moral panics elicited the response: 'What is the term "moral panic" doing in *the Spectator*? There are no "moral panics". As objective social phenomena they do not exist; they are just a self-regarding phantasm of the left-liberal imagination'.[1]

Such criticisms suggests that the term also serves a more pernicious purpose, namely to create the impression that certain people take a detached, rational, analytical approach to political and social problems, as opposed to those who exhibit a merely reflexive, knee-jerk response to challenges to received opinions and indeed to anyone who thinks differently from them. In that sense the term is more than just a conceit. It is also profoundly anti-intellectual because it attempts to stifle reasoned debate by portraying contrary points of view as simply subjective and irrational, if not indeed infantile and worthy of nothing but contempt. As such it represents not merely a serious misuse of language but a debasement of its purpose as a means of conducting reasoned argument.

The missing voice

If the concept of moral panic is to be of any theoretical and explanatory value, it must be possible to define a moral panic as a journalistic reaction to an episode or event which is demonstrably and empirically different from the reporting of an episode or event which is not defined as a moral panic. However, in the huge amount of literature on moral panics, I can find no substantive research which has taken into consideration the journalism practitioner's experience, and few practitioners are ever quoted. I find it remarkable that there appears to be no published communication between the theorists of moral panic and the very people who are generally accused of being the perpetrators of disproportionate reporting. I would argue that the moral panic concept is significantly flawed by the failure to take into consideration the practitioner's experience and the processes of journalism more generally.

As a practitioner, I believe that moral panic theory would greatly benefit if the following questions were asked:

- How do media practitioners think about stories identified as moral panics?
- Do journalists/editors write/publish a story with the intention of launching a moral panic?
- What work has been done to demonstrate that moral panics attributed to the media as something negative are different from campaigning journalism that tends to be regarded in a positive light?
- Does calling an episode a moral panic simply reflect the subjective or ideological position of the writer vis-à-vis a particular story or group of related stories?

Jock Young argued, admittedly a long time ago, that it is possible for the media 'rapidly to engineer a moral panic about a certain type of deviancy. Indeed, because of the phenomenon of overexposure – the glut of information over a short space on a topic so that it becomes uninteresting – there is institutionalised into the media the need to create moral panics and issues which will seize the imagination of the public' (1974: 243). But my personal experience as a practitioner is that journalists start with stories, not with the desire to ignite moral panics. When considering the role of the journalist in the creation of a moral panic, it is important to note that the identification of moral panics is almost invariably an ex post facto exercise. Of course, it is true that prior to publication or broadcast, the journalist can sometimes and to some degree judge whether a story is going to create a major reaction. But they rarely know the exact trajectory of any story, and generally have no idea whether the story will later be categorized as a moral panic, not least because the story has to go through several stages before it accrues that definition.

It would, of course, be fair to say that bias or exaggeration in the reporting and editing processes can result in news stories that can then be characterized as a moral panic. Nor would I dispute the fact that there are newspapers

the situation in which market forces were let rip across the media. In terms of broadcasting, this made competition for audiences far more fierce than it had ever been before, and threatened to make it much more like the national press in this respect. In both cases, the consequence was a significant increase in the amount of what has been termed 'market-driven' or 'dumbed-down' journalism or as Nick Davies puts it, the 'mass production of ignorance' (2008: 108). However, it also needs to be stressed that the picture is not entirely bleak, and that certain news organizations – new and old – are still delivering high-quality output and are prepared to undertake and fund investigative journalism which is genuinely in the public interest.

In his recent writing, Chas Critcher has attempted to come to grips with all of these changes in the news production process, in particular arguing against the over-simplification contained in the very concept of the *mass* media and warning of the danger of generalizing about the media as a monolithic whole. As he quite rightly puts it, 'It is important not to elide distinctions between different types of institutions (broadcasting and the press); newspapers (up-market, mid-market and down-market); constituencies (local and national); and genre (hard news and background exploration)' (2003: 131–2). But even Critcher does not investigate the experience of the news practitioner and the actual processes by which news is originated.

In the absence of any academic engagement with practitioners, factors that practitioners would consider key to any understanding of the news production process are thus still absent from theoretical discussions of the role played by the media in the moral panic process.

Facts versus opinion

When analysing media coverage, theorists rarely distinguish between the role of the reporter and the role of the commentator/columnist/pundit, and yet the relationship between the two is very important for understanding the trajectory of a story. While reporters tend to be involved from stage one of the story, columnists tend to become involved only when the story has achieved some level of traction with the audience and wider public, although it does have to be admitted that this is not true in all cases and that the increasing pace of news delivery has reduced the time between something being a news story and then the subject of comment.

On certain occasions commentators appear on the scene quickly, as in the James Bulger case – another story to have taken on the dimensions of a classic moral panic. The James Bulger murder story broke on 13 February 1993, and three days later there was an opinion-based piece by Melanie Phillips and Martin Kettle in *the Guardian*, headed 'The Murder of Innocence' and arguing that 'the case of James Bulger exposes once again our society's growing indifference and our own increasing isolation. He trusted a stranger and now he is dead'. This murder has become iconic in the moral panics canon as a story which, it is argued, should have been about the issue of children who had fallen through every safety net which should have stopped them from becoming killers, into a moral panic about (1) 'video nasties' (Barker and Petley 1997; Petley 2011: 87–114); and (2) evil children (Thompson 1998: 95–106).

The reporter/commentator, news/views contamination issue used to be unique to newspapers but it is has even spread into public service broadcasting where specialist reporters comment via blogs. Everybody, it seems, has an opinion, and not least when using the internet.

The audience

Thinking about moral panic in the way in which I am suggesting also leads onto a broader and yet again under-researched and under-theorized area – namely the relationship between journalists and their audiences. Journalists are keenly aware of their audiences because quite simply they depend for survival on fulfilling their requirements. When preparing their students for life in the news media, journalism academics teach them to be always aware of their audience. 'Who is your audience?' we ask, 'What is your audience's age, background and interests?', and 'Is your news report geared to your audience?' A news agenda aimed at the 18–25-year-old age group may have to be very different from a report aimed at a middle-aged audience. And yet the impact of this approach to news-making is still an under-researched area.

When one looks at *the Express* or *the Mail*, for example, one can see just how effectively they select material that will appeal to their audience. So when these newspapers run attacks on immigration, the EU, human rights, 'benefit scroungers' and so on; they are very carefully targeting their audience. Herein lies the $64 million question: at which point is the journalist ceasing to inform their audience (which is supposed to be journalism's raison d'être) and is instead merely confirming and reinforcing their prejudices, either in order to conform to the paper's ideological line or to deliver a story which the journalist knows will help sell the paper to its target readership?

Journalists tend to defend their profession by stating they have a duty to inform the population by delivering the truth. Yet practising spin and bias and delivering stories which may be only partly true (or indeed wholly untrue) merely in order to appeal to your audience is simply not journalism. As Richard Peppiatt said about his former employment at *the Daily Star* in his evidence to the Leveson Inquiry, 'The truth (and by this I mean a moral, as opposed to legalistic truth) is treated with such flippancy, and their motivations so capitalistic as opposed to journalistic, as to be a prime example of the gross irresponsibility that has engulfed this country's tabloid press, and for which I am ashamed to have been part' (2011: 5).

As gatekeepers, journalists make decisions about story selection and impose their agency at every turn. It is, of course, easy to decry *the Star* or *the Mail* for these practices, but to a greater or lesser degree all journalists practise these techniques. For example, *the Guardian* is very well aware of the interests of its readers. Are its stories selected in order to confirm their biases? How ready are *the Guardian*, *The Times* or *the Telegraph* to run stories that may conflict with their audience's beliefs and values, even if these stories are true? This area is under-researched and under-theorized by academics but is also ignored by practitioners, most of whom will simply argue that journalism is an instinctive process, thus avoiding difficult issues such as confirmatory bias and editorial power, not to mention the nature of truth.

The second point about audiences is that, once established, they rarely exercise their power in any orchestrated way. Every journalist is only too conscious that if the audience does not buy the newspaper its future is in peril. The audience thus has the ultimate sanction. Only once have I seen an audience exert real, if still limited, collective pressure on a newspaper. This was when, on 19 April 1989, four days after the Hillsborough football disaster in Sheffield in which 96 people lost their lives, *the Sun* used 'The Truth' as its front page headline, followed by three sub-headlines: 'Some fans picked pockets of victims', 'Some fans urinated on the brave cops' and 'Some fans beat up PC giving kiss of life', all thus alleging truly appalling behaviour by Liverpool FC fans. There was public outrage in Liverpool over what was seen as an outrageous smear and the newspaper was boycotted by most newsagents in the city. Many readers cancelled orders and refused to buy from shops that stocked it. The Hillsborough Justice Campaign also organized a less successful national boycott that nevertheless did have an impact on the paper's sales. The key question here, of course, is: who were the primary definers of the initial Hillsborough coverage? And, in particular, did the police feed the press with such stories in order to distract attention from their culpability for what happened? (Scraton et al. 1995)

Too often accounts of moral panic ignore the audience, and when they do acknowledge them they appear to regard them as all too readily duped. There is more than a whiff of the old Marxist approach here, with the audience conceptualized as monolithic, easily influenced and sheep-like. However, there is considerable evidence outside the domain of moral panic theorizing that audiences are plural, active and have varying levels of trust and belief in the various different media which they use. In the present context it is particularly worth noting that there is evidence that newspaper readers are well aware of the differences in the trustworthiness of different types of newspapers. For example, an Edelmann survey published in January 2012 showed that of the public sampled: 68 per cent of UK readers distrust tabloids and 47 per cent trust broadsheets (Table 3.1).

Barnett analysed YouGov data in 2008 that showed that slightly more than six in ten said that they trusted BBC news journalists a great deal or a fair amount. A little more than half gave the same response for Channel 4 and ITV journalists. At the other end of the scale came the print journalists, with fewer than one in six prepared to trust red-top journalists, and only slightly more for the mid-market titles (Barnett 2008).

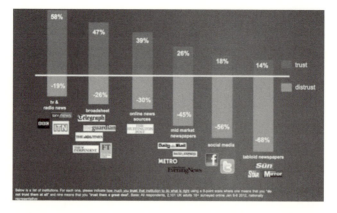

Table 3.1 Audiences have nuanced perception of which media can be trusted
Source: Curtis 2012.

Table 3.2 The audience trusts television journalists more than newspaper journalist counterparts

	% saying they trust a 'great deal' or a 'fair amount'	% saying they don't trust 'very much' or 'at all'	Difference
BBC news journalists	61	34	+27
Channel 4 news journalists	52	39	+13
ITV news journalists	51	43	+8
journalists on up-market newspapers	44	49	−5
journalists on local newspapers	39	55	−16
journalists on mid-market newspapers	19	75	−56
journalists on red-top newspapers	15	83	−68

Source: Barnett (2008: 8).

For most of my career, journalists and editors have been acutely aware that the media outlet for which they work has a degree of cultural capital, in this case a reputation accumulated over the years built based on the quality of the journalism which it produces. Reporting which can be shown to be inaccurate or disproportionate lowers the cultural capital of the outlet in which it is found, and this can have serious consequences for the up-market press in particular. It could be argued that this is not true of more down-market publications, but it should be noted that Rupert Murdoch closed the *News of the World* precisely because the revelation of its reckless journalistic methods expenditure not only caused readers and advertisers to desert it but threatened to put at risk both the cultural and financial value of the entirety of News Corp (Table 3.2).

Disproportionality

As we have seen, there are various models of moral panic, but common to all of them is 'disproportionality', the idea that public concern about something is not proportionate to its actual harmfulness. As Cohen puts it, 'The very usage of the term moral panic . . . implies that societal reaction is disproportionate to the actual seriousness (risk, damage, threat) of the event. The reaction is always *more* severe (hence exaggerated, irrational, unjustified) than the condition (event, threat, behaviour, risk) warrants'. However, he also recognizes that critics have had difficulties with the notion of disproportionality, in particular asking:

> Why is this just assumed? And on what grounds is the sociologist's view always correct, rational and justified? Even in these limited terms, the assumption of disproportionality is problematic. How can the exact gravity of the reaction and the condition be assessed and compared with each other? Are we talking about intensity, duration, extensiveness? Moreover, the argument goes, we have neither the quantitative, objective criteria to claim that R (the reaction) is 'disproportionate' to A (the action) nor the universal moral criteria to judge that T is an 'inappropriate' response to the moral gravity of A. (2002: xxviii)

In Cohen's view, however, 'this objection makes sense if there is nothing beyond a compendium of individual moral judgements. Only with prior commitment to "external" goals such as social justice, human rights or equality can we evaluate any one moral panic or judge it as more specious than another' (2002: xxviii). And, as he also notes, it is possible in certain cases to adduce empirical evidence in order to demonstrate that a panic is disproportionate to the danger posed by the cause of the panic. An example here would be having recourse to actual immigration figures in order to dispute the claim that the country is being 'flooded' by immigrants.

However, the question remains: how do journalists judge proportionality? This has not been asked. No one would, of course, disagree that media reporting is sometimes exaggerated or disproportionate. Some media moral positions are so contrived and attention-seeking that it has become common among certain comedians to satirize the media, and the experts and politicians on whom they draw, for their moral attitudinizing, and to accuse certain papers of whipping up moral panics in order to increase their sale. And an excellent example of just how easy it is to whip up is provided by Chris Morris in the episode of the series *Brass Eye* (Channel 4, 1997), in which he gets various assorted pundits and politicians to inveigh against the wholly fictional drug 'Cake'.

But who, ultimately, is the judge of disproportionately? We all have had the experience of thinking that something is disproportionate but how do we remove our own subjectivity and measure it, particularly if empirical evidence is unavailable or ambiguous? Again, as with the phrase moral panic itself, can the word 'disproportionate' be a code for something which we don't like for ideological or other reasons? Indeed, even empirically demonstrated cases of moral panics are all too rare. As Critcher notes of the study by Williams and Dickinson (1993) of newspaper crime reporting, '[This] is an example of a comparatively rare effort in moral panic analysis: to trace how far media coverage, in this case readership of particular newspapers, has discernible effect on how audiences view their social experience' (2006: 190).

Iconic and signal moments

Another aspect of journalism practice that does not seem recognized by moral panic theorists is what I would describe as iconic and signal moments and how these interact with moral panics.

Cohen argues in *Folk Devils and Moral Panics* that the media, police, local authorities, courts and the public overreacted to what was really a limited case of anti-social behaviour. He may well be right, and it could be an acute case of what moral panic theorists tend to call the 'deviancy amplification spiral'. But this jars with the fact that whenever the emergence of modern youth culture in the UK is discussed in print or on television it is usually illustrated by photographs of Mods and Rockers in confrontation. What happened on those beaches between 1964 and 1966 was an iconic moment in the development not simply of youth culture but of British society. If, as Cohen suggests, the conflict was minimal and was blown out of all proportion by the media and the authorities, why does it remain so iconic in the collective memory? Are these images iconic only because they are the product of a moral panic? Or are these images iconic because they capture a signal moment in time? These are obvious questions, but Cohen does not tackle them.

Journalists, on the other hand, are very aware of capturing the iconic or signal moment. They recognize that a particular event can represent to the public an important social or cultural moment. Therefore, the fact that an event is a one-off, or part of a series of linked events which is happening for the first time, does not make media coverage of it automatically disproportionate or moral panic-inducing. It may be symbolic of an important new trend in society, and the journalist works with the first draft of history not knowing which way it is heading.

Moral concern

The very phrase moral panic is problematic, as Cohen himself admits, 'because of its connotation with irrationality and being out of control' (2002: xxvii). As de Young puts it, 'The term "moral panic" has the most unfortunate tendency to conjure up images of folks frantically fending off more demons than hell can hold (2004: 1). Nor has it helped that the phrase has passed into certain areas of journalistic discourse where its 'loose and often ironic use has compounded the term's original ambiguities' (Critcher 2003: 132). 'Panic' is a colourful and exaggerated term used to make a point. But it needs to be noted that there are many media reports that create moral concern, and that the term 'moral concern' is quite different from and has none of the pithiness or rhetorical impact of moral panic.

The phrase moral panic may be a very convenient form of rhetorical shorthand, but it faces redundancy unless it can be fitted into a more nuanced, and also more empirically informed, framework. Thus I suggest that the stand-alone concept of moral panic needs to be replaced by a continuum of moral concern, which allows for factors such as disproportionality and panic but also justified moral indignation and outrage. It must also recognize, however, that one person's moral panic is another person's real concern, and that much great campaigning journalism is motivated by moral concerns. But what is it that makes one example of campaigning journalism an invitation to moral panic, and another an exposé of a social evil? Does our assessment depend simply on our political and ideological perspective? This was a problem addressed, albeit in a different context by former senior journalist at *The Times* and now Head of Journalism at City University, George Brock, in his 2010 inaugural lecture in which he warned of the increased use of 'synthetic' moral indignation by certain media outlets. In his view, this is poor journalism because it devalues the outlets' moral capital and does not resonate with the public, thus jeopardizing and undermining the very existence of the outlets in question.

Baby P: A case of moral panic?

As we have seen, the concept of moral panic is a very elastic one, and the term has often been used loosely and inconsistently. So, in an attempt to answer some of the points raised above, let us examine the case of Baby P as a possible moral panic.

Baby P was a 17-month-old boy who died in Haringey, North London, after suffering more than 50 injuries over an 8-month period, during which he was repeatedly seen by Haringey Children's Services and NHS health professionals. He was eventually killed by his mother's boyfriend. Baby P's identity, Peter

Connelly, was eventually revealed when his killers were named after the expiry of a court anonymity order on 10 August 2009.

However, the story as reported in the media, and especially sections of the press, soon turned out to be more about the incompetence of social workers rather than the degeneracy of a society where a child can be so brutally treated. Moral panic theorists tend to suggest that the social workers concerned (and, by extension, social workers in general) came to be represented as 'folk devils'. It has been suggested that the Baby P case was a moral panic in which the media response to a dreadful event was nonetheless disproportionate and with the wrong emphasis. As Ann Karpf pointed out, moral panic theorists such as Cohen suggested that the Baby P story bore 'all the hallmarks of a classic moral panic. Not because it isn't shocking, but as the attention is fixed on social workers, it switches attention from moral issues to technical decisions about risk (who should have intervened at this stage rather than that?) as a way of getting rid of our anxiety' (2008). It is also worth noting here that the idea that social workers are habitually demonized, and particularly at times of perceived societal failure, is not new (see in particular Franklin and Parton (1991) for detailed discussion of this pattern of reportage).

Moral panic theorists thus have tended to suggest that the media focus on the Baby P case was directed at the wrong issues. However, although it may well be true that papers such as *the Mail, the Express* and *the Sun* have a deep ideological dislike of social workers, does that make social workers the wrong target of media attention in this case? Or were they an integral part of the wider problem? In order to address some of these issues I thought it would provide a different perspective to talk to a practitioner, in the light of the central theme of this chapter, who reported in depth on the Baby P story and was critical of the actions of social workers. I thus interviewed James Oliver, a former colleague and a BBC *Panorama* producer who made two award-winning programmes on Baby P.[2]

First of all, I asked Oliver why the death of Peter Connelly became such a big story. He responded:

A small boy is dead. A small boy might have been murdered. The police are investigating whether the small boy was murdered by his mother, her boyfriend and a second man. This alone would almost certainly make the national press under normal circumstances. But it would not necessarily say much about our society other than there is cruelty and child abuse in it. The tabloids would cover it extensively, TV news less extensively, and it might be covered by a documentary on Channel 5.

However, he added, the fact that the boy was on the local authority's At Risk register made it a much bigger story, one that justified attention being focused on the social workers in the case:

> The story immediately has the potential to become much bigger. Why? – because immediately there are questions to answer. If a child who is on the At Risk register is murdered, then something has almost certainly gone wrong. It doesn't mean anyone could necessarily have done anything more to prevent it, or that the decisions made were wrong. But the net result was a dead child, where the state was involved in the role of that child's protector. So this story now has legs.

But why, I asked, did this story become quite so heavily covered? Why does *this* dead child become so significant when, sadly, there are many other dead children out there? Why does this one become iconic, and not the others? 'Because', replied Oliver, 'of another murdered child, Victoria Climbié'.

Victoria Climbié died in London in February 2000. She had been starved and tortured to death. At the trial of her murderers – her aunt and her boyfriend – and in the subsequent inquiry it was found that her death had been avoidable and that the local authorities, which included the London Borough of Haringey, should have protected her but had signally failed to do so. But the inquiry, headed by Lord Laming, did not confine itself to what had happened to Victoria, and made 108 recommendations for the reform of child protection, many of which were incorporated into the Children Act 2004. Thus, as Oliver pointed out, when it was realized that Peter died while on the At Risk register, it immediately raised the even bigger question of how a child care system which had supposedly been reformed failed him so completely:

> When we started investigating Peter's death and how the child protection system was working we were told by government, the NGO's, the local authorities, that all was well. In effect that this was just the horrendous murder of one child that had no implications for the system in place. But that was not true. The system was failing. Not only did it emerge that there had been systemic failures in Peter's case, but Haringey's social services were failing. And not just Haringey, Birmingham, Doncaster, and others, and even in those which were not failing we spoke to social workers who had major fears about the way the system was working.

What is interesting about this perspective from a news practitioner's perspective (although it is important to note that it is that of a BBC producer, who is bound by much stricter editorial guidelines – particularly those concerning impartiality – than those governing the press) is that it very clearly illustrates why he felt the story to be so important, and also why he believed it vital to focus on the aspect of the story which concerned the social services, and social workers in particular. It should also be noted that never once does he mention the notion of moral panic.

Conclusion

The failure of theorists to engage with practitioners when seeking to understand the moral panic concept is surprising. That, in the 40-year-old canon of moral panic theorizing, I cannot find any evidence of sustained interaction with news practitioners or any book or article which gives a news practitioner's perspective on the subject I find shocking. Admittedly, certain academics interested in the deviance school have interviewed journalists for a range of texts (e.g. Cohen and Young [1973]; Chibnall (1977); and Schlesinger and Tumber [1994]). But there is no major work on moral panics per se that includes practitioners' views or experience. Moral panic theorists are the first to cry conspiracy and bias when voices they deem important are left out of media reports. So why not interview journalists on moral panics?

Given the centrality of the media to moral panic theory the practitioners' view would seem to be well worth exploring. I would argue that experience on the news desk could reveal aspects of news production to which moral panic theorists seem oblivious. This would include observing that news production can on occasion be a bottom-up rather than a top-down process, particularly when the reporter identifies a new zeitgeist-defining event. I would also suggest that those who make use of the moral panic concept need to develop a better understanding of the news-making process in general. And, finally, I would like to re-iterate the idea of attempting to construct a continuum of moral concern, which would also involve devising an empirical framework within which to measure moral indignation, so that justified moral indignation can be distinguished from unjustified moral panic.

Notes

1 images.spectator.co.uk/alexmassie/3691056/the-pleasures-of-moral-panic.thtml
2 *Panorama*, 'What Happened to Baby P?' (BBC1, 17 September 2008); *Panorama*, 'Baby P: The Whole Truth?' (BBC1, 4 May 2009).

Bibliography

Aldrich, R. (2001), *The Hidden Hand: Britain, America, and Cold War Secret Intelligence*, London: John Murray.

Barker, M. and Petley, J. (eds) (1997), *Ill Effects: The Media/Violence Debate*, London: Routledge.

Barnett, S. (2008), 'On the Road to Self-destruction', *British Journalism Review*, 19(2): 5–13.

Chibnall, S. (1977), *Law and Order News*, London: Tavistock.

Cohen, S. (1972), *Folk Devils and Moral Panics*, St Albans: Paladin.

—([1972] 2002), *Folk Devils and Moral Panics*, 3rd edn, London: Routledge.

Cohen, S. and Young, J. (1973), *The Manufacture of News*, London: Constable.

—([1973] 1981), *The Manufacture of News*, 2nd edn, London: Constable.

Critcher, C. (2003), *Moral Panics and the Media*, Maidenhead, Buckingham: Open University Press

—(2006), *Critical Readings: Moral Panics and the Media*, Maidenhead, Buckingham: Open University Press.

Curtis, P. (2012), 'Why Has Trust in the Media Increased?', *Guardian*, 24 January, www.guardian.co.uk/politics/reality-check-with-polly-curtis/2012/jan/24/phone-hacking [accessed 23 October 2012].

Davies, N. (2008) *Flat Earth News*, London: Chatto & Windus.

de Young, M. (2004), *The Day Care Ritual Abuse Moral Panic*, Jefferson, NC: McFarland.

Ericson, R. V., Baranek, P. M. and Chan, J. B. L. (1987), *Visualizing Deviance: A Study of News Organization*, Toronto: University of Toronto Press.

Franklin, B. and Parton, N. (eds) (1991), *Social Work, the Media and Public Relations*, London: Routledge.

Goode, E. and Ben-Yehuda, N. ([1994] 2009), *Moral Panics: The Social Construction of Deviance*, 2nd edn, Oxford: Blackwell.

Hall, S., Critcher, C., Jefferson, T., Roberts, B. and Clarke, J. (1978), *Policing the Crisis: Mugging, the State and Law and Order*, London: Palgrave Macmillan.

Karpf, A. (2008), 'Our First Step towards Understanding the Death of This Child Should Be Not to Blame Social Workers but to Face the Mother's Experience of Childhood', *Guardian*, 15 November, www.guardian.co.uk/society/2008/nov/15/child-protection-social-care-babyp [accessed 23 October 2012].

Lashmar, P. and Oliver, J. (1998), *Britain's Secret Propaganda War 1948–1977*, Stroud: Sutton.

Leigh, D. and Lashmar P. (1985), 'Revealed: How MI5 Vets BBC Staff', *Observer*, 18 August.

McRobbie, A. and Thornton, S. L. (1995), 'Rethinking "Moral Panic" for Multi-mediated Social Worlds', *British Journal of Sociology*, 46(4): 559–74.

Moran, C. (2011), 'Intelligence and the Media: The Press, Government Secrecy and the "Buster" Crabb Affair', *Intelligence and National Security*, 26(5): 676–700.

Muncie, J. (1987), 'Much Ado about Nothing? The Sociology of Moral Panics', *Social Studies Review*, 3(2): 42–7.

Peppiatt, R. (2011), 'Evidence to the Leveson Inquiry. "Witness Statement"', www.levesoninquiry.org.uk/wp-content/uploads/2011/11/Witness-Statement-of-Richard-Peppiatt.pdf [accessed 23 October 2012].

Petley, J. (2011), *Film and Video Censorship in Modern Britain*, Edinburgh: Edinburgh University Press.

Schlesinger, P. and Tumber, H. (1994), *Reporting Crime*, Oxford: Clarendon Press.

Scraton, P., Jemphrey, A. and Coleman, S. (1995), *No Last Rights: The Denial of Justice and the Promotion of Myth in the Aftermath of the Hillsborough Disaster*, Liverpool: Liverpool City Council.

Thompson, K. (1998), *Moral Panics*, London: Routledge.

Young, J. (1974), 'Mass Media, Drugs, and Deviance', in P. Rock and M. McIntosh (eds), *Deviance and Social Control*, London: Tavistock, 229–59.

Williams, P. and Dickinson, J. (1993), 'Fear of Crime: Read All About It?', *British Journal of Criminology*, 33(1): 33–56.

4

'Are We Insane?' The 'Video Nasty' Moral Panic

Julian Petley

Are we insane? Are we bent on rotting our own society from within? Are we
determined to spur to a gallop the forces of decadence that threaten to drag us down?
                                                                    Daily Mail, 30 June 1983

In 1984 state censorship of video was imposed on Britain by the Video Recordings
Act. This required the British Board of Film Censors (BBFC) to classify every
feature film released on video. Because these classifications carry legal force –
unlike the classifications for cinema films handed out by the same body – it is a
criminal offence to distribute, rent or sell an unclassified video, and to rent or sell
a video to a person below the age stipulated in its certificate. Infringement carries
a hefty fine; between 1995 and 2007 there were 1,703 convictions under the Act,
and it is estimated that there was a similar number between 1984 and 1995. In
1994, the law was tightened still further, and the penalties for breaking it were
increased. The fact that other EU countries, with the exception of the Republic
of Ireland, managed to cope with the advent of home video without imposing
wholesale state censorship on the new medium makes the United Kingdom
something of an anomaly in this respect, and raises the obvious question of how
and why this state of affairs came about. A convincing answer is provided by the
notion of moral panic.

As Stanley Cohen famously explained in his seminal work on this subject:

> Societies appear to be subject, every now and then, to periods of moral panic.
> A condition, episode, person or group of persons emerges to become defined as
> a threat to societal values and interests; its nature is presented in a stylised and
> stereotypical fashion by the mass media; the moral barricades are manned by
> editors, bishops, politicians and other right-thinking people; socially accredited

experts pronounce their diagnoses and solutions; ways of coping are evolved or (more often) resorted to; the condition then disappears, submerges or deteriorates and becomes more visible. Sometimes the object of the panic is quite novel and at other times it is something which has been in existence long enough, but suddenly appears in the limelight. Sometimes the panic passes over and is forgotten, except in folk-lore and collective memory; at other times it has more serious and long-lasting repercussions and might produce such changes in legal and social policy or even in the way society conceives itself. ([1972] 2002: 1)

In this chapter I will attempt to demonstrate that the controversy over videos followed this trajectory remarkably closely. But, in the course of doing so, I also want to explore a number of issues which have arisen in moral panic theorizing since Cohen's book first appeared in 1972. In particular, the part played by the mainstream media in helping to ignite and perpetuate moral panics, the question of whether such panics necessarily require folk devils, the role of these episodes of panic within their broader political and ideological contexts, the problem of agency (and in particular the extent to which highly mediated panics can be said to represent 'public opinion') and, finally, the 'post-modern' challenge allegedly posed to moral panic theory by the development of new and interactive forms of media. But first a little background information is necessary.

Video as threat

Home video took off rapidly in Britain in 1979 and soon became an extremely popular medium. However, because the major distributors were worried both about video piracy and denting their theatrical audiences (which in 1981 dropped by fifteen million on the previous year) they at first steered clear of the fledgling industry, which was thus dominated by a plethora of small independents. UK video rights could be bought for as little as £1000, and the video shelves were soon well stocked with cheap exploitation fare, including soft-core pornography, housed in particularly garish and lurid covers. But, most important of all, video at this point was not subject to censorship by the BBFC. What cannot be over-estimated here is the shocking impact on the censoriously minded of the sudden availability, in a domestic medium, of a range of images which the combined forces of the Obscene Publications Act (OPA), Customs and Excise, the police and the BBFC had, for decades, done their very utmost to shield from British eyes. As BBFC Director James Ferman put it remarkably presciently in 1979:

Audiences in Britain never see the worst the world's film-makers have to offer. Films glorifying rape, the torture of naked women, the degradation of adolescent girls, the infliction of serious bodily harm through easily copied weapons, the casual slaughter of animals – such things are habitually cut or rejected in the British cinema. If they were permitted, I believe the public would demand that the police and the courts and Parliament take a far tougher line with cinema than they have so far. (66)

Uncensored home video thus rapidly emerged as a 'threat to societal values and interests'. The first complaints about video advertising were made to the Advertising Standards Authority in 1981. The first national press story about the dangers of domestic video appeared in the *Mail* under the headline 'The Secret Video Show' on 12 May 1982. This warned thus:

More and more children, well used to video recorders in school, are catching on to the fact that their parents' machine can give them the opportunity to watch the worst excesses of cinema sex and violence . . . The problem arises because video is now the fastest growing part of the home entertainment industry – and yet is too young to have developed its own controls.

And so there entered the second of Cohen's actors, the media, in the shape of the newspaper which would later play the leading role in the video panic and its attendant campaign for statutory control of the new medium. The article also introduced the first of those manning Cohen's 'moral barricades', Scarborough teacher Richard Neighbour, who expressed concern that 'video gives the children access [to] something that the parents may not be able to control'.

The *Mail*'s intervention was followed on 23 May by another paper which played a key role in sparking off the video panic, *The Sunday Times*, with an article headlined 'How High Street Horror is Invading the Home'. This was the first time that the term 'video nasties' was used in the national press. The article warned that 'uncensored horror video cassettes, available to anybody of any age, have arrived in Britain's High Streets . . . They exploit extremes of violence, and are rapidly replacing sexual pornography as the video trade's biggest moneyspinner.' It also explains that 'the nasties are far removed from the suspense of the traditional horror film. They dwell on murder, multiple rape, butchery, sado-masochism, mutilation of women, cannibalism and Nazi atrocities.' Specific titles singled out included *The Driller Killer, SS Experiment Camp, Cannibal Holocaust, I Spit on Your Grave* and *Snuff* (which is described, wholly inaccurately, as 'horrifyingly convincing'). The presentation of these videos in Cohen's 'stylized and stereotypical fashion' is thus already well underway. The article also introduced another fighter at the barricades, the Tory MP Peter Lloyd, at that time piloting through parliament a private member's bill to toughen up the censorship of films shown in cinema clubs, who laments the arrival on video of these 'really harmful sadistic films with details of violence, especially against women', and warns that 'these video sales and rentals will be the problem of next year and the year after'.

All of these, bar *The Driller Killer*, but with the addition of *The Texas Chainsaw Massacre, Cataclysm* and *Macabre,* turned up on 28 May in a full-page article in the *Express* headed 'This Poison Being Peddled as Home "Entertainment"', which elaborates on *The Sunday Times'* litany by describing the films as showing 'castration, sadistic attacks on women, and violence including the use of chain-saws and electric drills'. Moral warrior Richard Neighbour is quoted again, but is also joined by Lord Chief Justice Lane, whose maiden speech in the Lords the previous year, we are reminded, warned about what he called 'positive incentives' to commit crime offered by scenes of violence 'depicted on various screens of all sizes'. But this article also introduces the next set of actors in Cohen's schema, the 'socially accredited experts', in the shape of the BBFC which, we are told, 'has set up a working party to investigate the possibility of giving certificates to video films. If a film was deemed too horrific to get a certificate it would then be illegal to sell it'. We also receive here the first hints at 'ways of coping' with the newly emergent video problem; these take the form of a suggestion that video shops should, like sex shops, be licensed by local councils, and the 'exclusive' revelation that the Metropolitan Police Obscene Publications Squad has seized a copy of *SS Experiment Camp* and sent a report to the Director of Public Prosecutions (DPP) with a view to his bringing a possible test case against the video under OPA. Detective Chief Superintendent Kruger of the squad looms large in another *The Sunday Times* article on 30 May, in which he states that 'horror videos are a new concept, and I think we're going to get involved in them more and more'. The article also reveals that the BBFC and the British Videogram Association (BVA, the video distributors' body) have set up a working party to devise a video classification system similar to that used in the cinema. In the following week's paper it is revealed that *The Driller Killer* and *I Spit on Your Grave* have been referred to the DPP. From June 1982 onwards, politicians begin to man the moral barricades, with a number of questions about videos being asked in both the Commons and the Lords.

On 8 August 1982 *The Sunday Times* reveals that 'prosecutions against the distributors of video nasties – the horror and terror cassettes first exposed in

The Sunday Times – are to be made this week'. In the event, charges were successfully brought against *Death Trap* and *The Driller Killer*, and, in a separate case, *I Spit on Your Grave*, but both the police and the veteran moral campaigner Mary Whitehouse clearly thought that the charges were not sufficiently serious.[1] Whitehouse, the head of the 'clean up TV' campaigning body the National Viewers' and Listeners' Association, was then given a great deal of largely uncontested space in the press to call for the resignation of the DPP, lambast the hearings as a 'farce' and a 'public scandal' and label the videos (which she admitted she hadn't seen) as 'appalling and utter filth'. Whitehouse is the classic example of the kind of 'moral entrepreneur' who plays a key role in driving moral panics forward, and, as we shall see below, performed this role to the hilt in helping to whip up the next stage of the video nasty panic, frequently in concert with the *Mail*. However, the DPP made it clear that now it had been established that violent videos could be classified as obscene under the OPA, which had hitherto been invoked mainly against pornography, future prosecutions would be brought under section 3. Police forces up and down the land then began raiding video distributors and seizing thousands of tapes which they claimed breached the OPA, a frightening process which is chillingly described by several of its victims in extras in the DVD sets *Box of the Banned* and *Video Nasties: The Definitive Guide*. Thus the final part of Cohen's narrative fell into place: an extension of the law, specifically of the remit of the OPA. These ongoing raids and subsequent court actions are also a good example of what Cohen calls *escalation*, in which existing laws are enforced more harshly by the relevant authorities, a process which is legitimized by the initial and ongoing 'exaggeration and negative symbolization' of the panic-inducing objects ([1972] 2002: 67).

What we have here, then, is in fact a classic moral panic, only in miniature, but it is one which mirrors in every respect the far bigger (and better known) offspring to which it would give birth the following year. Particularly significant here is the key role played by the press, and particularly *The Sunday Times*, in actually helping to ignite the panic in the first place. In its reports of the developing story, the paper repeatedly draws attention to itself as a leading actor in the events which it is describing, and it is particularly notable that its early stories *precede* the parliamentary questions and police actions noted above, which can thus be seen partly as *responses* to its journalistic efforts. Similarly, as we shall see later, it was a campaign by the *Mail* which actually *pushed* politicians into creating and then supporting the Video Recordings Bill. Thus before progressing any further we need to examine, in general terms, the crucial role played by the media, and particularly the press, in the process of moral panic fomentation.

'Populist guardians of public morality'

The media always play a crucial (though by no means the sole) role in helping to shape people's perceptions of social reality, although the extent to which this is the case is all too frequently under-estimated. People have all sorts of thoughts and views about public figures whom they have never personally met and about events which they have not themselves experienced at first hand, and the ultimate source of many of these, even though mediated via friends, family, work-mates and the like, can only be the press, radio, television and now the internet. Such figures and events are thus, on the whole, not experienced directly but via a whole series of processed images and coded representations, and in the case of panic-inducing events reported by the media it is largely on the basis of these that, as Cohen argues, 'people become indignant or angry, formulate theories and plans, make speeches, write letters to the newspapers' ([1972] 2002: 18). Cohen refers to the early stages of the media's presentation of panic-inducing events as comprising an *inventory*, whose ingredients are crucial in determining the later stages of the reaction to these events. These are, first, *exaggeration and distortion*. These consist primarily in the 'mode and style of presentation characteristic of most crime reporting: the sensational headlines, the melodramatic vocabulary and the deliberate heightening of those elements of the story considered as news' ([1972] 2002: 20). Thus, for example, in the *Mail*'s 'Secret Video Show' article we are warned of children watching 'the worst excesses of cinema sex and violence' and 'torrid sex and violence sessions', the *Express* headline speaks of 'perversion and violence' and 'poison', while *The Sunday Times* and the *Express* construct, as noted above, a particularly lurid litany of the contents of the generality of horror videos (which, in fact, is based on the highlights of an extremely small number of titles). The second ingredient of the inventory is *prediction*: the dire warning that the events in question will not only recur but actually get worse if nothing is done. Cohen also refers to this as the 'prophecy of doom' ([1972] 2002: 38). We have already encountered the Tory MP Peter Lloyd warning that 'these video sales and rentals will be the problem of next year and the year after', while the *Express* argued that any delay in introducing legislation would be 'giving more time for horror video to tighten its grip'. The final ingredient is *symbolization*, which denotes the process whereby certain words come to acquire wholly negative meanings and connotations, which is but one aspect of a wider process of the creation of what Cohen calls 'unambiguously unfavourable symbols' ([1972] 2002: 28). And here we need look no further for an example than the invention, apparently by a *Sunday Times* journalist, of the highly resonant and evocative phrase video nasty.

As noted above, the media play an extremely important role in helping to construct people's perceptions of social reality, and it can further be argued that they play a particularly important one in defining and shaping social problems. As Cohen argues: 'The media have long operated as agents of moral indignation in their own right: even if they are not self-consciously engaged in crusading or muck-raking, their very reporting of certain facts can be sufficient to generate anxiety, indignation or panic' ([1972] 2002: 7). This, it should be added, is particularly true of the British press, and especially of its moralistic and populist mode of crime reporting, into which journalistic domain much reporting of panic-inducing events falls. As Cohen puts it, 'Such "news" . . . is a main source of information about the normative contours of a society. It informs us about right and wrong, about the boundaries beyond which one should not venture and about the shape that the devil can assume' ([1972] 2002: 9). It is for this reason that Stuart Hall et al. (1978) aptly describe the press as 'the populist guardians of public morality' (239) and the 'range riders of discipline' (Hall et al. 1978: 242). As Steve Chibnall puts it, in a critical account of crime reporting which deserves to be better known:

> Crime and the processing of offenders offers an opportunity by redefining the moral boundaries of communities and drawing their members together against the threat of chaos . . . Crime news may serve as the focus for the articulation of shared morality and communal sentiments. A chance not simply to speak *to* the community but *for* the community, against all that the criminal outsider represents, to delineate the shape of the threat, to advocate a response, to eulogise on conformity to established norms and values, and to warn of the consequences of deviance. In short, crime news provides a chance for a newspaper to appropriate the moral conscience of its readership . . . The existence of crime news disseminated by the mass media means that people can no longer need to gather together to witness punishments. They can remain at home for moral instruction. (1977: x–xi)

Newspaper stories, especially those about crime, are thus peopled less by 'real' characters than by emblematic heroes and villains, personifications of good and evil acting out roles in a symbolic drama. This drama becomes particularly heightened – melodramatic even – at times of crisis for the agencies of social control. Specific anxieties tend to become generalized and rolled into one over-arching panic about the breakdown of law and order and 'the end of life as we know it'. Discrete social problems come to be represented as symptoms of an underlying social malaise, signs of a generalized moral decline. Thus is provided a simple explanation of diverse and perplexing social phenomena, which all too frequently leads to the resort to hasty 'solutions' which are both ill founded and badly thought out, the Video Recordings Act, which was the direct outcome of the video nasty panic, providing a particularly acute example of such a measure.

Thus let us now return to the development of the video nasties saga and continue our examination of it as an example of a moral panic. (For more detailed accounts of the nasties narrative, see Barker (1984), Kerekes and Slater [2000: 7–67], Martin [(1993) 2007: 14–34] and Petley [2011: 17–48].)

'Ban the sadist videos'

During the autumn of 1982, questions about videos continue to be asked in both the Lords and Commons. On 15 December the Labour MP Gareth Wardell introduces, with all-party support, a Ten-Minute Rule Bill which would make it an offence to rent or sell adult videos to children and young people. He describes a video recorder as 'a potential weapon that may be used to attack the emotions of our children and young persons' (quoted in the *Telegraph*, 16 December 1982), and condemns certain (unnamed) videos as a 'distasteful fricassee of pornography, rape and murder' and 'a slur on British life' (quoted in the same day's *Guardian*). Meanwhile work continues on developing a voluntary system of regulation by the BBFC and the BVA. As is usually the case with such measures, Wardell's bill fails to win government support and falls by the wayside at its second reading on 18 February 1983. Crucially, it is *this* which sparks off what would become the *Mail*'s 'Ban the Sadist Videos' campaign, with an article on 25 February headlined 'We Must Protect Our Children *Now*'. The article castigates home secretary William Whitelaw's unwillingness to contemplate statutory regulation as 'ludicrous' (twice) and his faith in the BBFC/BVA measures as manifesting merely a 'pious hope'. On 2 March the *Telegraph* reveals that in a letter replying to Mary Whitehouse's request for stricter obscenity regulation, Mrs Thatcher had stated: 'Like you I deplore those who seek to profit out of exploiting the weakness of others, and in doing so undermine our traditional standards of decency and respect for family life.'

By the beginning of April 1983, Norman Abbott of the BVA was expressing the fear that because of the growing hysteria being whipped up by sections of the press and the consequent pressure on MPs, the voluntary classification scheme would not be given a fair chance to prove itself. Interviewed in the trade magazine *Broadcast*, 4 April, he stated:

> The Minister specified that while prepared to wait a *reasonable* time, the Government will go ahead and prepare legislation so there is a ready-made Bill prepared in all its pre-legislative details that can be rushed through immediately the Government deems the voluntary scheme to have failed. The indications are that *reasonable* may only mean months. The Government believes the problem can be controlled in a stroke of the pen but that is impossible whether by our scheme or legislation. The problem of policing will still be exactly the same.

The *Telegraph*, 8 April, reveals that in March, Mary Whitehouse had written to all MPs asking for support and that 150 had replied that they would back video legislation. *The Times*, 11 April, also quotes her as urging the Tories to include proposals for stricter obscenity laws in their manifesto for the general election which had just been called. As she put it, in yet another example of the 'prophecy of doom': 'No party can afford to ignore the threat, and if the law is not changed, the spread of pornography via video and cable television will do our children terrible damage'. In the event, the Tory manifesto stated that the government would respond to 'the increasing public concern over obscenity and offences against public decency, which often have links with serious crime. We propose to introduce legislation to deal with the most serious of these problems, such as the dangerous spread of violent and obscene video cassettes.'

The BBFC/BVA regulatory scheme is announced on 14 April (and is promptly denounced by Whitehouse as 'unworkable'). On 16 May, *Broadcast* reports that if the Tories win the election, statutory censorship of videos is highly likely, basing its forecast on remarks by Tory MP Timothy Sainsbury at a Video Traders Association (VTA, the body representing video retailers) meeting at which he announced that junior Home Office minister Patrick Mayhew was actively considering proposals for legislation. He called the industry's efforts 'well-intentioned' but continued: 'They are not good enough – primarily because they lack the power to ensure that the regulations will be respected. The industry will not be persuaded just by moral arguments or a code of conduct, and respectable dealers will be damaged by outlets that ignore the system.' However, Derek Mann of the VTA, whose members had continued to be at the sharp end of the police raids mentioned above, is quoted to the effect that although in his view voluntary classification was a step in the right direction, 'government legislation may not be a bad thing for the retailer'.

The Tories win the general election on 9 June. On 27 June there takes place
the inaugural meeting of what would become the Parliamentary Group Video
Enquiry (which is discussed at length in Brown (1984) and in the DVD set *Video
Nasties: The Definitive Guide*). During the summer, the papers report various
cases (discussed below) in which defendants argue that watching nasties had
made them commit violent crimes. Police raids continue. On 30 June, the *Mail*
publishes its lengthy editorial, 'Rape of Our Children's Minds' (of which more
below), and on the same day, and by no means coincidentally, Mrs Thatcher
tells the Commons that 'It is not enough to have voluntary regulation. We must
bring in a ban to regulate the matter.' Similarly, home secretary Leon Brittan
announces to MPs that:

> I am not satisfied with the current state of the law. The Government fully accepts
> the need for more effective control of the sale and rental of objectionable video
> cassettes, as we made clear in our election manifesto. I welcome the proposed
> introduction by the video industry of voluntary controls, but I do not consider
> that, by themselves, such controls will be sufficient. There will certainly have to be
> statutory controls and I am urgently considering what form they should take.

It then became readily apparent that a draft bill on the subject had *already*
been nearly completed by the Home Office and would now be taken up by a
Conservative backbencher, Graham Bright, who had just topped the ballot for
private members bills. The use of this particular parliamentary device (one which
normally fails very early in its progress through parliament) clearly demonstrated
the government's desire for speed, as it circumvented any need to consult the video
industry. However, the absence of a timetable and of any mention of legislation
in the current session of parliament angered the ever-impatient the *Mail*, which
headlined its front page on 1 July: 'MPs Back *Mail* Campaign and Tell Premier:
Ban Video Sadism Now'. Sure enough, on 14 July the broad outlines of the bill
were announced, and the following day's *Express* felt confident enough to run
the headline 'Video Nasties Face Total Ban'. That month the DPP also issued a
full list of videos which had been subject to court action and made it clear that
his office would recommend prosecution of any dealer stocking them.

The Bill was scheduled for its second reading on 11 November; all that was now
necessary was to ensure that it would be supported on the day, and, therefore, the
fuelling of the moral panic continued apace, particularly in the press. (It needs to
be stressed that the articles cited here are but a tiny fraction of those published
on this subject during this period, as can be gauged from Martin [(1993) 2007:

17–34].) Stories about violent crimes committed allegedly under the influence of nasties continued to appear in newspapers at regular intervals (see below), but the two most important drivers of the panic were, first, Graham Bright's screening at the House of Commons on 1 November of a farrago of extracts, compiled by Chief Superintendent Kruger, from various nasties. Shown to MPs, many of whom had probably never seen even a recent 'X'-certificated horror film, it succeeded admirably in its own terms and provided the next day's papers with an absolute field day: 'Video Nasties Show Stuns MPs: Many Quit in Disgust' (*Sun*), 'Film Show Sickens MPs' (*Mail*), and 'Video Nasties Leave MPs Reeling With Horror' (*The Times*). With remarkably good timing, Bright's bill is published two days later.

The second key driver was the publication on 23 November of the first report of the Parliamentary Group Video Enquiry mentioned above. The entirely phony statistic (see Brown 1984) that four out of ten children over the age of six had seen a video nasty was the stuff of hysterical front pages right across the press, a press which, incidentally, is normally highly dismissive of academic research, which it likes to characterize as the work of 'boffins' or inhabitants of the ivory tower. The *Mail*, 24 November, headlined its front page 'Sadism for Six Year Olds', with the strap-line, 'Videos replace baby sitters . . . and the children's party conjuror', while the *Sun* heralded the 'Birth of the "Video Nasty" Generation'. Thus aided, by the end of the month, the bill had sailed unopposed through both its second reading and committee stage, although by now a very few critical voices were being raised in papers such as *The Times*, the *Telegraph*, the *Financial Times* and the *Guardian*, in particular questioning the bona fides of the above-mentioned report, and pointing out that the proposed new law would cover a great deal more than simply a few nasties, most of which had anyway vanished from the market thanks to police and court actions under the OPA. Such interventions, however, were to absolutely no avail. On 7 March 1984 the second report of the Parliamentary Group Video Enquiry was published, to coincide with the bill being debated in the Lords. Again the results claimed by the research are highly questionable (to put it at its mildest) and again press coverage is not simply uncritical but entirely unquestioning: thus the headline 'Half of Children See Film Nasties' (*Mail*, 8 March). On 17 March the bill is given an unopposed third reading in the Commons.

And so it was that a measure which, throughout its parliamentary trajectory had received little serious discussion and met with almost no opposition, completed its journey through parliament and received the Royal Assent in July 1984. (For a useful discussion of its remarkably easy passage see Marsh, Gowin and Read [1986].) And yet it was a draconian, wide-ranging and far-reaching piece of legislation. The Video Recordings Act, as it now was, gave the BBFC statutory powers in the field of video, and required every feature film released on video, including those currently in distribution, to be classified and, where necessary, cut or even banned outright. It would be an offence to sell or rent an unclassified feature film on video, or to sell or rent a video to someone younger than the age stipulated in its classification certificate. Documentary and non-fiction films of one kind or another were exempt from classification, provided that they did not deal with certain specified subjects. Thus, returning to Cohen's opening schema, the video nasty panic brought about not simply the extension of the scope of an existing law – the OPA – but the creation of an entirely new one, a process which Cohen refers to as *innovation*, whereby social control is extended not only in degree but also in kind, this extension being legitimated by reference to the threat to society allegedly posed by the objects of panic.

The signification spiral

Indeed, one of the most remarkable aspects of the video nasty panic was the speed at and intensity with which a few horror videos came to be seen as nothing less than harbingers of the apocalypse. The way in which one phenomenon becomes linked to others and all of them come to be seen as working insidiously together to pose a threat to 'life as we know it' is referred to by Cohen as the 'it's not only this' syndrome ([1972] 2002: 39). However, in order to analyse this aspect of the video nasty panic I will have recourse to what Hall et al. usefully call the *signification spiral* (which is not dissimilar to the notion of *amplification* employed by Cohen). This they define as 'a way of signifying events which also intrinsically escalates their threat . . . The activity or event with which the signification deals is *escalated* – made to seem more threatening – within the course of the signification itself' (1978: 223). Such a spiral consists of the following elements:

1.　the identification of a specific issue of concern;
2.　the identification of a subversive minority;
3.　'convergence', or the linking, by labelling, of this specific issue to other problems;
4.　the notion of 'thresholds' which, once crossed, can lead to an escalating threat;
5.　the prophesy of more troubling times to come if no action is taken; and
6.　the call for 'firm steps'. (Hall et al. 1978: 223)

I want to concentrate here specifically on the notions of *convergence* and *thresholds*, since the other elements have effectively already been discussed, albeit under different headings, via Cohen. *Convergence*, according to Hall et al., occurs when

> two or more activities are linked in the process of signification so as to implicitly or explicitly draw parallels between them . . . Another, connected, form of convergence is listing a whole series of social problems and speaking of them as 'part of a deeper, underlying problem' – the 'tip of an iceberg', especially when such a link is also forged on the basis of implied common denominators. In both cases the net effect is *amplification*, not in the real events being described, but in their 'threat potential' for society. (1978: 223)

In the case of *thresholds*, Hall et al. note that 'in the public signification of troubling events, there seem to be certain thresholds which mark out symbolically the limits of societal tolerance. The higher an event can be placed in the hierarchy of thresholds, the greater is its threat to the social order, and the tougher and more automatic is the coercive response' (1978: 225). They set out three thresholds: the moral, the legal and the violent, and the *echt* moral panic (like the nasties one) moves inexorably from the first to the last as the signification spiral gathers momentum. The moral threshold is concerned with questions of 'permissiveness', and events which cross it contravene conventional moral norms, thus mobilizing moral sanctions and social disapproval. However, if any of these acts breaks the law (or if new laws are passed which criminalize some hitherto legally permissible but morally frowned upon activity) then the legal threshold is crossed. This transgression raises the threat potential of any action, challenging not simply the moral consensus but the legal order and the social legitimacy which it enshrines. Usually such acts involve crossing (or are signified as leading inexorably across) the violence threshold, and violent acts are frequently construed as constituting a threat to the future existence of the very state itself. Thus every action which can be signified as violent or leading to violence can be represented as a symptom of widespread social disorder, the tip of an iceberg, and any form of action thus identified immediately becomes a law-and-order issue. Hall et al. conclude that:

> The use of convergences and thresholds together in the ideological signification of societal conflict has the intrinsic function of escalation. One kind of threat or challenge to society seems larger, more menacing, if it can be mapped together with other, apparently similar, phenomena – especially if, by connecting one

relatively harmless activity with a more threatening one, the scale of the danger implicit is made to appear more widespread and diffused. Similarly, the threat to society can be escalated if a challenge occurring at the 'permissive' boundary can be resignified, or presented as leading inevitably to a challenge at a 'higher' threshold. By treating an event or group of actors not only in terms of its/their intrinsic characteristics, aims and programmes, but by projecting the 'anti-social potential' across the thresholds to what it *may* cause (or, less deterministically, lead to), it is possible to treat the initial event or group as 'the thin end of a larger wedge' . . . The important point is that, as issues and groups are projected across the thresholds, it becomes easier to mount legitimate campaigns of control against them. When this process becomes a regular and routine part of the way in which conflict is signified in society, it does indeed create its own momentum for measures of 'more than usual control'. (1978: 226)

The video nasty panic was particularly rich in convergences. For example, the videos were linked to the anti-social family. Thus in the *Mail* story about the 'video rapist' (see below) the director of the National Society for the Prevention of Cruelty to Children reveals that 'I had a case where a worker was not able to interview a family until all of them, including children, had finished viewing the rape scene in *I Spit on Your Grave*'. And according to the social commentator David Holbrook in *The Sunday Times*, 2 January 1983, in an article whose headline 'The Seduction of the Innocent' irresistibly recalls the campaign against US horror comics in the early 1950s, 'children are actually deliberately being shown films of buggery, rape and mutilation'. (In a further example of convergence, Holbrook, like many other commentators, here simply lumps together pornographic and horror films, which in fact belong to entirely different genres and frequently appeal to different audiences.) He also links children viewing videos (although it is quite unclear which kinds he actually means) to their being taken to the London Dungeon museum,[2] as well as their being exposed to the sex education book *Talking Sex*; in his view, 'One cannot but see such manifestations as forms of coarse seduction of the innocent. But what is more startling is the total absence of protest on part of teachers, parents or the authorities'. Thus the net is widened – this is not just a problem of bad parenting on the part of the usual culprits, namely working-class families. A similar line was taken by Tory MP Jerry Hayes in the Commons on 11 November 1983, when he stated that 'I bitterly regret that those middle-class people who sit on beanbags wearing Gucci accessories in their Hampstead flats which are bedecked with Laura Ashley decorations and talk about world affairs should allow their children to see the type of video films with which we are dealing.'

Nasties are also linked to fears about the spread of organized crime, for example in the *Mail*'s 'We Must Protect Our Children *Now*' article on 25 February 1983, which cites the above-mentioned MP Gareth Wardell as referring to 'evil video gangsters', and as having 'a conversation with a Welsh video dealer who came to say "Look, take care. You are dealing with some pretty tough customers. You might even get visits from some who carry shooters"'. Similarly, the *News of the World*, 13 November 1983, lambasts the 'evil sex-kings' and 'get-rich-quick gangsters' of the video trade. Meanwhile, the *Mail*'s remarkable 'Rape of Our Children's Minds' editorial, 30 June 1983, which is one of the clearest examples of 'the end of life as we know it' trope in the whole nasties saga and is reproduced in full in Barker (1984: 28), compares the contents of nasties to real-life events in the Third Reich (a regime which, incidentally, the *Mail* ardently supported right up until the outbreak of the Second World War), and asks: 'are we insane? Are we bent on rotting our own society from within? Are we determined to spur to a gallop the forces of decadence that threaten to drag us down?' Similarly in an article for the *Mail* on 1 February 1984, Mrs Whitehouse paints the nasties as symptoms of 'the corruption and gross exploitation which has invaded our culture'. At another point these videos are linked with another favourite newspaper folk devil, the National Union of Mineworkers, when both the *Mail* and the *Telegraph*, 4 July 1983, revealed that the miners' pension fund held shares in a company which distributed nasties; this was Centre Video, but even a cursory reading of the text beneath the screaming headlines reveals that only eight (*Telegraph*) or six (*Mail*) of the 3,000 videos which it distributed were nasties, that the pension fund trustees had no idea of the contents of the videos in which the company traded, and that the manager of the firm had offered to withdraw the offending titles as soon as his attention was drawn to them. And at times the process of convergence threw up 'links' which can only be described as ludicrous; thus when the highly sanitized US TV movie about the after-effects of a future nuclear war, *The Day After*, was shown on British television, Roger Scruton in *The Times*, 13 December 1983, hitched it to the right-wing campaign against those opposed to nuclear weaponry by stating that '*The Day After* is, by report [he hadn't seen it] a particularly disgusting video nasty, larded with the moralising cant that one must expect from people who let their thoughts dwell upon the image of human suffering'. But even this absurdity was outdone by an article headed 'Pony Maniac Strikes Again', in the *Mirror*, 3 January 1984, in which a series of sexual attacks on ponies elicits the comment from a police spokesman that 'the maniac could be affected by video nasties or a new moon'.

In terms of *thresholds*, we saw at the start of this article how rapidly the nasties crossed the moral and legal thresholds, but what I want to concentrate on here is how they were portrayed as crossing the violence threshold as well. Our discussion of convergences has already shown how the distribution of nasties was linked by commentators to organized crime, and thus to violence, but what I want to concentrate on here is how they were portrayed as potential or actual *causes* of violence.

In the *Telegraph*, 5 September 1982, David Rosenberg reports that 'the social impact of the "nasties" is infinitely more menacing [than that of pornography], said top policemen and psychologists I talked to last week'. Chief among these is the ubiquitous Superintendent Kruger, who states that 'the police are here to prevent violence for violence's sake, which is precisely what these films glorify. The prospect of just one person mimicking *Driller Killer* is horrifying'. In his *Sunday Times* article quoted above, David Holbrook cites a study carried out for the US government by the National Institute of Mental Health into the effects of violence on television, which, he states, 'came to the conclusion that the evidence is overwhelming that it leads to aggressive behaviour in young people'. What he fails to mention, however, is that its results, like those of so much research of this kind undertaken in the States, are highly questionable, as are the findings of H. J. Eysenck, also quoted approvingly in the article. (For critical accounts of 'media effects' see Cumberbatch and Howitt [1989], Barker and Petley [1997, 2001] and Gauntlett [2005].)

On 28 June 1983, under the headline 'Fury over the Video Rapist' and the strap 'Boy, 18, attacked women after seeing films', the *Mail* reported that 'demands for action on video "nasties" mounted last night following the case of a teenage rapist who struck twice after watching pornographic films'. However, according to the article, it was not pornographic but horror videos that the rapist liked to watch, and it also quotes his defence lawyer as saying that his client 'lived out the fantasy brought on by the videos, which often portrayed women as enjoying rape'. However, the only video actually mentioned in the article is *I Spit on Your Grave*, in which a raped woman murders all her assailants! The *Mail* does admit that Austin was emotionally immature, had a low IQ and was a habitual glue-sniffer, but omits the fact that he had seven previous offences for theft and burglary and that he had raped two women shortly after being released from a detention centre. However, the shakiness of this story did not deter the *Mail's* Lynda Lee-Potter, another key player in the nasties saga, from using her column on 29 June to warn that 'the impact that this sick, beastly money-making corruption is having on innocent minds is going to make previous anxieties about violence on television look like worries about the impact of Enid Blyton!' She also warned that 'if video censorship of the most stringent kind isn't brought in pretty damned quick we're going to have an upsurge in violence and terror and abuse in our land and homes the like of which we never suspected in our wildest terror'.

Further 'proof' that violent videos actually cause violence was apparently offered by the case of Christopher Meah. On 5 August 1983, under the headline 'Rapist "Was Addicted to Video Nasties"', *The Times* reported his wife as saying that 'he was loving, kind and considerate until he became addicted to watching an endless string of horrifying video films containing detailed scenes of the most depraved and vicious kind . . . I am convinced that they changed his personality and that they should be banned'. However, in the same day's *Mail* it is revealed that his two favourites were *The Thing*, which has an all-male cast and features no sex at all, and *The Last House on the Left* which, though certainly unpleasant, does not contain 'multiple sex attacks', as the paper suggests. Rather more to the point was that Meah had undergone a severe personality change after suffering brain damage in a car crash in 1979, had taken a cocktail of drink and drugs before the rape, and at the time of the offence was on bail – which had been strongly opposed by the police – for two previous assaults.

The *Mail* also found judicial backing for its journey across the thresholds in the shape of Lord Chief Justice Lane. Proudly announcing on 9 November 1983 that 'The Lord Chief Justice Backs Our Fight against Corrupting Films', it quoted him as stating that 'what our legislators seem not to realise is that it is not merely children who need to be prevented from seeing these frightful publications. There are others upon whom the effects may be even more disastrous'. He warned that unless strict censorship was imposed on videos, 'it will not be long before these scenes are enacted in real life . . . Human beings are imitative, and the less strong-minded the more imitative they are'. And, bringing us back neatly to convergence, he concluded that 'so long as permissiveness increases, so will crime, both in quantity and nastiness'.

A question which frequently arises in discussions of moral panics is whether such episodes must by definition involve folk devils if they are to be considered *echt* panics. For those who argue that this is indeed the case, video nasties might appear at first sight not to fit the bill, since the objects of panic are inanimate video tapes, not demonized human beings. But as this section in particular has demonstrated, the video nasty panic is actually awash with groups habitually demonized by the press (and by conservative opinion in general) such as irresponsible parents, trade unionists, anti-nuclear campaigners and so on. But the most pervasive folk devils here are those who simply watch the kind of films which became stigmatized as video nasties, and what is particularly significant about the way in which they are habitually represented is the element of class-dislike which permeates the discourse. Thus, for example, on 28 June 1983 in the *Mail*, Lynda Lee-Potter bemoaned 'the impact that this sick, beastly, money-making corruption is having on illiterate minds', while in a debate on the Video Recordings Bill on 16 March 1984, the Conservative MP for Ealing North, Harry Greenaway, complained that videos 'are often a higher priority in the homes of people who are not particularly articulate, and who do not read books or listen to music very much. In some homes videos even take priority over food and furniture'. Here the viewers of video nasties are implicitly identified as members of that most stigmatized of all social groups – the 'underclass'. (For further discussion of this topic see Petley [2001].)

Nasties in context

In the preceding pages, drawing on the work of both Cohen and of Hall et al., I have attempted to map the nasty saga, as it developed between 1982 and 1984, as a moral panic. However, it needs to be stressed that moral panics do not simply appear out of the blue, but have deep social and historical roots. As some of the sentiments quoted in the course of this article indicate, the nasty panic drew on a very considerable reservoir of fears about popular culture and its supposedly corrupting effects. As Geoffrey Pearson puts it in his seminal history of 'respectable fears':

> Popular entertainments of all kinds have been blamed for dragging down public morals in a gathering pattern of accusation which remains essentially the same even though it is attached to radically different forms of amusement: pre-modern feasts and festivals; eighteenth-century theatres and bawdy-houses, mid-nineteenth-century penny gaffs; the Music Halls of the 'Gay' Nineties; the first flickering danger-signs from the silent movies; the Hollywood picture palaces between the wars; and television viewing in our own historical time. Each, in its own time, has been accused of encouraging a moral debauch; each has been said to encourage imitative crime among the young. (1983: 208)

And, of course, each successive panic simply deepens the reservoir of fears upon which subsequent panics draw – thus within hours, literally, of the massacres at

Hungerford in 1987 and Dunblane in 1996, and of the conclusion of the trial of the two boys who murdered James Bulger in 1993, the papers were once again awash with stories blaming horror videos for these crimes. Indeed, so great was the renewed outcry against nasties in the aftermath of the Bulger case that it led to the Video Recordings Act being tightened still further. (For full accounts of this process see Barker and Petley [1997] and Petley [2011: 87–114].)

The nasty panic also has to be understood within its contemporary political and ideological contexts. It took place near the start of the Thatcher regime, one quite overtly committed to rolling back the tide of what it perceived as 1960s 'permissiveness' and imposing what it liked to refer to as 'Victorian values', a crusade in which it was daily cheered on by the majority of Britain's newspapers. As James Curran has put it, the 1960s

> symbolised for some all the negative changes that had taken place in the recent past: the country's decline in the world, the rise of crime, the erosion of a sense of community, young people with more money than sense, the decline of courtesy and respect. Indeed, a growing legion of folk devils – black muggers, punk rockers, flying pickets, Irish terrorists, football hooligans, single parents, illiterate youngsters, and 'race' rioters – came to be viewed as facets of a common problem: the loss of authority and erosion of tradition that had begun in the 1960s. (Curran et al. 2005: 23–4)

In such a situation, moral panics, which, given the nature of the British press, are not exactly difficult to ignite, are a useful means of attempting to gain the consent of the population, or at least significant sections of it, to the imposition of increasingly coercive measures on the part of the state, thus lending democratic legitimacy to exceptional or 'more than usual' exercises of control and containment on the part of the authorities. As Hall et al. note, in the later stages of this process, discrete moral panics tend to become 'mapped together' into a more general panic about the collapse of the social order and the onset of anarchy, with the result that 'minor forms of dissent [such as distributing or watching nasties] seem to provide the basis of "scapegoat" events for a jumpy and alerted control culture; and this progressively pushes the state apparatus into a more or less permanent "control" posture' (1978: 222). The cycle of moral panics thus issues directly into the law-and-order society, in which at the 'expense of certain of those liberties which, in more relaxed times, we enjoyed . . . the state has won the right, and indeed inherited the duty, to move swiftly, to stamp fast and hard, to listen in, discreetly survey, saturate and swamp, charge or hold without charge, act on suspicion, hustle and shoulder, to keep society on the straight and narrow' (1978: 323).

The short-circuit of communication

This is not to suggest in some conspiratorial fashion that moral panics are simply 'got up' by state agencies in order to extend their powers over the population. Indeed, in the case of the nasties it is abundantly clear from the narrative advanced in this chapter that it was reactionary newspapers and moral entrepreneurs, frequently acting in concert, which played the major role in igniting the panic in the first place and prodding the police and DPP into action, with the government unwilling to become involved until impelled to do so by the intense pressure generated by newspapers, backbenchers and the Whitehouse brigade. However, the important point to grasp here is that *all* of these, and not simply the state agencies, constitute the 'control culture', which, as Cohen explains, 'contains not just official institutions and personnel but also typical modes and models of understanding and explaining' the forms of deviance which give rise to moral panics ([1972] 2002: 57).

It may well be objected that the one element which has not been explored in this article is public opinion in the matter of nasties and video censorship. There are two reasons for this. First, there is actually very little evidence of any such opinion being gathered, although what little there is does not support the idea that the nasty panic was widespread in the population at large. Thus a *What Video/Popular Video* survey in 1982 showed that for 60 per cent of those who rented or bought videos, horror and science fiction were their favourite category; a MORI poll[3] in October 1983 revealed that 92 per cent of those polled had never been offended by the contents of a pre-recorded video cassette; while another MORI poll in March 1984 showed that 65 per cent of those interviewed were opposed to the government deciding which videos were available for home viewing. However, in the matter of moral panics, as indeed in all other matters, newspapers habitually claim to represent or speak for public opinion, in a process which Hall et al. call 'taking the public voice' and the 'enlisting of public legitimacy for views which the newspaper *itself* is expressing' (1978: 63). Never mind that the opinions thus presented by newspapers, whose values are predominantly reactionary and illiberal, may be anything but representative of the views of the population as a whole, these are the opinions which, in Britain at least, carry the greatest weight with politicians of all parties. Given that this is demonstrably the case, it doesn't actually matter what the public really think about subjects which have been given the moral panic treatment by the press. Chas Critcher argues: 'In moral panics, support from the public is a bonus, not a necessity. In any case, it can be constructed, largely by the media' (2003: 137). Similarly Ericson, Baranek and Chan argue that the media are an integral part of a 'deviance-defining elite', with everyone outside this elite simply being left to 'watch, listen to, or read the distant representations that form this symbolic spectacle' (1987: 351).

What we have here, then, is less a *circuit* of communication between the press, the public and politicians than a process involving, for the most part, just two sets of actors: the press and politicians. In other words, it is a *short-circuit* of communication. Thus, in the case of the nasties at least, it is possible to resolve the problem identified by David Miller and Jenny Kitzinger with moral panic theorizing, namely its alleged lack of agency. According to them:

> It is never very clear who is doing the panicking. Is it the media, the government, the public, or who? One reason for this lack of clarity is that distinctions between the media and the state, between the media and public belief, and between the state and other social institutions and groups are dissolved into Cohen's notion of the control culture. (1998: 216)

Here, as noted above, it was very clearly newspapers and moral entrepreneurs which actually made most of the running, particularly in the early stages of the panic. Indeed, in the case of the *Mail* the distinction largely collapsed anyway, but what this episode all too clearly illustrates is the quite remarkable power which a stridently populist press has managed to exert over the British political class for decades, although it needs to be added that this is largely because politicians have allowed it to do so.

It is for this reason that it is impossible to accept, in the UK context at least, what one might call the 'post-modern' critique of moral panic theory put forward by Angela McRobbie and Sarah Thornton. In their view:

> The proliferation and fragmentation of mass, niche and micro-media and the multiplicity of voices, which compete and contest the meaning of the issues subject to 'moral panic', suggest that both the original and revised models are outdated in so far as they could not possibly take account of the labyrinthine web of determining relations which now exist between social groups and the media, 'reality' and representation. (1995: 560)

McRobbie also notes that:

> The moral panic is the right's campaigning arm, but the right has increasingly had to contend with the pressure groups which have become the campaigning arm of the opposition. No sooner does a moral panic emerge than it is angrily

disputed, and its folk devils are fiercely defended by any one of a range of pressure groups which have emerged as a key force in opposing the policies of the new right during and after the Thatcher years. (1994: 199)

So far, so unproblematic, apart from the revealingly po-mo bracketing-off of 'reality' in the first quotation. After all, no one would disagree that new, and indeed older, forms of media have mushroomed in the past 20 years, and that the authoritarian turn taken by both the Tories and 'New Labour' has produced an extra-parliamentary oppositional backlash. It is also the case that the oppositional forces have well understood the important role played by the media, and especially the national press, in helping to whip up moral panics and create folk devils, and have attempted to intervene in and defuse moral panics by providing information and analysis which run counter to dominant media representations. But the operative word here is 'attempted', since most of the mainstream media, and in particular the vast majority of the national press, have remained resolutely closed to such incursions. McRobbie and Thornton argue that 'when Labour and Conservatives take the same line on law and order, arguing for "effective punishment" and the need for the moral regeneration of society, many media are inclined to give voice to other, sometimes dissenting, groups' (1995: 566). But the truth is quite the opposite, in that the shifting of the parliamentary consensus sharply to the right has served only further to naturalize the thoroughly illiberal worldview pedalled by most national newspapers, and to narrow the range of voices heard on radio and television, since the broadcasters (in spite of recent protestations to the contrary by the BBC) still appear to believe that the impartial stance on political matters which are required by law to adopt is best achieved by 'balancing' the views of the mainstream parties at Westminster. Extra-parliamentary views thus tend to find themselves at best marginalized, at worst demonized or simply silenced.

However, as indicated earlier, McRobbie and Thornton also draw attention to the presence of minority and specialist media, observing that 'folk devils now produce their own media as a counter to what they perceive as the biased media of the mainstream' (1995: 568). They also note that:

Moral panic is a favourite topic of the youth press. When the mass media of tabloids and TV become active in the 'inevitable' moral panic about 'Acid House', the subcultural press were ready. They tracked the tabloids every move, re-printed whole front pages, analysed their copy and decried the misrepresentation of Acid House. Some 30 magazines now target and speak up for youth. (1995: 568)

But while the proliferation of alternative media of one kind or another is undeniable, and indeed thoroughly welcome, the question of its political effectivity, particularly in defusing and contesting moral panics, simply has to be addressed. Thus in the case of raves, the subcultural press, and even the liberal rump of the national press (*Guardian*, *Observer*, *Independent*), may have done their best to counter the hysteria and disinformation pumped out on a daily basis by politicians and illiberal newspapers, but this did precisely nothing to stop the passing of the Criminal Justice Act and Public Order Act (POA) 1994, Section 63 of which criminalizes raves, in so doing revealing the depths to which the bureaucratic mind can sink by stating that '"music" includes sounds wholly or predominantly characterised by the emission of 'a succession of repetitive beats'. One has little idea of what people actually thought of such a blatantly authoritarian measure, but nor in the present context does it actually matter, since the Act was the result not of a plebiscite nor of a referendum but of an entirely circular, self-reinforcing process involving newspapers and politicians. (For accounts of the genesis of the Act see McKay [1996] and Collin [1997].)

McRobbie and Thornton argue that:

> In the old models of moral panic, the audience played a minor role and remained relatively untheorised. With few exceptions, they were the space of consensus, the space of media manipulation, the space of an easily convinced public. A new model need embrace the complex realm of reception – readers, viewers, listeners and the various social groups categorized under the heading of public opinion cannot be read off the representation of social issues. (1995: 572)

And, from a theoretical perspective, they are indeed quite correct: moral panic theory certainly does need to take on board modern work on audiences and how they read actual media texts. But, in terms of contemporary political reality, the inescapable fact is that, as noted at the start of this section, either politicians believe that the opinions expressed by the majority of newspapers do indeed reflect public opinion, or these are the opinions to which politicians are most highly sensitized and thus liable to react in policy terms. Consequently, what the public actually thinks counts for little. (For a chilling and remarkably well-detailed account of this process in action see Dean [2012].)

However, at long last, the fall-out from furore over the phone-hacking at the *News of the World* has shone a spotlight onto the true nature of the relationship between the press and politicians, one in which the former, far from acting in the public interest as a 'Fourth Estate' or a watchdog over the latter, has behaved far more like an attack dog, bullying and threatening politicians into supporting policies which gel with its own extreme and narrow ideological views and, in the case of the Murdoch press in particular, policies which facilitate the untrammelled expansion of its owners' media interests. The fact that the Tory government in 1983 finally acceded to the loud and insistent demands for statutory video censorship expressed both through and by papers such as *the Mail* should not be allowed to obscure the fact that they first attempted to resist these demands. It should also be noted that this process was repeated in every detail in the events leading to the toughening of the Video Recordings Act in 1994 in the wake of the Bulger murder. It has suited both sides in this unhealthiest of relationships to swathe it in thoroughly mystificatory rhetoric about press freedom, public accountability and so on, but thanks to the Leveson Inquiry the cat is now well and truly out of the bag, and it will be extremely difficult to stuff it back in again, however hard newspapers and politicians may try to do so. As a consequence, moral panics, one profoundly hopes, may be rather more difficult to ignite in the future.

Notes

1   The charges were brought under section 2 of the OPA, which meant that the cases were heard in magistrates courts and concerned only the videos themselves, rather than the distributors of the videos. These were forfeited and destroyed, but had the cases been brought under section 3, which requires a trial by a judge and jury, the distributors themselves would have been in the dock, and, if found guilty, could have faced imprisonment.

2   On its website, the London Dungeon describes itself thus: '1000 years of London's darkest and most gory history, 14 actor led shows and 3 scary rides make the London Dungeon attraction an educationally chilling experience and a great day out for the whole family'.

3   MORI was one of Britain's leading public opinion survey companies. In 2005 it merged with another such company, Ipsos UK, to form Ipsos MORI, which is the second largest market research organization in the United Kingdom.

Bibliography

Barker, M. (ed.) (1984), *The Video Nasties: Freedom and Censorship in the Media*, London: Pluto Press.

Barker, M. and Petley, J. (eds) (1997), *Ill Effects: The Media/Violence Debate*, London: Routledge.

— (eds) (2001), *Ill Effects: The Media/Violence Debate*, 2nd edn, London: Routledge.

Box of the Banned (2005), DVD extra 'Ban the Sadist Videos', Anchor Bay.

Brown, B. (1984), 'Exactly What We Wanted', in M. Barker (ed.), *The Video Nasties: Freedom and Censorship in the Media*, London: Pluto Press, 68–87.

Chibnall, S. (1977), *Law and Order News*, London: Tavistock.

Cohen, S. ([1972] 2002), *Folk Devils and Moral Panics*, 3rd edn, London: Routledge.

Collin, M. (1997), *Altered State: The Story of Ecstasy Culture and Acid House*, London: Serpent's Tail.

Critcher, C. (2003), *Moral Panics and the Media*, Maidenhead, Buckingham: Open University Press.

Cumberbatch, G. and Howitt, D. (1989), *A Measure of Uncertainty: The Effects of the Mass Media*, London: John Libbey.

Curran, J., Gaber, I. and Petley, J. (2005), *Culture Wars: The Media and the British Left*, Edinburgh: Edinburgh University Press.

Dean, M. (2012), *Democracy Under Attack: How the Media Distort Policy and Politics*, Bristol: Policy Press.

Ericson, R. V., Baranek, P. M. and Chan, J. B. L. (1987), *Visualising Deviance*, Milton Keynes: Open University Press.

Ferman, J. (1979), 'Censorship Today', *Films Illustrated*, October, 62–7.

Gauntlett, D. (2005), *Moving Experiences: Media Effects and Beyond*, Eastleigh: John Libbey.

Hall, S., Critcher, C., Jefferson, T., Clarke, C. and Roberts, B. (1978), *Policing the Crisis: Mugging, the State and Law and Order*, London: Macmillan.

Kerekes, D. and Slater, D. (2000), *See No Evil: Banned Films and Video Controversy*, Manchester: Headpress.

Marsh, D., Gowin, P. and Read, M. (1986), 'Private Members Bills and Moral Panic: the Case of the Video Recordings Act (1984)', *Parliamentary Affairs*, 39(2): 179–96.

Martin, J. ([1993] 2007), *The Seduction of the Gullible: The Curious History of the British "Video Nasties" Phenomenon*, 2nd edn, Liskeard: Stray Cat.

McKay, G. (1996), *Senseless Acts of Beauty: Cultures of Resistance Since the Sixties*, London: Verso.

McRobbie, A. (1994), 'The Moral Panic in the Age of the Postmodern Mass Media', in A. McRobbie (ed.), *Postmodernism and Popular Culture*, London: Routledge, 198–219.

McRobbie, A. and Thornton, S. L. (1995), 'Rethinking "Moral Panic" for Multi-mediated Social Worlds', *British Journal of Sociology*, 46(4): 559–74.

Miller, D. and Kitzinger, J. (1998), 'AIDS, the Policy Process and Moral Panics', in D. Miller, J. Kitzinger, K. Williams and P. Beharrell (eds), *The Circuit of Mass Communication*, London: Sage, 213–22.

Pearson, G. (1983), *Hooligan: A History of Respectable Fears*, London: Macmillan.

Petley, J. (2001), 'Us and Them', in M. Barker and J. Petley (eds), *Ill Effects: The Media/Violence Debate*, London: Routledge, 170–85.

— (2011), *Film and Video Censorship in Modern Britain*, Edinburgh: Edinburgh University Press.

Video Nasties: The Definitive Guide (2010), DVD extra 'Video Nasties: Moral Panic, Censorship and Videotape', Nucleus Films.

Part Two

Lifestyle, Risk and Health

5

Theorizing Alcohol in Public Discourse: Moral Panics or Moral Regulation?

Henry Yeomans

Introduction

In recent years, politicians, police chiefs, journalists and medical professionals have been vocal in their condemnation of excessive alcohol consumption. Newspapers routinely refer to a 'binge drinking epidemic' (*Daily Mail*, 2 June 2010), Prime Minister David Cameron has spoken of drink-induced 'mayhem on the streets' (UK Government, 2012) and Work and Pensions Secretary Iain Duncan-Smith has claimed alcohol is 'damaging the fabric of the nation' (*The Times*, 23 January 2010). Despite the widespread belief that we live in new and difficult times, the 'drink problem' in Britain is nothing new. From the eighteenth century 'gin craze' and the Victorian temperance movement to the more current debates over 24-hour licensing and minimum pricing, acute public concern about drinking has been a regular feature of British history. Are these recurrent anxieties the result of successive episodic outbursts of irrational anxiety about different social changes, as classic moral panic theory might postulate? Or can other theoretical frameworks, particularly moral regulation theory, improve our understanding of the British relationship with alcohol?

Various academics have examined the connection of alcohol consumption to social anxiety or moralization (Gusfield 1996; Valverde 1998; Yeomans 2011a). This chapter brings fresh insights in two main ways: first, by focusing on British history, a neglected area in the sociology of drinking; and second, by bringing enquiries up to date with an examination of recent public discourse on drink, which has been largely preoccupied with the idea of alcohol as a health problem. Drawing on the work of Alan Hunt and Chas Critcher, this chapter uses the history of British concerns about drinking to shed new light on the question of whether moral panic theory is still relevant, and, if so, in what form.

Theoretical background

Ben-Yehuda defines a moral panic as 'the creation of a situation in which exaggerated fear is manufactured about topics which are seen (or claimed) to have a moral component' (2009: 49). Similarly, Jenkins states that 'moral panic' denotes an official reaction to a certain social phenomenon that is out of all proportion with the actual level of threat posed (Jenkins 2009). In Cohen's 'classic' version of moral panic theory, the official reaction is targeted at specific groups of people, such as Mods and Rockers, who are transformed into 'folk devils'. This reaction is not a straightforward response to the target group's behaviour; instead, social anxiety caused by broader societal changes comes to be directed, by the media, politicians and other members of the establishment, at these folk devils. The end result of this panic, according to Cohen, is that 'ways of coping are evolved or (more often) resorted to' and consequently 'the condition disappears, submerges or deteriorates and becomes more visible' (Cohen 1972: 9). Since the 1970s, this typical form of moral panic theory has proved popular among academics seeking to explain episodes during which mainstream society becomes fearful, angry and moralistic about a certain group or type of behaviour to an extent that is disproportionate to the level of danger, or probability of harm, actually faced. But in recent years, moral panic theory has taken something of a critical battering. It has been accused of being politically biased, unfairly critical of public reactions and epistemologically and ontologically flawed (Hunt 1999; Cohen 2009; Jenkins 2009). Clearly there are some fundamental questions relating to the continuing viability of moral panic theory which need to be answered.

It is not possible to examine all of these debates, so this chapter will concentrate on the issues most relevant to the author's own research in historical social science. These relate mainly to the utility of the moral panic concept as a means through which to explain certain historical events and also locate these events within longer-term processes. Moral panic theory has been criticized due to its classically episodic approach which depicts these phenomena as, in Cohen's words, rising up 'every now and then' (Cohen 1972: 9) before submerging again as some form of equilibrium is reached or restored. Each panic, therefore, appears as an independent event. This point has been disputed by, among others, Rowbotham and Stevenson (2003) who argue that these moral panics are not episodic but a regular, if not routine, feature of social life. Typically, these phenomena are attributed to social anxiety; but this notion is deemed by Alan Hunt to be too causally vague to be useful (Hunt 1999). In order to explain the actions of social actors, Hunt argues we need a more discursive understanding of how social problems and their proposed solutions are constructed. Hunt develops a form of moral regulation theory which encapsulates both a Gramscian concentration on the reproduction of certain forms of social order as well as a Foucauldian focus on the construction of knowledge and the ethical subjectivity of individuals (Ruonavaara 1997; Hunt 1999). Moral regulation theory is thus concerned with the problematization of certain types of behaviour over the course of history, and the relation, through (legal and moral) regulation, of this normative process to the governance of human behaviour. Does Hunt's discursive and processual theory of moral regulation provide a more useful theoretical lens through which to conduct research in historical sociology?

Explaining the 'drink problem': Anxiety or discourse?

Moral panic and moral regulation theories encourage concentration on differing means, anxiety and discourse, through which to explain the emergence of social problems. Which is more suited to studying the 'drink problem'?

Moral panics and social anxiety are clearly relevant to the subject area of drinking. Indeed, these heuristic devices have been employed numerous times since Joseph Gusfield (1962) highlighted the causal importance of status anxiety within the emerging middle class in producing the American temperance movement. More recently, Peter Borsay's (2007) discussion of the Georgian 'gin panics' cited contextual factors, such as rapid urbanization, increasing working-class affluence and concerns about the breakdown of the family, as factors instrumental in producing the social unease which came to be directed at the consumption of spirituous liquor.[1] Gin was a relatively new substance, having been introduced to Britain from the Netherlands after the Glorious Revolution, and historians generally accept that its consumption was on the rise in London during the first half of the eighteenth century (Nicholls 2009). But, according to Borsay, it was 'the capacity to yoke the rise in gin drinking to the wider concerns of society that transformed a potential social problem into a full blown "moral panic"' (2007) – a panic which saw William Hogarth famously depict the criminal and immoral depravities of 'Gin Lane'. Nicholls describes how it is common to see the Licensing Act 1751, which raised the licence fee for gin-sellers and restricted the type of premises which could hold a licence, as making the gin trade respectable and thus ending the gin panics (Nicholls 2009: 46–8).[2] The 'gin panics' thus seem to lend themselves readily to explanation through moral panic theory: social changes created anxiety which became focused on a new substance and a new social group (emerging urban working class); Hogarth and others 'manned the barricades' before legal changes restored some sense of equilibrium.

But the utility of social anxiety as an explanatory concept is not universal. In his study of the Black Act 1723, E. P. Thompson criticized the idea that this repressive law, which condemned many people to death for relatively minor criminal offences, could be explained simply by the wave of public concern unleashed by social unrest. A widespread perception of crisis may have led to a consensus that something needed to be done, but 'If we agree that "something" needed to be done this does not entail the conclusion that *anything* might be done' (Thompson 1977: 195). In terms of explaining the particular nuances of legal and political responses to certain social problems, the notion of anxiety is insufficient. Hunt (1999), Jenkins (2009) and others have extended this argument to ask why certain types of behaviour come to be seen as problematic in the first place. Why did social anxieties in the 1960s become fixed on youth culture? Or, to return to Thompson's example, why were poaching and the felling of trees seen to be such potent threats to the dominant social order? How were agitators recruited and support mobilized? For Hunt (1999), a crucial object of enquiry must be the process of problematization, whereby a normative judgement is made about the immorality or unacceptability of certain types of conduct. As an explanatory matrix, social anxiety sheds limited light on why certain things become social problems, or what is done about them once they are problematized.

This point can be elucidated with reference to the 'drink problem' during the First World War, which has also been termed a 'moral panic' (Greenaway 2003: 97). The outbreak of war led to an intensification of concerns for national efficiency; the currency of discipline and order was inflated by recognition of a need to maximize productivity (both industrial and military). Alcohol was swiftly represented as detrimental to this efficiency drive and, in May 1915, Lloyd George declared that 'we are fighting three foes, Germany, Austria and Drink: and as far as I can see the greatest of these deadly foes is Drink' (Nicholls 2009: 154). Although Lloyd George's statement reeks of hyperbole, he was not alone in singling out alcohol as an especially virile threat to the nation. The government tightened legal restrictions on drink during the war, for example, by restricting opening hours, limiting the strength of alcoholic drinks and going as far as experimenting with nationalization of the drinks industry in certain strategically important areas. In addition, a campaign to persuade people to make and uphold patriotic teetotal pledges for the duration of the war was backed by King George V, Lord Kitchener and senior Anglican clergy (Yeomans 2011b). During the First World War, therefore, the menace of drink seems to have been exaggerated, and the barricades were manned by distinguished representatives of the status quo. So, considering the grave military threats being faced, why was alcohol identified as 'the greatest foe'? And why, despite concerns that it would deprive the British state of much-needed tax revenue and starve our wine-exporting allies of national income (Yeomans 2011b), was teetotalism seen by many as the solution?

In order to explain some of the peculiarities of the debates about alcohol during the First World War, it is necessary to consider how the 'drink problem' was conceived at the time. Was alcohol seen as entirely problematic? Did it pose moral as well as practical questions? In what terms did people argue for greater regulation? It is evident that the simple existence of anxiety about efficiency and national security are not explanation enough. Although moral panic theory may have been suitable for investigating the 'gin panics', in the First World War and beyond a more discursive approach to the drink question is necessary.

Episodes and processes: Is a synthesis necessary?

So, a discursive approach to debates about alcohol, more in line with moral regulation theory, is required. The 'gin panics' and the First World War have already been mentioned, but these are far from the only instances of heightened public alarm about drink. Indeed, to understand discourse on alcohol during 'the Great War', it is necessary to consider the nineteenth century and the development of the temperance movement. As in moral regulation theory, a longer-term focus on historical processes is required.

The emergence of the temperance movement might be construed through the rubric of moral panic theory. The early movement crystallized around opposition to the Beer Act 1830, a liberalizing piece of licensing legislation which led to a large increase in the number of premises selling beer and an accompanying increase in the number of arrests for drunkenness (Wilson 1940; Harrison 1971). People's drinking habits thus became the focus of much moral disquiet and the number of active temperance societies greatly expanded. This was particularly the case in the emerging heartlands of the temperance movement, Yorkshire and Lancashire where, perhaps due to the pace and extent of industrialization, anxieties about drinking appeared most acute (Harrison 1971). The ingredients of a moral panic are present: anxiety about 'deeper' social changes, a liberal legal stimulus and an angry, vocal reaction. However, the first British temperance societies were founded prior to the Beer Act; John Edgar's Belfast based group and John Dunlop's Renfrewshire society were both founded in 1829 (*Belfast News Letter*, 14 August 1829). Moreover, they were inspired by the widely reported establishment of American temperance groups (*Morning Chronicle*, 5 August 1829). These parallel events in America imply that the emergence of the temperance movement was not driven by local or national factors, such as legal or social changes. The temperance movement appears part of a trans-Atlantic attitudinal transformation which produced a project to reform the behaviour of drinkers.

More than just a worried reaction, the temperance movement came to embody a whole new discourse of anti-alcohol sentiment. Consistent with Georgian concerns for gin, early temperance groups promoted moderate drinking or abstinence from spirits only. But attitudes began to change in the early 1830s and people increasingly began to identify alcohol itself, rather than drunkenness, as the source of sinful behaviour. It was no longer the case that drinking may lead to temptation and immorality; alcohol itself was 'a terrible evil' (*Preston Guardian*, 26 October 1872a) of such magnitude that there was not 'anything to compare' (*Preston Guardian*, 16 November 1872b). To temperance activists, alcohol was an evil substance and, in Preston in 1832, Joseph Livesey demonstrated the salience of these discursive changes when he began administering the first teetotal pledges. The pledge was a routine of self-disciplined avoidance of all alcoholic drinks and, therefore, a means to avoid the sinful act of drinking entirely. As an idea and basis for organized campaigning, teetotalism spread rapidly across Britain and America. Livesey's British Association for the Promotion of Temperance (BAPT) and the London-based New British and Foreign Society for the Suppression of Intemperance were both established in 1835 to advance teetotalism and, by 1840, even moderationist pioneer John Dunlop had joined the teetotal ranks (Harrison 1971). Based around abstinence, the temperance movement developed a discourse about alcohol which was conceptually distinct from its historical precursors.

Unlike during earlier outbursts relating to drinking, anti-alcohol sentiment from the late 1820s onwards was highly organized. Groups such as Livesey's BAPT, later the British Temperance League (BTL), were national organization with numerous local branches. Livesey describes their activities as based on 'kindly Christian-like teaching and admonition . . . visiting the back slums, holding temperance meetings everywhere, and circulating sound information and temperance tracts and publications' (*Preston Guardian*, 26 July 1873). These efforts, to persuade people to adopt the teetotal pledge, earned the BTL and similar groups the title 'moral suasionists'; but they were not only concerned with new initiates. For those already pledged, temperance societies sought to aid continued abstinence through providing fraternal support and a social life not centred on the local pub (Shiman 1988). Teetotal groups were highly evangelical and, with a missionary zeal, they spread the gospel of temperance to various parts of the globe. Eriksen (1989) describes how Sweden, whose attitudes and laws continue to exhibit a heightened mistrust of alcohol, was introduced to temperance by British and American missionaries. For the Band of Hope, formed in Leeds in 1847, the crucial frontier was a generational one and they aimed to inculcate teetotal habits in children (Shiman 1988). Prohibitionist temperance groups, such as the UK Alliance, were organized on a similar system of local branches and national leadership. Prohibitionists, however, directed their campaigning efforts at governments rather than individual drinkers in an effort to affect restrictive legal reform. They were highly organized and well-funded; Brown (1972) reports that, in the 1880s, the UK Alliance had much higher revenues than either of the main political parties. Whether employing suasionist or prohibitionist tactics, highly organized temperance campaigns spanned the whole of the Victorian period.

The British temperance movement is, therefore, difficult to classify as a moral panic. It was not an outburst of alarm prompted by anxiety about social changes, but a sophisticated, organized campaign against the use of alcohol which was sustained until well into the twentieth century. Unlike the 'gin panics', the temperance movement engendered the discursive development of abstinence, which replaced older sentiments based around moderation or avoiding drunkenness. In addition, the level of mobilization clearly distinguishes these two examples of mass anti-alcohol sentiment. The temperance movement, therefore, much more easily fits the mould of a moral regulation movement. Hunt (1999: 28) states that moral regulation projects require a target, agents, tactics, discourses and a political context – all characteristics the temperance movement clearly possessed. Alcohol, the target of this moral regulation project, was thus problematized, and extensive efforts were made to increase legal or personal (via the pledge) regulation of its use. The temperance movement corresponds to many other characteristics of moral regulation movements which Hunt identifies, for example, it was a campaign 'from below' which involved working-class but mainly middle-class agents. Equally, it is positioned on the interface between what Foucault refers to as 'governance of the self' and 'governance of others' (Hunt 1999: 2); it was clearly not enough for men like Livesey to abstain from alcohol themselves and they felt compelled to spread this habit among others. As a long-term mobilization based on discursive developments, the temperance movement appears much better suited to study through the theoretical lens of moral regulation theory.

But, amidst the long-term development of temperance mobilization and subsequent, ongoing debates about the effect of drink on crime and health, there were/are clear high points in concern. For example, in the early 1870s parliamentary consideration of licensing reforms coincided with a frenzy of temperance activity as well as mobilization of the drinks industry. It was even commented at the time by William Harcourt MP that the government appeared to be operating in 'a state of moral panic' (*The Times*, 31 December 1872a). Equally, drink debates during the First World War were perhaps the zenith of the temperance movement. Temperance activists had long predicted that national intemperance would cause collective decline and, in the context of total war and dependence on military and industrial efficiency, this fear became wildly acute. Moreover, in both these episodes lasting legal reforms emerged from the discursive fever-pitch. The Licensing Act 1921 made permanent certain wartime restrictions, such as morning and afternoon closure of licensed premises, which endured until relatively recently, and the Licensing Act 1872 established licensing requirements and drunkenness offences which continue to shape the legal governance of alcohol (Yeomans 2011a). Although heated moral debates may not be exceptional (as Cohen claimed), it does seem feasible to see singular episodes of panic as high points of concern or formative events within longer processes of problematization and regulation. This reasoning echoes Critcher, who has argued that moral panics are an extreme and temporary form of moral regulation, high points in an established current of moral concern. Critcher goes on to argue that, although constituent of moral regulation projects, moral panics still stand out as significant events and thus require their own conceptual identity (Critcher 2009).

Critcher's synthesis of moral panics and moral regulation sits well with the topic of drinking, debates about which are not exceptional but are punctuated by episodes of extreme concern. This historical changeability of debates about drink could equate with what Sean Hier refers to as 'the volatility of moralization' (Hier 2008). Hier uses this concept as a substitute for moral panics, a way to denote 'sensational, inflammatory, and spectacular discourses that articulate moral transgressions on the part of diverse individuals and/or social groups' without labelling these discourses as irrational, disproportionate or exceptional (Hier 2008: 174). While Hier manages to conceptually embed these periods of heightened concern within more usual processes of moralization, he offers little or no mechanism through which discourse on social problems can be linked to external social events. Hier's attempts to move moral panic theory away from the traditional comparison of representation and reality and towards a focus on wider practices of governance leads to a near-total concentration on discursive forms; indeed, the very term 'volatility' implies that discursive changes are the result of internal instabilities within a given discourse. This may be a suitable tool with which to characterize, for example, developments in the 1850s which saw the American concept of prohibition become popular among temperance advocates in Britain. However, explaining other discursive developments can require the acknowledgement of broader political, social and economic factors. The outbreak of the First World War was a geo-political event, ontologically separate to alcohol discourse, which nevertheless provided a stimulus which led to alterations in the problematization and regulation of drinking. While the concept of social anxiety has been criticized as a vague explanatory tool, it does provide a means through which social problems are related to their historical context. In stressing the need for discursive research, Hier risks throwing the explanatory baby out with the bathwater of anxiety.

To summarize, a theoretical synthesis is required. In addition to moral regulation theory's discursive approach, this section has highlighted the applicability of its long-term, developmental focus. However, there is still a need for a conceptual category of extreme or unusual events which occur within longer-term processes of moral regulation, as well as an accompanying need to link both moralization processes and extreme episodes to their wider contexts. To return to where we began, the furore about drink during the First World War must be seen as both a reaction to external geo-political events and the culmination of decades of abstinence-based temperance campaigning. The new outbreak of war, mediated through older understandings of alcohol, produced an episode of moral panic – an intense, heightened drive for moral regulation over a short period of time. Aspects of moral panic theory should, therefore, be incorporated into moral regulation approaches to historical social science.

The moral inheritance of temperance

Critcher's theoretical synthesis allows the temperance movement to be conceived as a long-term moral regulation project, albeit punctuated with shorter episodes of more alarmed discourse. But the issue of how certain chronological points within this current of moralization relate to each other remains problematic; hence this section explores the issue by investigating what happened to the moral discourse on alcohol after the decline of temperance. This research jars somewhat with the dominant neo-liberal logic of alcohol regulation. Classically, liberal behavioural governance focused on facilitating informed decision making; the state must educate people and thus empower them to make choices about their own lifestyle. Neo-liberalism constructs these choices around risk and harm, requiring that we each become involved in the management of the personal risks we face in order to minimize the probability that we are harmed in some way (Haggerty 2003). These neo-liberal choices, in theory, draw on contemporary, rational forms of knowledge; they are individual, calculative and informed by expert advice. Moral panic theory, however, is not well-placed to critique neo-liberalism; Haggerty (2003) has argued that, in seeking to expose disparities between perceived and actual probabilities of harm, moral panic theory operates through the same rational, calculative logic. As they are typically seen as exceptional and temporary, moral panic theory also finds it difficult to conceptually marry episodes of panic with the notion that one outburst of anxiety may influence subsequent ideas or shape the next episode of moral panic. Moral panic theory could, therefore, be seen as ahistorical or 'presentist', and similar again to the dominant logic of neo-liberalism. So, what can historical perspectives add to our knowledge of concepts of risk and harm? How should contemporary behavioural choices be understood? This section will investigate these questions with reference to recent debates on alcohol and actions of public health lobby groups.

Taking exception to historical exceptionalism

Alarmed, vocal complaints about the drinking habits of the British population intensified massively in 2003–2004 and have remained prominent since (Critcher 2008; Yeomans 2012). Tony Blair labelled excessive drinking a 'new British disease' (*BBC News*, 20 May 2004), David Cameron stated that binge drinking 'drains resources in our hospitals, generates mayhem on our streets and spreads fear in our communities' (UK Government 2012) and public health professionals Anna Gilmore and Jeff Colin claimed that 'drinks companies spread liver disease as surely as mosquitoes do malaria' (*Guardian*, 21 February 2011). As Gilmore and Colin indicate, recent debates have been particularly concerned with issues of health and some commentators, especially those connected to medical professions, have called for a minimum price on alcohol. Tough regulation is seen as necessary because, as *the Daily Mirror* put it, 'UK alcohol consumption is out of control' (*Daily Mirror*, 22 July 2009). Indeed, alcohol consumption did rise for much of the late twentieth century and liver disease mortality has followed a similar upward trajectory. However, in 2004, the World Health Organisation (WHO) found British alcohol consumption to be still only middling in European terms and, similarly, liver disease mortality rates are not comparatively high (2004, 2006). Most interestingly, the explosion of public anxiety about drinking in 2004 actually coincided with the early stages of a sustained decline in average British alcohol consumption which amounts, in some estimates, to 13 per cent over 2004–10 (Robinson and Bulger 2008; *BBC News*, 3 September 2010). It is, therefore, difficult to defend the claim that drinking is 'out of control' or agree with *the Guardian*'s 'expert' judgment that Britain's drinking problem is 'pre-eminent in Europe' (*Guardian*, 11 September 2009). The reaction to British drinking habits seems disproportionate and it would certainly be possible, therefore, to diagnose a severe case of moral panic.

However, classifying the events as a typical moral panic risks neglecting the importance of the historical dimension of attitudes to alcohol. It has already been discussed how, classically, the term 'moral panic' denotes exceptional events which, after some social rebalancing, disappear or submerge. But, since the beginning of the temperance movement, anxieties about alcohol have not disappeared; Greenaway discusses how drink has proven an ever-changing and near-omnipresent feature of public and political debate (Greenaway 2003). From the First World War and the Mass Observations of the 1930s to drink-driving reforms in the 1960s and the all-day opening of public houses in the late 1980s, alcohol has rarely avoided the public and political gaze for long. This persistent unease or borderline neurosis is not exclusive to Britain; Levine (1993) identifies a similar prevalence of public concern about drinking in the United States, Canada, New Zealand, Australia, Sweden, Finland, Iceland and Norway. Interestingly, these Anglo-Saxon and Nordic countries were all home to sizeable, abstinence-based temperance movements in the nineteenth and early twentieth centuries, and all seem to have retained a preoccupation with drink. The United States, for example, may have repealed prohibition, but its strict laws still forbid the sale of alcohol to those under the age of 21 and enable many states to establish 'dry counties'. Sweden is also notable as its historical concentration on the municipal control of the liquor trade continues to be evident in the operation of a state alcohol retail monopoly on off-licence sales. So, in the wake of large-scale abstinence-based social movements, anxieties about drink are endemic rather than exceptional in Britain as well as in Levine's other temperance cultures.

Outbursts of alcohol-related public concern are not temporary, unique or exceptional events, but regular, if not constant, features of public life. The relative importance attributed to alcohol and the type of comment it provokes may vary over time, but, at any given time from the Victorian period onwards, some level of anxiety can be expected. The previous section employed Critcher's theoretical synthesis to argue that the Victorian temperance movement constituted a distinct project to morally regulate drinking which was punctuated with episodes of heightened alarm. Given the chronological and international association of contemporary unease about alcohol and temperance movements, it is, therefore, worth considering whether modern medical anxieties about drink are connected in any way to the temperance project. I have argued elsewhere that the near-hysterical public reaction to the implementation of 24-hour licensing in 2005 was an episode of moral panic that should be understood with reference to the discursive legacy of the temperance movement (Yeomans 2009). Based on a similar incorporation of episodes of panic into long-term discursive processes, the next section will investigate the historical development of the ideas and attitudes which support the alarming medical discourse of the present day.

Congruity in moral and medical discourses

Since 2008, there have been calls for the government to tackle alcohol-related social problems by introducing a minimum price per unit of alcohol (usually 40–50p). This plan was actively promoted by a variety of medical and public health groups, many of which, including the British Liver Trust, the Royal College of Physicians and the Institute of Alcohol Studies, are coordinated under the umbrella of the Alcohol Health Alliance. Subsequently, formal plans to introduce minimum pricing have been announced in Scotland as well as England and Wales. While this represents a new departure in policy terms, the origins of minimum pricing lie in much older discursive frameworks.

Sir Liam Donaldson, who served as Chief Medical Officer (CMO), 1998–2010, has been one of the major exponents of minimum pricing and used his annual reports in 2008 and 2009 to advance the measure. Donaldson justified this intervention by referring to what he calls 'passive drinking', defined as the direct or indirect effects of one person's drinking on the rest of the society (Donaldson 2009: 17–23). This 'collateral damage' includes drunken violence, vandalism, sexual assault, child abuse and foetal alcohol spectrum disorder. It is important to note that the problems do not lie purely with alcohol dependence or binge drinking; Donaldson explains how drinking above the recommended weekly limits increases the risk of heart disease and stroke, how any amount of drinking is linked to osteoporosis and reduced fertility, and, in regard to the risk of cancer, 'there is no safe alcohol limit' (Donaldson 2009: 19). Hence, 'a huge health burden carried by both the NHS and the friends and families who care for those damaged by alcohol' (Donaldson 2009: 17) is identified as part of England's 'drinking problem'. The effects of drinking go beyond damage to the health and well-being of the individual drinker, this is 'a problem for everybody' which affects 'many spheres of life and leaves no communities untouched' (Donaldson 2009: 22). Donaldson conforms to the 'availability theory' of alcohol consumption, which states that availability is the primary determinant of levels of consumption and levels of consumption are the primary determinant of alcohol-related harm (Plant and Plant 2006: 124). Thus, if availability is reduced through a measure to make alcohol less affordable, consumption and harm will also decrease. It is on these grounds that the CMO advocates minimum pricing as the best means to tackle this dire national situation.

The discourse of the modern public health lobby echoes that of the prohibitionist strand of the temperance movement. In 1856 Samuel Pope, the Secretary of the UK Alliance, claimed that alcohol 'destroys life, it imperils property, it wastes food, it tempts to crime, it engenders poverty, it increases taxation, and it weakens the power and impedes the progress of the people' (*The Times*, 2 October 1856). Just as Donaldson sees alcohol as inextricably linked to a variety of problems, prohibitionists saw drinking as responsible for a huge range of social ills. Moreover, prohibitionists were keen to point out that these were social, rather than purely individual, problems. Pope explained that alcohol

> destroys my primary right of security by constantly creating and stimulating social disorder. It invades my right of equality by deriving a profit from the creation of misery I am taxed to support. It impedes my right to free moral and intellectual development by surrounding my path with dangers, and by

weakening and demoralising society, from which I have a right to claim mutual aid and intercourse. (*The Times*, 2 October 1856)

For both Donaldson and the prohibitionists, alcohol-related harm is extensive and varied in form, as well as being inevitably social or communal in its effects. Donaldson avoids the explicitly moral language of prohibitionists but shares many of the same discursive features.

An additional and important similarity is that, for both groups in question, alcohol is regarded as inherently problematic. This problematization results, first, from the belief that the consumption of alcohol leads to other harms. Just as Pope claimed that drinking 'tempts to crime', others linked it to 'the worst cases of murder, street robbery, housebreaking, seduction, and suicide' (*The Times*, 4 January 1830). Alcohol was understood as predisposing people to inflict harm on either themselves or others, and so was commonly referred to as a 'temptation' or a 'temptation under sanction of law' (*Preston Guardian*, 23 August 1873c). An equivalent notion, regarding the propensity of drink to predispose towards harm, is identifiable in contemporary discourse. Writing in *The Times*, Alcohol Concern's Nicolay Sorensen stated that 'people who binge drink or drink excessively are more likely to be victims of violent crime, require emergency treatment or damage their health in the long term' (*The Times*, 28 November 2008). In 2004, the *Alcohol Harm Reduction Strategy for England* highlighted how binge drinkers expose themselves to a higher risk of accidents, alcohol poisoning and sexual assault, as well as making themselves more likely to both suffer from and commit violent crime. In addition, the report describes how 'chronic drinkers' are threatened by a high risk of, for example, cirrhosis, cancer and suicide, at the same time as increasing the risk that they will commit drink-driving or domestic violence (UK Government 2004). In modern parlance, it is the *risks* rather than *temptations* to which alcohol exposes its consumers which is troubling. Despite linguistic change, the underlying discursive feature remains intact.

The classification of alcohol as inherently problematic derives, second, from a perceived lack of safety in moderation. Dawson Burns and other prohibitionists believed that drinking was a slippery slope; it may begin as a moderate habit, but eventually a person will become intemperate. Intemperance was considered sinful and so, if all drinking leads to intemperance, all drinking is, therefore, sinful (and hence abstinence is required) (Cook 2006). In a similar vein, Donaldson's insistence that there is no 'safe limit' below which alcohol consumption does not increase the chances of developing cancer displays an interesting problematization of alcohol per se (rather than excessive drinking). Similarly, the New Labour government's 'Units – They All Add Up' TV campaign aimed to encourage lower consumption among moderate, regular drinkers whose health may be threatened in the long term. One of the adverts featured a middle-aged, apparently middle-class woman who managed to exceed her recommended daily limit of 2–3 units through seemingly harmless activities such as enjoying a gin and tonic with a friend at lunchtime and sharing a bottle of wine with her partner on Friday evening. We were told at the end of the advert that such routines of regular consumption 'could add up to a serious health problem' (Department of Health 2008). Lowe and Lee's (2010) investigation of the somewhat baffling decision in 2007 to advise teetotalism among pregnant women found that uncertainty about the probability of harm is increasingly viewed as dangerous. Their conclusion resonates with the broader picture on alcohol; in the absence of scientific certainty to the contrary, alcohol is once again regarded as essentially problematic. In addition to relating to other risks or temptations, alcohol itself is reproduced as a dangerous substance. In explicitly secular medical discourse, drinking no longer endangers the mortal soul but it does threaten long-term well-being by positioning the drinker within a temporal spectrum of lethal eventualities.

The modern public health lobby also arrive at similar policy conclusions as prohibitionists. There was much debate among Victorian temperance groups about how best to achieve societal abstinence from alcohol. Prohibitionists saw the suasionist idea of achieving national sobriety through the spread of teetotal pledges as fanciful; some would never take the pledge and those that did may not keep to it. In light of this, prohibitionist Dawson Burns mockingly asked suasionist Joseph Livesey 'Had all the residents of Preston who have signed kept their pledge, what would have been the temperance condition of Preston to-day?' (*Preston Guardian*, 19 July 1873b). Burns believed that, essentially, many people are deficient in moral fortitude and hence 'there are millions to whom the traffic is a terrible temptation' (*Preston Guardian*, 26 July 1873a). This was a popular Victorian idea, evident in 1872 when *The Times* declared that 'there never was a time when the hard-working but thriftless and improvident Englishman was not notorious for want of self-control' (*The Times*, 9 August 1872b). Nowadays, a similar lack of faith in the population's capacity for self-control is apparent; in 2010, *Express* columnist Theodore Dalrymple argued that Britain is rapidly becoming 'a nation without sufficient self-respect to control itself' (*Express*, 13 August 2010). Largely as a result of the American experience, prohibition has been discredited as a policy and so the modern public health lobby pursue a more sophisticated agenda based around minimum pricing. But the implication is identical; it is only through legal intervention that the dream of national sobriety can be realized.

The clear overlap of modern medical discourse on alcohol and older, explicitly moral discourses is not a recent development. Temperance campaigners had often sought medical evidence to support their stance; W. Hunt (1841) made the claim, highly dubious by modern standards, that alcohol is an indigestible poison that remains in the body until death. But from the late nineteenth century onwards, a more developed 'scientific' strand of the temperance movement began to emerge. Valverde (1998) describes how this movement defined heavy drinking as a disease (or a 'disease of the will'), meaning it is not the fault of the individual. But this de-stigmatizing effect went hand-in-hand with treatment programmes which usually possessed a distinctly moral component, such as the fostering of willpower. This juxtaposition of the medical and the moral was not, Valverde argues, seen as contradictory by most contemporaries, who believed habits of consumption were related to aspects of morality. She describes how the *British Journal of Inebriety* allowed adverts for non-alcoholic drinks in its pages 'as if by drinking Cadbury's cocoa one directly imbibed moral resolve along with nutritious matter' (Valverde 1998: 63–4). The most striking example of Valverde's point is Alcoholics Anonymous (AA), which espouses the belief that alcoholism is a disease at the same time as prescribing the profoundly religious '12 Steps' treatment programme. This programme, written in the 1930s, still includes such steps as making 'a decision to turn our will and our lives over to the care of God as we understood him' (2010). AA is now a respected, multinational organization, regarded as possessing considerable authority on the subject of addiction. It is not simply the case that modern medical discourse parallels temperance discourse; a fusion of medical and moral ideas has long characterized understandings of alcohol.

So, there are considerable discursive affinities between the views of Victorian prohibitionists and the modern public health lobby. For both groups, alcohol is an inherently problematic substance responsible for a variety of personal and social harms. These harms are constructed as practically inevitable; the 'slippery slope' of the Victorian period has been reinterpreted as a continuum of probability within which the chances of developing cancer or becoming a victim of crime become more real with every sip. Temptation, that omnipresent moral danger, has been translated into the secular concept of risk which, given the personal deficiencies of the population, most people are unable to effectively manage. In the absence of sufficient internal controls, the state must create external regulations that curb the tempting or risky availability of alcohol. Despite minimum pricing and risk discourse appearing as new, secular phenomena, there is, therefore, ample discursive evidence that contemporary understandings of drink are constructed within older heuristic frameworks. Recent alarm about alcohol is not, therefore, exceptional as a historical event, and nor is it independent from older historical episodes and processes.

Agency and the construction of behavioural choices

The new urgency in alcohol discourse comes mainly from the Alcohol Health Alliance. This coalition of groups has pursued a reasonably unified agenda, typified by Nicolay Sorensen's piece in *The Times* in 2008. After describing how alcohol increases various risks, Sorensen stresses that without sufficient information about these risks people will be unaware of the potential dangers of alcohol and so unable to 'make the choice' (*The Times*, 28 November 2008). But are choices about drinking as individual and calculative as Sorensen suggests? And can moral panic theory add anything to our understanding of this area?

Behavioural choices about alcohol are constructed, in no small part, by legal frameworks. Where alcohol can be sold, at what time and to whom are all aspects of drinking behaviour which are legally regulated. The punitive sanctions which can be applied to those found to be drunk and disorderly in a public place or driving a car while under the influence also shows that what people can and cannot do during or after consuming alcohol is also regulated by law. Many of these legal frameworks find their origins in the Licensing Act 1872. Among other things, this statute confirmed the basic requirement that all sellers of alcoholic drinks possess a licence (which had been scrapped for beer in 1830), it created earlier closing times for public houses and gave the police the power to enter licensed premises without the invitation of the landlord/landlady. I have highlighted elsewhere that temperance societies played an important role in both stimulating and shaping this licensing reform, and so it is not outlandish to suggest that they continue to exert some posthumous influence over the regulation of drinking (Yeomans 2011a). Perhaps more potently, through statutory provision, judicial precedent and the actions of certain local authorities, such as police forces and local councils,[3] a variety of more contemporary actors also play significant parts in the delineation of the legal boundaries of permissible behaviour. Through law and policy, a variety of actors are involved in constructing the legal regulation of drinking.

Beyond these legal constraints, individuals are left with a certain amount of behavioural freedom. It is not contrary to the law for adults to choose to drink alcohol and nor, in principle, is drunkenness illegal. When individuals make these types of choices, neo-liberalism requires them to do so 'rationally' with reference to assessments of probability of harm; but information and experts may, as Burgess has stressed, possess an agenda that is ulterior to simply facilitating choice. Liam Donaldson, who classifies binge drinking as a 'high-risk behaviour' and has been instrumental in promoting the idea of passive drinking (Donaldson 2009: 13), was on the government's payroll until 2010 in his position as Chief Medical Officer (CMO). Sorensen, quoted earlier, represents Alcohol Concern, whose campaigns for policy changes have, since their formation in 1985, been largely funded by the Department of Health (Burgess 2009). Certain key players in the public health lobby are, therefore, engaged in the project of behavioural regulation on a daily basis. The Institute of Alcohol Studies (IAS), which aims to improve scientific understandings of alcohol and produce policy, is not government-funded and so proudly proclaims its own independence (2010). However, the IAS was formed and continues to be largely funded by Alliance House Foundation. This group, previously known as the UK Temperance Alliance, was formed in the mid-twentieth century by the Victorian prohibitionist behemoth the UK Alliance and is committed to spreading total abstinence from alcohol. The IAS may be independent but, as with the CMO and Alcohol Concern, there are clearly questions about the impartiality of the apparently scientific understandings of alcohol which they champion. Legal choices about drinking are, therefore, partially structured by discursive agents involved in behavioural regulation or linked to historical temperance.

In addition to being delineated by legal parameters of permissible conduct and sometimes based on the prescriptions of potentially partial medical actors, behavioural choices can also be regulated in a more abstract way. Public health groups seek primarily to influence behavioural choices with reference to frightening risk assessments which encourage individuals to make a certain decision; but other agents, commonly politicians, give further moral direction. To elaborate, David Cameron describes binge drinking as 'a serious problem' responsible for a 'scourge of violence' (UK Government 2012) and Iain Duncan-Smith believes that excessive drinking 'is damaging the fabric of the nation' (*The Times*, 22 January 2010). These statements show that, even if we ignore the sometimes skewed information on risk, 'the choice' to drink (or, indeed, to binge drink) which Sorensen refers to is clearly not a free or individual one. Cameron, Duncan-Smith and others are clearly communicating to individuals which type of behaviour is normatively preferable and which will attract moral censure. Just as temperance groups asked people to choose between the sinful habit of drinking and the virtuous practice of abstinence, modern choices about drink are constructed within a moral framework which clearly designates which choice is good and acceptable, and which is bad, irresponsible, damaging and risky. So, medical professionals, politicians, campaign groups and others ensure that individual choices about drinking are legally and morally weighted.

As Burgess (2009), Hunt (2003) and others have described, risk discourse often encapsulates and thus continues older, morally driven discursive positions. Notions of risk and harm are, therefore, subsumed within a broader moral discourse which serves to regulate behavioural choices about alcohol made within the parameters of the law. This conclusion is entirely consistent with moral regulation approaches to social problems, although the means through which it was arrived at are not. Examination of who is generating and disseminating risk-based knowledge and who is morally structuring choices about alcohol embodies a concern with agency. Moral regulation theory is, generally speaking, weaker on this aspect of historical explanation; the discursive focus of research concentrates on how knowledge is constructed rather than who is constructing it. Hunt, interestingly, does recognize the role of group agency; he sees it as crucial to understand how groups of people come to see the world and try to influence it. But his group-focus and his suspicion of addressing the intentions of agents (Hunt 1999, 2004) suggest that individual agency remains beyond the pale. This discussion of various politicians, the CMO, Sorensen and others suggests that certain individual and group agents do possess a degree of discursive influence or public profile. This concern with agency has been embodied in this piece; who is 'manning the moral barricades' throughout history, and what their particular situational or ideological motives are, have been crucial concerns. Again, this concern with agency demonstrates the utility of certain aspects of the moral panic approach when transplanted into the more historical and discursive strategy of moral regulation theory.

Neo-liberalism and moral inheritance

Moral panics are not exceptional, temporary events that are chronologically isolated and qualitatively independent of each other. This section has explored how modern, primarily medical alarm about alcohol is linked, both discursively and to a degree organizationally, to the moral regulation project of the temperance movement. Legal and moral frameworks within which choices about alcohol are made have been identified and their historical development, influenced by temperance campaigns, has been described. Understandings of alcohol are, therefore, historically animated ideas, based on the long-term fusion of moral and medical perspectives. In neo-liberal society, choices may be explained largely with reference to risk but, when placed in historical perspective, this concept appears as a secular rendering of older understandings based on temptation or sin, instead of an ahistorical, value-neutral and probabilistic gauge of the likelihood of harm. These enduring discursive frameworks show that knowledge of alcohol does not exist in a historical vacuum but has been shaped over time by various actors (notably the temperance movement). How we understand alcohol and what we do about it are not decisions reached in an atomistic way; there is a moral inheritance in law, science and popular discourse, passed from one generation to the next, which plays a crucial role in the comprehension and regulation of drinking.

This idea of a moral inheritance is intended to supplement Critcher's synthesis of the two theoretical approaches by providing a means with which to understand how certain chronological points within a longer moral regulation project relate to each other. This argument is based, mainly, on the moral regulation approach to historical social science. The idea of a 'moral panic' is, perhaps, conceptually limited as a tool for historical study. But in addition to other utilities identified earlier, the capacity for moral panic theory to focus on agency, on who exactly is manning 'the moral barricades', has proved useful.

Conclusion

The intention of this chapter has been to explain how both moral panic and moral regulation theories have informed my research, and to reflect upon the lessons which the history of Britain's 'drink problem' may have for both theories. The main theoretical implications of this chapter are that we need a means through which to study social problems which is historical, discursive and processual as well as episodic. Moral regulation theory has generally been the more applicable and insightful of the two theories within my research, although aspects of a moral panic approach have been usefully integrated. Critcher's synthesized model, in which moral panics are presented as high points within longer-term processes of moralization, has been highlighted as particularly useful. This model has been supplemented with a discursive appreciation of the moral inheritance, both attitudinal and legal, which one episode of anxiety about alcohol may bequeath to posterity. In addition, this chapter has found that moral panic theory's valuations of agency as well as its ability to relate moral discourse to external social, political or economic events are helpful empirical tools when integrated into a longer-term discursive research strategy. Despite the critical battering it has taken, moral panic theory still, therefore, has something to offer social science.

Notes

1 Chas Critcher (2011) has also examined this period with reference to moral panic theory.
2 Although, it must be noted, Nicholls questions this historiographical orthodoxy.
3 Local authorities were given control over licensing in the Licensing Act 2003. Hence, who can sell alcohol, where and between what hours, is decided locally. Police and local authorities have other powers too – for example, the ability to create 'alcohol-free zones' where officers have the power to stop people consuming alcohol.

Bibliography

Alcoholics Anonymous (AA) (2010), *The Twelve Steps of Alcoholics Anonymous,* www.aa.org/en_pdfs/smf-121_En.pdf [accessed 13 September 2010].

BBC (2004), 'Alcohol the "New British Disease"', *BBC News,* 20 May.

— (2010), 'Alcohol Consumption "Continues to Fall"', *BBC News,* 3 September.

Belfast News Letter (1829), 'To the Editor of the News-Letter', 14 August.

Ben-Yehuda, N. (2009), 'Moral Panics – 36 Years On', *British Journal of Criminology,* 49(1): 1–3.

Borsay, P. (2007), 'Binge Drinking and Moral Panics: Historical Parallels?', *History and Policy,* www.historyandpolicy.org/papers/policy-paper-62.html [accessed 1 December 2010].

Boseley, S. (2009), 'Expert Blames UK Drink Culture for Youth Deaths', *Guardian,* 11 September.

Brown, J. B. (1972), 'The Temperance Career of Joseph Chamberlain, 1870–1877: A Study in Political Frustration', *Albion,* 4(1): 29–44.

Burgess, A. (2009), 'Passive Drinking: A Good Lie Too Far?', *Health, Risk and Society*, 11: 527–40.

Burns, D. (1873a), 'Dawson Burns and the Permissive Bill', *Preston Guardian*, 26 July.

— (1873b), 'The Permissive Bill Movement – Dawson Burns to the Rescue', *Preston Guardian*, 19 July.

— (1873c), 'The Permissive Bill Question', *Preston Guardian*, 23 August.

Cohen, S. (1972), *Folk Devils and Moral Panics*, London: MacGibbon and Kee.

— (2009), 'Carry On Panicking', Address given to the *British Society of Criminology Annual Conference,*, Cardiff, 29 June.

Cook, C. (2006), *Alcohol, Addiction and Christian Ethics*, Cambridge: Cambridge University Press.

Critcher, C. (2008), 'Moral Panics: A Case Study of Binge Drinking', in B. Franklin (ed.), *Pulling Newspapers Apart*, Abingdon: Routledge, 154–62.

— (2009), 'Widening the Focus: Moral Panics as Moral Regulation', *British Journal of Criminology*, 49(1): 17–34.

— (2011), 'Drunken Antics: the Gin Craze, Binge Drinking and Political Economy of Moral Regulation', in S. Hier (ed.), *Moral Panics and Politics of Anxiety*, Abingdon: Routledge, 171–89.

Dalrymple, T. (2010), 'Our Binge Drinking Culture Is a Living Hell for Everyone', *Daily Express*, 13 August.

Department of Health (2008), 'Units – They All Add Up', TV Advert, www.guardian.co.uk/media/video/2008/may/19/alcoholunits [accessed 1 December 2010].

Donaldson, L. (2009), *Annual Report of the Chief Medical Officer 2008 – On the State of Public Health*, Department of Health: London: Department of Health.

Eriksen, S. (1989), 'Drunken Danes and Sober Swedes? Religious Revivalism and the Temperance Movements as Keys to Danish and Swedish Folk Cultures', in B. Strath (ed.), *Language and the Construction of Class Identities*, Gothenburg: Gothenburg University Press, 55–94.

Gilmore, A. and Colin, J. (2011), 'Drinks Companies Spread Liver Disease as Surely as Mosquitoes do Malaria', *Guardian*, 21 February.

Greenaway, J. (2003), *Drink and British Politics since 1830*, Basingstoke: Palgrave.

Gusfield, J. (1962), 'Status Conflicts and the Changing Ideologies of the American Temperance Movement', in D. J. Pittnan and C. R. Snyder (eds), *Society, Culture and Drinking Patterns*, New York: John Wiley and Sons, 101–20.

— (1996), *Contested Meanings: The Construction of Alcohol Problems*, Wisconsin: University of Wisconsin Press.

Haggerty, K. (2003), 'From Risk to Precaution: The Rationalities of Personal Crime Prevention', in R. V. Ericson and A. Doyle (eds), *Risk and Morality*, Toronto: University of Toronto Press, 193–214.

Harrison, B. (1971), *Drink and the Victorians*, Pittsburgh: University of Pittsburgh Press.

Hier, S. P. (2008), 'Thinking Beyond Moral Panic: Risk, Responsibility, and the Politics of Moralization', *Theoretical Criminology*, 12(2): 173–90.

Homo (1830), 'Abuse of Spirituous Liquor', *The Times*, 4 January.

Hope, J. (2010), 'Set a Minimum Price for Alcohol, Watchdog Pleads', *Daily Mail*, 2 June.

Hunt, A. (1999), *Governing Morals*, Cambridge: Cambridge University Press.

— (2003), 'Risk and Moralization in Everyday Life', in R. V. Ericson and A. Doyle (eds), *Risk and Morality*, Toronto: University of Toronto Press, 165–92.

— (2004), 'Getting Marx and Foucault in Bed Together!', *Journal of Law and Society*, 31(4): 596–609.

Hunt, W. (1841), *History of Teetotalism in Devon*, Western Temperance Advocate Office.

Institute of Alcohol Studies (IAS) (2010), *About Us*, www.ias.org.uk/aboutus/who_we_are.html [accessed 1 December 2010].

Jenkins, P. (2009), 'Failure to Launch: Why Do Some Social Issues Fail to Detonate Moral Panics?', *British Journal of Criminology*, 49(1): 35–47.

Levine, H. (1993), 'Temperance Cultures: Concern about Alcohol in Nordic and English-Speaking Countries', in M. Lader, G. Edwards and D. C. Drummon (eds), *The Nature of Alcohol and Drug-Related Problems*, Oxford: Oxford University Press, 16–36.

Livesey, J. (1873), 'The Alliance and the Permissive Bill', *Preston Guardian*, 26 July.

Lowe, P. K. and Lee, E. J. (2010), 'Advocating Alcohol Abstinence to Pregnant Women: Some Observations about British Policy', *Health, Risk and Society*, 12(4): 301–11.

Morning Chronicle (1829), 'Temperance Society', 5 August.

Nicholls, J. (2009), *The Politics of Drink*, Manchester: Manchester University Press.

Plant, M. and Plant, M. (2006), *Binge Britain*, Oxford: Oxford University Press.

Pope, S. (1856), 'Further Reply by the Honorary Secretary', *The Times*, 2 October, 8.

Preston Guardian (1872a), 'Annual Tea Meeting of the Fisher-Gate Chapel Band of Hope', 26 October.

— (1872b), 'Conference on the Reform of Temperance in the Corn Exchange', 16 November.

Robinson, S. and Bulger, C. (2008), *General Lifestyle Survey*, Newport: Office for National Statistics.

Rowbotham, J. and Stevenson. K. (2003), *Behaving Badly*, Ashgate: Aldershot.

Ruonavaara, H. (1997), 'Moral Regulation: A Reformulation', *Sociological Theory*, 15(3): 277–93.

Shiman, L. L. (1988), *Crusade against Drink in Victorian England*, Basingstoke: Macmillan.

Sorensen, N. (2008), 'Should Alcohol Carry Health Warnings?', *The Times*, 28 November.

Stoppard, M. (2009), 'Save Teens from Alcohol Tragedy', *Daily Mirror*, 22 July.

Sylvester, R. and Thomson, A. (2010), 'Iain Duncan-Smith on Power, Alcohol Abuse and Britain's Broken Society', *The Times*, 22 January.

The Times (1872a), 'Public Meeting in Oxford', 31 December.

— (1872b), 'That Portion of the British Public . . .', 9 August.

Thompson, E. P. (1977), *Whigs and Hunters*, Harmondsworth: Penguin.

Thomson, A., Sylvester, R. and Leroux, M. (2010), 'Raise Drink Prices and Defy "Immoral" Supermarkets, Tory Strategist Demands', *The Times*, 23 January.

UK Government (2004), *Alcohol Harm Reduction Strategy for England*, London: Cabinet Office.

— (2012), *Alcohol Strategy 2012*, London: Home Office.

Valverde, M. (1998) *Diseases of the Will: Alcohol and the Dilemmas of Freedom*, Cambridge: Cambridge University Press.

Wilson, G. B. (1940), *Alcohol and the Nation*, London: Nicholson and Watson.

World Health Organisation (2004), 'Global Status Report on Alcohol', Singapore: WHO.

— (2006), 'European Status Report on Alcohol and Health', Denmark: WHO.

Yeomans, H. (2009), 'Revisiting a Moral Panic: Ascetic Protestantism, Attitudes to Alcohol and the Implementation of the Licensing Act 2003', *Sociological Research Online*, 14(2), www.socresonline.org.uk/14/2/6.html [accessed 25 October 2012].

— (2011a), 'Providentialism, the Pledge and Victorian Hangovers: Investigating Moderate Alcohol Policy in Britain, 1914–1918', *Law, Crime and History*, 1: 95–107.

— (2011b), 'What Did the British Temperance Movement Accomplish? Attitudes to Alcohol, the Law and Moral Regulation', *Sociology*, 45(1): 38–53.

— (2012), *'Spirited Measures and Victorian Hangovers: Public Attitudes to Alcohol, the Law and Moral Regulation'*, Unpublished PhD thesis, University of Plymouth, UK.

6

Moral Panics, Governmentality and the Media: A Comparative Approach to the Analysis of Illegal Drug Use in the News

Jeremy Collins

Introduction

The moral panic thesis has been defended as continuing to offer worthwhile insights into the social construction of deviance and risk while also being criticized on a number of levels (Thornton 1994; Critcher 2003, 2008). It has been suggested that moral panic analysis might benefit from an encounter with other perspectives and theoretical approaches, such as the governmentality approach. This chapter represents an attempt to apply moral panic analysis and certain ideas derived from theories of governmentality to a specific case study in order to examine how the latter can inform and support the former.

This particular case study concerns the news coverage of an apparently new 'designer drug' officially called mephedrone but known to users by a number of nicknames including 'meow meow', 'm-cat' and 'bubbles'. The drug is a 'cathinone' chemically similar to amphetamine, and it has been suggested that its recent prevalence is due to a reduction in the purity and availability of other drugs such as ecstasy (Release.org.uk). Mephedrone became a subject of mainstream news attention in 2009 as a 'legal high', and was banned in April 2010.

This chapter comprises two key sections. The first applies a well-known model of moral panic analysis to the mephedrone coverage in order to set out certain key features of the case study and to illustrate the value of the model, as well as to highlight some problematic issues. The second section briefly describes a number of relevant ideas from the governmentality literature, drawing in particular on O'Malley's (1999, 2001) understanding of drug policy as a form of moral regulation. This then provides the framework for a discussion of mephedrone and the alternative discourses surrounding it.

Timeline

Critcher's attempt to revise Cohen's ([1972] 2002) seminal moral panic model in the light of Goode and Ben-Yehuda's ([1994] 2009) 'attributional model' produced a process comprising eight key elements (2003: 151–3). The discussion below is an attempt to map the details of the 2009–10 mephedrone UK news coverage onto Critcher's model, identifying those elements which are consonant alongside those which are not present in the current case study. However, it is first worth mentioning the timeline in which the mephedrone coverage emerged in UK newspapers.

The first mentions of mephedrone in the British press emerge in Spring 2009 with broadsheet concerns over its legal status and consequent availability 'over the counter' and online (*Guardian*, 12 March 2009; *Observer*, 26 April 2009). There are sporadic references in tabloid newspapers to mephedrone as a 'club drug' (*Star*, 19 April 2009; *Sun*, 24 July 2009), and in September 2009 a tenuous link to a specific UK death is made when it is reported that a teenager had hanged himself a few days after taking pills which might have contained mephedrone (*Sun*, 8 September 2009).

This linkage provides a useful example of the news values involved, whereby other possible explanations are minimized and the drug link is emphasized. The *Sun* reported that the boy had left a note referring to 'seeing an angel' and 'being with Jesus', and that his mother blamed the drug. The role of parents in the coverage is important and will be highlighted later.

Towards the end of 2009, the coverage becomes more frequent, with references to mephedrone as a 'new drug craze among teenagers' (*Mail*, 28 November 2009) and other deaths linked to its use. In particular, the death of 14-year-old Gabi Price (*Telegraph*, *Express*, *Mail*, *Sun*, 25 November 2009) gained widespread coverage. She was reported to have taken the drug with ketamine at a party and to have died of heart failure. Later coverage, however, noted a pathologist's report which found that she died of 'natural causes' due to pneumonia following a throat infection (*Star*, *Sun*, 17 December 2009).

This kind of story allows the moral panic thesis to construct a 'discourse of misinformation' in which deaths are misattributed to drugs and the 'real' causes

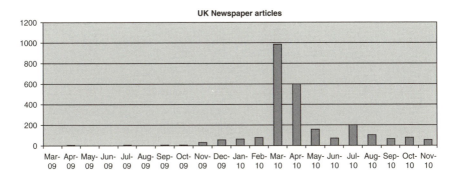

Figure 6.1 Stories about mephedrone in the national press, March 2009–November 2010

are ignored. This may be the case here, but it is interesting that both the *Sun* and the *Star* later acknowledged the pathologist's report.

From the end of 2009, there were around 50–80 articles per month until a spike in coverage in March and April, when Home Secretary Alan Johnson announced a ban on the drug 'within weeks' (*Telegraph*, 29 March 2010). During the run-up to the ban, two members of the Advisory Council on the Misuse of Drugs (ACMD – the body which advises the government on drug policy) resigned in protest against the way in which the ban was being introduced (*Telegraph*, 3 April 2010); this followed previous resignations due to concerns around the classification of ecstasy. The political ramifications of this, along with a number of other key themes, generated the bulk of the press coverage during March and April 2010. From the highpoint of March and April 2010, the coverage declined to a level which suggested that the issue had become a background news topic, with stories concerning mephedrone-linked deaths and references to other 'legal highs' comprising the main themes represented towards the end of 2010. Figure 6.1 sets out the contours of the coverage.

Mephedrone as moral panic

The following section sets out the eight key elements of moral panic analysis and applies them to the UK newspaper coverage of mephedrone from March 2009 to November 2010. Examples of the coverage are set out below.

Emergence

The initial concerns around mephedrone followed established patterns around drugs and young people and were not particularly 'fragmented' (Critcher 2003: 17), as the 'sense-making processes' that might be relevant to entirely novel scares are not necessary. Previous news frames surrounding 'dance drugs', 'designer drugs', youth culture in general, and concerning ecstasy in particular (Thornton 1994; Thompson 1998; Cohen 2002: xiii–xiv) provide a clear perspective through which an apparently new substance can be understood and positioned.

These, however, are inflected in specific ways. First, via the 'legal high' discourse, in which the availability of mephedrone is problematized: '"Legal high" Sold on Internet Should be Banned in Britain, Say Psychiatrists' (*Telegraph*, 30 April 2009). This article quotes a Glasgow doctor who has treated an addicted 'young professional man' to the effect that 'there are hundreds of websites [. . .] selling these so-called "legal highs". It is a poorly regulated industry with consumers having little knowledge of ingredients or their effects'.

The lack of consumer knowledge concerning a legal commodity is presented here as a problem whose solution can be found not, for instance, in a market-based solution involving educating the consumer, but in a ban. The reference in the headline to the internet represents a further, by now well established, frame of representation, and is linked in much of the coverage to the availability and lack of regulation of mephedrone. The internet here represents an uncontrolled and to some extent unknowable terrain into which young people are venturing, unaware of the risks involved.

Mephedrone is also represented as a 'threat to societal values or interests' (Cohen [1972] 2002: 1) in the sense of being a threat to particular notions of the family as a social value; this is evident in the emphasis in much of the coverage concerning children and schools: 'Meow Drug Floors 180 Kids in 1 School; Two Pupils a Day Off Sick after Taking "Legal High"' (*Sun*, 9 March 2010) and 'Teen Girls on Killer Meow during Class; Pupils Suspended over Drug' (*Star*, 31 March 2010). The novelty of the issue lay partly in the composition of mephedrone as a 'new' synthetic/designer drug, and more generally in its legal availability compared with the illegal drugs to which it was compared (both in terms of its effect and its chemical composition): a *Sun* article, 'New Club Drug Fear', states 'police last night issued a warning to clubbers over a new legal designer drug which health experts want banned' (*Sun*, 24 July 2009).

Inventory

Different social groups involved in the mephedrone news coverage were stereotyped in different ways, with 'clubbers' in particular constructed as irrational and reckless, victims presented as (previously) innocent and happy, and, therefore, other drug users implicitly presented as unhappy and abnormal. Nevertheless, there is no clear evidence of a recognizable folk devil emerging, and in this respect Critcher (2003: 150) is surely right that it is a mistake to insist, as Goode and Ben-Yehuda do, that any moral panic must include a folk devil. Instead, the drug itself became a mythical threat to the social order. Within moral panic studies, the notion of exaggeration and distortion can often rest on problematic assumptions about a benchmark reality which cannot easily be accessed (Cohen 2002: xxviii). Nevertheless, the risks of mephedrone were exaggerated at least to the extent that the deaths of a number of young people were attributed either tentatively or explicitly to mephedrone when little evidence was available to this effect, and often when the official toxicology results eventually found otherwise. The death of Gabi Price mentioned above is one example of this, but there were a number of others.

In March 2010, two young men, Louis Wainwright and Nicholas Smith, were reported to have died after taking mephedrone during a 'night out' in Lincolnshire (*Mail*, 17 March 2010). Reports included warnings from a police officer that the drug was dangerous, and descriptions of the drug's alleged side effects (*Star*, 17 March 2010). Most of the coverage was relatively circumspect in making a link, while others were more direct; thus the headline in the *Express*, 17 March, '"Legal High" Kills Two Teens' was followed by the line: 'A town was last night put on alert after two teenagers died from taking a controversial legal party drug'. However, reports which appeared later suggested they had not taken mephedrone (*Belfast Telegraph, Guardian, Independent*, 29 May 2010).

The death of 24-year-old Lois Waters was linked to mephedrone in various reports on 24 March 2010. While the *Express* called her the fourth victim, the *Mail* headline asked: 'Is Lois Victim No.6 of "Legal High" Drug?' (24 March 2010). The headlines in other newspapers apparently confirmed that she was 'Woman, 24, Is Sixth Person to Die after Taking "Miaow Miaow"' (*Telegraph*, 24 March 2010); '6th Victim of Meow Is Normal Happy Girl' (*Sun*, 24 March 2010). This latter headline also, of course, signifies the presumed abnormality and unhappiness of 'typical' drug users. In July, the inquest into her death reportedly found that mephedrone may have contributed to her death in combination with anti-depressant use and an 'underlying undetected heart condition' (*Independent*, 2 July 2010).

On April 16 – the day mephedrone was made illegal – the inquest into the death of Laura Main, a 24-four-year-old trainee solicitor, was reported.

Her death was apparently due to the mixture of alcohol and GHB which she had consumed, but some headlines emphasized the 'meow meow' which she had also used (*Mail*, *Sun*, 16 April 2010), while her work as an escort and a DJ increased the news value of her story. Indeed, the framing of these stories primarily around the deaths of attractive, young, middle-class, and often female, drug users suggests a very particular discursive approach.

The apparent suicide of a former premiership footballer's daughter was reported on 22 July. Sibylle Sibierski hanged herself after taking mephedrone and alcohol, and was depressed due to the breakdown of a relationship. Again, certain headlines emphasize one particular aspect of the story, as in the case of 'Meow Drug Victim' (*Mail*, 22 July 2010). Similarly, the Scottish *Metro*'s headline: 'Footballer's Daughter in "Legal Drug Suicide"' (22 July 2010) is presumably intended to refer to mephedrone rather than alcohol.

These examples illustrate not just the exaggerated nature of the coverage, but also the extent to which the press, sensitized to mephedrone as a social problem, alleged that the drug was a causal factor in many deaths that could more reasonably be ascribed to other causes, such as alcohol consumption or personal health problems. One further news item, concerning self-mutilation rather than a death, underlines these points, as depicted in the following newspaper stories: 'Me-Ouch Drug Hell' (*Star*, 27 November 2009), 'Sex-Tear Injury on "Cat" Drug' (*Sun*, 27 November 2009) and 'Drug User Ripped Off His Own Scrotum' (*Sunderland Echo*, 27 November 2009).

The headlines above introduced a news item concerning a mephedrone user who had apparently mutilated himself following an '18-hour bender' which brought on hallucinations. This story, reported as fact, was attributed to Durham police, and a later *New Scientist* article tracked down the author of the police report from which the story emerged. The police officer concerned explained that some parts of the report had been 'cut-and-pasted' from websites, and that the owner of the source website suggested that the story was effectively an anonymous online joke. The *New Scientist* described the story as a 'miaow-miaow myth' (Fleming 2010).

Moral entrepreneurs

Critcher suggests that public concern can be constructed by the media (2003: 137), and the evidence described in this chapter suggests that, in the particular case of mephedrone the press in particular became a focus for moral entrepreneurialism. There were also, however, non-media moral entrepreneurs involved.

Because of the pre-existing frame surrounding drug stories, the police were already positioned as key claims-makers in the mephedrone coverage: 'Police Alert over Dangers of New Drug Taken by Teenagers. At a meeting of Banchory Community Council this week, Constable Wilson told residents: "The way people source it, they don't know what they are getting. They don't know what effects it has"' (*Aberdeen Press and Journal*, 13 January 2010). This particular example is interesting in that it takes a problem often associated with illegal drugs – the fact that their composition is often unknown – and applies it to a substance which (at the time) was perfectly legal, and about which clear information could, at least potentially, be disseminated to users.

Parents were also allocated a key role as actors in the mephedrone coverage as they described the negative impacts of the drug on their children: 'My 16-Year-Old Son is Addicted to Mephedrone. I just hope that people start to sit up and listen because this drug is getting out of control' (*York Press*, 22 January 2010), and in 'Ban Deadly Drug that Killed My Son', Ms Kiltie said, 'Nobody knows the long-term effects. How many more kids is this going to kill? How many more mums will have to go through this?' (*Express*, 20 March 2010). In these examples, parents become legitimized as sources on account of their proximity to those directly affected by mephedrone, and their calls for action, therefore, carry a specific moral weight.

Cohen's original formulation listed bishops as one kind of the 'right-thinking people' manning the moral barricades. There is some evidence of moral entrepreneurship from this source here: 'Pastor Calls for Immediate Ban. The scourge of mephedrone is "10 times worse" than what has been publicly revealed, a north Belfast pastor claimed last night' (*Sunday Life*, 28 March 2010). The clergyman quoted here is Pastor Brian Maddon of North Belfast, who described the hospital visits he had made to mephedrone users; his call for a ban is supported by his personal interaction with users as well as by his moral authority.

Experts

The key group of experts involved here were the members of the ACMD who were reported as supporting a ban on mephedrone. In part, this position is legally sanctioned as the government is statutorily required to take their advice before enacting legislation, and the coverage reported the observation of the committee chair, Les Iversen, that the drug was 'amphetamine by any other name' and should be appropriately classified ('Experts to Seek "Miaow" Drug

Ban', *Express*, 29 March 2010; 'Ban Mephedrone, Experts Tell Home Secretary', *The Times*, 29 March 2010). A particular complication in the presentation of expert perspectives emerged when a member of the council, Polly Taylor, resigned, apparently over the pressure applied to the council by government. This followed other resignations in protest at the dismissal of the previous chair of the ACMD, David Nutt, whose 'harm minimization' approach to drug classification was incompatible with government policy. This schism between experts and government allowed an alternative perspective to be reported in places: 'Johnson to Ban Sale of the Legal High Mephedrone. Professor David Nutt, who was sacked as chairman of the ACMD, urged the Government last week not to ban the substance until there was a full body of evidence. He suggested allowing adults to take the drug under close supervision rather than driving it underground' (*Independent*, 29 March 2010). These perspectives were, however, largely restricted to broadsheet outlets, and much of the comment elsewhere made no clear reference to the reasons for Polly Taylor's resignation, but focused on the impact of the resignation on the possibility of an immediate ban, and how this reflected on the competence of the government: 'Expert Quits to Sink Meow Meow Ban' (*Mail*, 29 March 2010), and 'Resignation Could Derail Drugs Ban' (*Evening Times* [Glasgow], 29 March 2010). One explanation of this emphasis could be that as a structural issue – specifically the terms of reference of the ACMD and its relationship with government, which were the apparent cause of Taylor's resignation – this element of the story was simply less newsworthy than its political implications, particularly in a pre-election period.

A further expert group could arguably consist of (ex-) users: 'I Nearly Died After Taking Mephedrone' (*Plymouth Evening Herald*, 23 February 2010). First-person stories provide both a moral position (as warnings) but also a kind of authority, not of a formal rationality but a kind of emotional rationality. This could be argued to be part of a rejection of traditional authority derived perhaps from the risk society (Mythen 2004: 56–9), whereby the erosion of public belief in scientific rationality allows lay actors themselves to become 'private alternative experts' (Beck quoted in Mythen 2004: 59).

Elite consensus

This is difficult to judge, but the confusion around the position of the Liberal Democrat Party on this particular issue suggests an attempt to make political capital despite remaining within the consensus: 'Adviser Quits After Drug

Ban Decision. Liberal Democrat home affairs spokesman Chris Huhne said Government "meddling" in the advisory council had delayed earlier investigations into the drug' (*Newcastle Journal*, 3 April 2010). This argument seems rather contorted in that it is an attempt to criticize the government's position regarding the ACMD while nevertheless essentially supporting their intention to impose a ban. Party politics aside, a wider elite consensus is evident largely in the negative sense of an absence of any clear and organized opposition to the furore over the drug, notwithstanding occasional broadsheet concerns about the wisdom of a ban, supported by David Nutt in particular (see above).

Coping and resolution

As Critcher suggests (2003: 153), one of the most consistent elements in moral panics is a change in the law as a resolution of the apparent social problem concerned. In this case, a legal ban on the drug was proposed from the very first mainstream news reports about it, and this was finally implemented in April 2010. In the case of most such drug bans, the assumption that legal proscription will in some sense deal with the problem is rarely examined in any detail. Alternative solutions, as we have suggested, were rare in the press, but there were nonetheless a few examples of authored comment pieces by journalists and experts which took a different line from the mainstream: 'Let's Keep this High Legal: Criminalising Users of Mephedrone Could Have Unwanted Consequences. We Need a Class D Answer' (David Nutt, *Guardian*, 18 March 2010), and 'No Law Will Stop People Wanting to Get High; Selling Small Amounts of Drugs in Clubs Is Not Shocking. It's a Responsible Idea' (Melanie Reid, *The Times*, 1 April 2010). Nutt suggests a number of alternatives to an outright ban, including a 'class D holding category' which allows regulated access to the drug, and argues that more research into the drug needs to be done. Meanwhile Reid's argument supports the 'normalization thesis', whereby for many young people drug use is an unexceptional part of everyday life (Manning 2007), and supports Nutt's contention that regulation together with education is the most 'honest, logical and responsible thing to do'.

Fade away

Figure 6.1 suggests that the coverage of mephedrone has fallen substantially since the ban was implemented, and in terms of news value the novelty of mephedrone as a 'legal high' is clearly reduced as it becomes one of many restricted substances.

Forsyth's study (2001) of the reporting of drug deaths suggested that certain drugs – ecstasy in particular – gain relatively more coverage than others, and it is possible that the news value of continuity (or 'follow-up') and the newspapers' own campaigns and agendas (Harcup and O'Neill 2001) contributed to substantial continuing coverage in the latter half of 2010.

Legacy

It is perhaps too early to find any clear evidence regarding the legacy of a moral panic which has only recently been 'resolved'. We might speculate that the category of 'legal high' has been problematized or moralized, in the sense that such substances are now more likely to be treated (in media accounts) as potentially dangerous. The legal change has, of course, criminalized users of the drug, and this in itself is an important 'material effect' (Critcher 2003: 153) on users. However, this may be less important than the more generalized impact on the discourses around illegal drugs and prohibition as a solution.

The above analysis suggests that the moral panic thesis allows a worthwhile discussion of such social issues and their mediation. Nevertheless, it is worth noting that the specific political context of this case study – the build-up to the 2010 United Kingdom general election – inflects much of the coverage, and this suggests that much of the coverage can be understood through a party political prism. So the criticisms of the slow speed at which the ban was being introduced (often from right-wing/Conservative newspapers) and the 'chaos' of the resignations from the ACMD can be characterized (at least in part) as attempts to destabilize the then home secretary Alan Johnson and the Labour government more generally.

More fundamentally, the analysis above reflects wider concerns about certain aspects of the moral panic thesis. Goode and Ben-Yehuda insist on the need for any moral panic to generate a folk devil, a 'suitable enemy', constructed in order to 'arouse emotions'. As they put it, 'All moral panics, by their very nature, identify, denounce, and attempt to root out folk devils' ([1994] 2009: 28). However, it seems clear that mephedrone did not provide a specific folk devil in the sense of a social 'outgroup' which could be demonized and denounced. But as Critcher has suggested, in many cases of moral panic no such social group is constructed; thus, for example, in child abuse scandals and scares about ecstasy and 'video nasties', the folk devil either becomes a largely abstract, 'mythical' threat or is found in an object rather than a deviant social group (2003: 150).

A further criticism of the moral panic approach concerns the emphasis which it places on exaggeration, and on the idea that the response to the perceived problem – by moral entrepreneurs, in media accounts and then on the part of policy-makers – is demonstrably excessive. According to these critics, moral panic theory 'implies that public concern is in excess of what is appropriate if concern were directly proportional to objective harm' (Springhall 1998: 5). In this view, moral panic scholars are claiming to be in possession of an objective measure of the 'appropriate' level of concern in each case, one which can then be compared with the 'excessive' news coverage. Some have argued that, at least in particular cases, the term 'moral panic' implies a lack of justification for genuine public concern, and that this is unhelpful and misleading (Kitzinger 1999: 212), suggesting that such anxieties are 'an ersatz compound manufactured by the media, a few odd bishops, strident voices from the left and the right, moralists and nostalgists of all kinds' (Springhall 1998: 8). While some have defended the need for recognition of the role played by disproportion in media panics (Critcher 2003: 151; Goode 2008), there remains a suggestion that this approach can implicitly uncover the 'hidden truth' of a perceived problem (in this case drug consumption) by exposing the ideological exaggerations of those moral entrepreneurs and claims-makers promoting the scare. I will argue below that the notion of governmentality can problematize and provide a useful corrective to this element of the moral panic thesis.

Mephedrone and governmentality

It should be noted that while the moral panic thesis (at least in Cohen's conception and in its development by Critcher and others) makes the media a central concern, the governmentality approach adopts a much wider perspective in its analysis of (self-) regulation and social control. Nevertheless, it is linked to the themes of interest to moral panic theorists not just via its Foucauldian origins in the understanding of criminality and deviancy (Critcher 2008: 1139) but also in its applicability to questions of public understandings of risk and hazard (Lupton 1999b; Mythen 2004: 167) which also come under the purview of moral panic analysis.

Foucault's insistence on the body as the locus of struggles over social power might usefully be linked to moral panics such as that about mephedrone as they reflect the 'struggle over rival discourses and regulatory practices' (Thompson

1998: 25). Critcher similarly notes the potential explanatory value of the concept of governmentality and highlights research which applies it to the control of drug users. Disciplinary surveillance and regulation identify two categories of drug use: the disorganized, chaotic lifestyle of the addict and the recreational user (Critcher 2003: 170). This suggests a need to understand not just the discourses of those wishing to ban mephedrone, but also of those wishing to avoid such legal restrictions.

The theory of governmentality is derived from a Foucauldian concern with the discursive construction of reality (Lupton 1999a: 6). In particular, it engages with government as an attempt to understand and act on human activity: 'From the perspective of those who seek to govern, human conduct is conceived as something that can be regulated, controlled, shaped and turned to specific ends' (Dean [1999] 2010: 18). The rationalities of government are about the 'conduct of conduct', and in this way government is understood as being not just about the regulation or control of others, but also about how we govern ourselves as individual. We are, therefore, made responsible for ourselves through 'technologies of the self', as contemporary liberal government acts on the assumption that the regulation of human activity is 'best achieved through (rather than acting on) the actors involved' (Garland 1999: 21). Those who consume illegal drugs are, on this account, encouraged to avoid 'problematic' drug use by making the correct (normative) decisions based on rational information. The neo-liberal harm minimization approach presupposes the ability to provide 'factual', non-judgemental information to users. This link between the study of governance in modern democracies and the self-regulation of individual subjects becomes pivotal in the analysis of drug policy.

Conservative and neo-liberal approaches

The predominance of actuarial risk management models in the neo-liberal regimes of European and Anglophone nations has, in O'Malley's view, influenced policy to the extent that ostensibly pragmatic harm minimization strategies for drug use have been developed. Such strategy 'normalizes illicit drug use in the sense that it *subordinates* criminal law, with its exclusionary, coercive and denunciatory techniques to the inclusionary "technical" and ostensibly amoral techniques of harm minimization' (1999: 195). In this case, the notion of 'normalization' refers not to the attitudes of users but to the way in which the state attempts to position the user as a legitimate subject rather than as a criminal or deviant 'other'. In cases where harm may be done to others, O'Malley suggests that a kind of 'strategic moralization' occurs in which, for instance, drunk drivers or drug traffickers are constructed in moral terms; these groups can effectively be understood as (potential) folk devils. For drug use which need not be considered inappropriate, users are constructed as rational, responsible individuals and the harm minimization approach adopted by certain neo-liberal governments emphasizes the need to provide information and advice which supports 'responsible' drug use and encourages the user to calculate their own risk profile. In this way, users become 'self-regulating' citizens, monitoring their own behaviour.

This harm minimization perspective assumes that users can be rendered socially and economically viable providing that the relevant and appropriate information is supplied to them in order for them to position themselves in alignment with the needs and aims of government. They are, therefore, 'responsibilized' only in the sense that they are required to 'choose' the correct behaviour and thus regulate themselves and their drug use. This is what O'Malley (1999: 210) describes as the 'dark side' of neo-liberal governmentality; drug users are constructed as rational, self-governing actors, making the appropriately state-aligned decisions via the information provided. Thus, government will allow citizens to choose, provided that the choices made concurs with the requirements of the government. As Dean suggests: 'The state is constituted by a promise: "We will assist you to practise your freedom, as long as you practise it in our way"' ([1999] 2010: 188). The ineffectiveness of prohibition is recognized in the harm minimization approach, as are the health risks associated with drug use; the goal, therefore, is not to eliminate drug use, but to align users with the objectives of the state by offering the opportunity to become rational, economically active citizens.

While this approach to drug use has been implemented in certain countries, elsewhere it has been challenged by a conservative agenda which is perhaps dominant in many Western liberal democracies. It has been argued that many such states have, since the 1980s, become 'governmental hybrids' of conservatism and neo-liberalism (Stenson 2001: 22), with the latter element's emphasis on individuals, markets and minimal international boundaries in an uneasy alliance with conservative preferences for socially integrative moral frameworks and social structures, and concern for the national interest. The conservative approach to drugs excludes users as immoral, promotes prohibition and abstinence, emphasizes the connections between drug use and crime and defends moral values centred around 'family, religion, rationality, sobriety, independence, respect for law and authority and so on' (O'Malley 2001: 93). This is most evident in the 'war on drugs' approach found most conspicuously in the United States, but it can also be observed in other countries and in other contexts. Garland (1999: 32), for instance, has argued that the conflict between conservative and neo-liberal policy options was fought out in the 1990s in the United Kingdom's approach to the prison service; while the service was reorganized as an autonomous executive agency along neo-liberal, managerialist lines, in practice politicians intervened in policy for conservative political purposes. This suggests a need to examine the specific ways in which different governmental approaches are applied in particular political and social contexts.

According to the governmentality approach to risk, in modern neo-liberal regimes responsibility for social risks is transferred to individuals, and personal identity is 'managerialized' to produce the subject as 'the entrepreneur of himself or herself' (Gordon 1991: 44). The responsibilized individual is then required to make the 'correct' rational risk decisions, potentially across a whole range of life choices. This O'Malley calls 'private prudentialism' and it allows a moralization of risk, in which poor decisions are seen as representing moral failure and a lack of self-discipline. In this way, risk regulation becomes a matter of promoting the government of the self.

O'Malley has suggested that harm minimization strategies applied to drug regulation in neo-liberal societies can be understood as reflecting a more individualizing, responsibilizing approach. The drug user as a rational actor who makes informed decisions becomes an 'amoral', 'normal' consumer, and the harm minimization approach emphasizes the attempt to restore the user to the position of an economically functioning citizen, as opposed to aiming at the elimination of drug use; but in this, the user becomes responsible for the decisions which they make and culpable for the consequences of their actions.

Mephedrone and neo-liberal governmentality

In the mephedrone press coverage, the discourse of harm minimization is muted, but is nevertheless evident. David Nutt (2009) has explicitly proposed a harm reduction approach to drug use elsewhere (Nutt et al. 2007), and in his *Guardian* article suggesting alternatives to a legal ban he argues the need for clear evidence of harm before making such a decision, on the grounds that a ban might lead to users switching to other more dangerous drugs. His suggestion of a 'class D' which would enable users to access 'quality-controlled' drugs along with information and advice directly echoes the neo-liberal emphasis on responsibilizing the user, who is 'protected but not criminalized' (2010). Further suggestions of testing facilities for users and of wider drug education similarly suggest movement towards a position in which users become accountable for their mephedrone use via a (neo-)liberalized information policy.

An *Independent* comment piece on 18 March 2010 by the newspaper's health editor Jeremy Laurance referred to Nutt's suggestion that a ban is unwise because 'a criminal conviction could be more damaging than the drug itself'; this is, first, framed as an issue of rational measurement of different harms (as part of a managerialist neo-liberalism) as well as, second, suggesting that avoiding the criminalizing of users is a key objective of drug policy.

The managerialism of the harm minimization approach – exemplified in the discursive emphasis on 'evidence-based policy' derived from scientific research – insists that drug policy should be freed from the distortions of politics and public opinion. Thus, a *Telegraph* comment piece on 18 March 2010 by Andrew M. Brown suggested that Nutt 'has only ever argued that policy should be based on solid scientific evidence. Drugs, though, is an area where most politicians are not thinking of the evidence only. They are also trying to look robust and impressive in tomorrow's headlines.'

This perspective is arguably evident in certain approaches to moral panics, in that it can be suggested that moral panic analysis unveils the ideological distortions of media accounts and can allow a dispassionate view of the topic in question. Understood as a form of governmentality, however, the harm minimization approach is not an alternative to ideological policy-making but, rather, an alternative discourse of moral regulation. Similarly, Melanie Reid's (2010) *The Times* comment piece quoted earlier suggests that 'accurate, non-judgmental, harm reduction information' is required: 'Arm young people with the facts, and they are at least better equipped to decide about risks for themselves.' Young people are encouraged to internalize the risk analyses of experts through the information provided; the user is then regulated not via overtly moral proscription, but via the mechanism of choice, with the (largely unspoken) proviso that, as Dean suggests, this freedom is exercised 'in our way' ([1999] 2010: 188).

Despite the above examples, there are no sustained 'anti-ban' discourses evident in the mephedrone newspaper coverage, and there are a number of possible reasons for this absence. Although it has been argued by McRobbie and Thornton (1995) that moral panic analysis ignores the emergence of subcultures in which groups cast as folk devils fight back in order to reclaim the public agenda, in this case there was no clear folk devil, and no obvious substantial opposition from any subcultural group emerged into the news coverage. Second, it could be argued that the novelty of mephedrone made it difficult for the notion of the 'responsible user' to gain traction, given that its effects, more so than in the case of other legal and illegal substances, were simply unknown.

O'Malley (2001: 93) acknowledges that neo-liberal harm minimization strategies fight for acceptance within various national governments against conservative values which stress collective moral positions on drug use and its links to criminal activity, as represented in discourses around the 'war on drugs'. This conflict is similarly evident in the case of mephedrone, where harm minimization was discussed as a response to the drug, but was drowned out by more explicitly moralizing conservative discourses.

Conclusion

It has been argued that many of those who study moral panics have generated their critiques from a 'liberal, left-leaning, or radical' perspective (Goode and Ben-Yehuda [1994] 2009: 46), and as Cohen (2002: xxvii) has noted, conservative critics of such studies have accused them of selectivity in the attention given to certain kinds of disproportionate media coverage. Framing an issue as a moral panic provides for the construction of a 'discourse of misinformation' linked to a notion of disproportionality in news coverage, and taken together this allows for an explicit critique of certain attempts to regulate and control public behaviour while implicitly down-playing or even endorsing regulatory activities of other kinds.

The value of the governmentality approach to understanding the social construction of risk issues such as drug use lies, at least in part, in the way in which it allows a critique not just of those conservative ideologies which are often identified within moral panic studies, but also of the alternative discursive strategies which are always already part of an (alternative) framework of moral regulation.

In the case of mephedrone, a standard moral panic critique of the coverage might well expose the exaggerations and distortions through which a moralizing conservative discourse presented an opportunity for official agencies and legal or regulatory bodies to provide a 'solution' to a social problem via bringing into being a new legal power. This, however, would be at best a partial analysis, given that the alternative position presented (admittedly in muted form) in the media – that drugs should be subject to a harm minimization approach which acknowledged a more rational, liberal and scientifically informed understanding of drug use – is not addressed. An analysis derived from the governmentality perspective allows for this alternative discourse to be fully interrogated, not as simply a benign absence of regulation or as an expression of scientific objectivity, but as a specific framework of (neo-liberal) 'responsibilization', a form of moral (self-) regulation in its own right.

Clearly, the applicability of this perspective to the wide range of issues and topics to which the moral panic label has been applied is questionable, and needs to be tested on a case-by-case basis. Nevertheless, in terms of the public debates around recreational drug use, the evidence presented here suggests that it can provide a useful additional perspective on the role of the media in the discursive construction of moral risk.

Bibliography

Cohen, S. ([1972] 2002), *Folk Devils and Moral Panics*, 3rd edn, Abingdon: Routledge.

Critcher, C. (2003), *Moral Panics and the Media*, Maidenhead, Buckingham: Open University Press.

— (2008), 'Moral Panic Analysis: Past, Present and Future', *Sociology Compass*, 2(4): 1127–44.

Dean, M. ([1999] 2010), *Governmentality: Power and Rule in Modern Society*, 2nd edn, London: Sage.

Fleming, N. (2010), 'Miaow-Miaow on Trial: Truth or Trumped-up Charges?', *New Scientist*, 29 March, www.newscientist.com/article/dn18712-miaowmiaow-on-trial-truth-or-trumpedup-charges.html?full=true [accessed 10 December 2010].

Forsyth, A. J. M. (2001), 'Distorted? A Quantitative Exploration of Drug Fatality Reports in the Popular Press', *International Journal of Drug Policy*, 12(5): 435–53.

Garland, D. (1999), '"Governmentality" and the Problem of Crime', in R. Smandych (ed.), *Governable Places: Readings on Governmentality and Crime Control*, Aldershot: Ashgate, 15–43.

Goode, E. (2008), 'Moral Panics and Disproportionality: The Case of LSD Use in the Sixties', *Deviant Behavior*, 29(6): 533–43.

Goode, E. and Ben-Yehuda, N. ([1994] 2009), *Moral Panics: The Social Construction of Deviance*, 2nd edn, Chichester: Wiley-Blackwell.

Gordon, C. (1991), 'Governmental Rationality: An Introduction', in G. Burchell, C. Gordon and P. Miller (eds), *The Foucault Effect: Studies in Governmentality*, Chicago: University of Chicago Press, 1–51.

Harcup, T. and O'Neill, D. (2001), 'What Is News? Galtung and Ruge Revisited', *Journalism Studies*, 2(2): 261–80.

Home Office, *Advisory Council on Misuse of Drugs*, www.homeoffice.gov.uk/drugs/ acmd/ [accessed 10 November 2010].

Kitzinger, J. (1999), 'The Ultimate Neighbour from Hell? Stranger Danger and the Media Framing of Paedophiles', in B. Franklin and N. Parton (eds), *Social Policy, the Media and Misrepresentation*, London: Routledge, 207–21.

Lupton, D. (1999a), 'Introduction: Risk and Sociocultural Theory', in D. Lupton (ed.), *Risk and Sociocultural Theory: New Directions and Perspectives*, Cambridge: Cambridge University Press, 1–11.

— (1999b), *Risk*, London: Routledge.

Manning, P. (2007), 'Introduction: An Overview of the Normalization Debate', in P. Manning (ed.), *Drugs and Popular Culture: Drugs, Media and Identity in Contemporary Society*, Cullompton: Willan, 49–55.

McRobbie, A. and Thornton, S. L. (1995), 'Re-thinking "Moral Panic" for Multi-mediated Social Worlds', *British Journal of Sociology*, 46(4): 559–74.

Mythen, G. (2004), *Ulrich Beck: A Critical Introduction to the Risk Society*, London: Pluto Press.

Nutt, D. J. (2009), 'Equasy – An Overlooked Addiction with Implications for the Current Debate on Drug Harms', *Journal of Psychopharmacology*, 23(1): 3–5.

— (2010), 'Let's Keep This High Legal: Criminalising Users of Mephedrone Could Have Unwanted Consequences. We Need a Class D Answer', *Guardian*, 18 March.

Nutt, D. J., King, L. A., Saulsbury, W. and Blakemore, C. (2007), 'Development of a Rational Scale to Assess the Harm of Drugs of Potential Misuse', *The Lancet*, 369: 1047–53.

O'Malley, P. (1999), 'Consuming Risks: Harm Minimization and the Government of "Drug-users"', in R. Smandych (ed.), *Governable Places: Readings on Governmentality and Crime Control*, Aldershot: Ashgate, 191–214.

— (2001), 'Risk, Crime and Prudentialism Revisited', in K. Stenson and R. R. Sullivan (eds), *Crime Risk and Justice: The Politics of Crime Control in Liberal Democracies*, Cullompton: Willan, 89–103.

Release.org.uk, *Mephedrone & Methylone*, www.release.org.uk/drugs-law/drugs-a-to-z/ mephedrone-methylone [accessed 10 November 2010].

Springhall, J. (1998), *Youth, Popular Culture and Moral Panics: Penny Gaffs to Gangsta Rap 1830–1996*, Basingstoke: Macmillan.

Stenson, K. (2001), 'The New Politics of Crime Control', in K. Stenson and R. R. Sullivan (eds), *Crime Risk and Justice: The Politics of Crime Control in Liberal Democracies*, Cullompton: Willan, 15–28.

Thompson, K. (1998), *Moral Panics*, London: Routledge.

Thornton, S. (1994), 'Moral Panic, the Media and British Rave Culture', in A. Ross and T. Rose (eds), *Microphone Fiends: Youth Music and Youth Culture*, London: Routledge, 176–92.

7

'He Who Buries the Little Girl Wins!' Moral Panics as Double Jeopardy: The Case of *Rule of Rose**

Elisabeth Staksrud and Jørgen Kirksæther

The term 'moral panic' was evidently first used by Marshall McLuhan.[1] He observed how 'highly literate people' perceived new (electric) media – at the time, TV and radio – as a threat to the written word ([1964] 2001: 82), making it difficult for them to examine the question of new media's effect on 'our Western values' without 'getting into a moral panic'. McLuhan connected the concept of moral panic directly to the development of what he describes as 'electric media'. Today, the idea that new media technology can lead to a moral panic is, while not yet a fully developed theoretical concept, still timely and fitting to subsequent studies. This is equally evident in the next step of the media-evolutionary ladder, the shift from electric to electronic media.[2]

For the past decades, the fear that new media – the internet, mobile phones and computer games – cause harm to and affect the moral values of the general public, and children in particular, has been a central part of the public and political discourse in the Western world. Risk perceptions connected with new technology and new innovations might frighten people, and lead to a (heavy) refusal of the use and acceptance of these technologies. Since its formative years, the internet has been linked with pedophilia, pornography, bomb-making, abuse and general indecency, creating public fears directed towards the technology itself. This has led to a strong advocacy to control access to and content on the internet, resulting in various legal initiatives aimed at protecting the public in general, and children in particular, from harm (see, for instance, Sutter 2000; Staksrud 2002; Marwick 2008). Similarly, electronic games have undergone the same type of public treatment, starting out small, blossoming, becoming the target of public fears and then finding themselves at the receiving end of a series of legislative and regulatory motions.

Double jeopardy

Such developments are one of the key elements of Stanley Cohen's well-known definition of a moral panic: it leads to the feeling that 'something should be done' and 'measures should be taken' (Cohen 1972). At the same time the use of new technology has become an everyday activity for European citizens, young and old.

Goode and Ben-Yehuda ([1994] 2006) developed Cohen's concept further, identifying five crucial elements that define a moral panic: a heightened level of *concern* over the behaviour of a certain group and the consequences that behaviour presumably causes for the rest of the society; *hostility* against that group, creating stereotyping and a division between 'them' and 'us'; a widespread *agreement* or *consensus* in society or segments of the society that the threat is real; *disproportionality*, meaning that the public concern is 'in excess of what is appropriate if concern were directly proportional to objective harm' (Goode and Ben-Yehuda [1994] 2006: 53); and, finally, that moral panics are *volatile*, for they erupt and subside fairly suddenly.

For Critcher (2006), the key concept from Goode and Ben-Yehuda's argument is that of disproportionality: moral panics are by definition *disproportionate reactions to perceived threats*. This definition is in itself an invitation to descriptive analysis, linking studies on a broad range of issues together under what Critcher calls 'the common characteristics of those social problems which suddenly emerge, cause consternation among powerful institutions and seem to require exceptional remedies' (2006: 2). Such remedies are often in the form of legislation and law enforcement. As described by Goode and Ben-Yehuda, a moral panic is almost inevitably accompanied by the questioning of the appropriate social and legal control of the responsible parties ([1994] 2006).

Thus, for the past three decades, the concept of moral panic has provided a framework for the study of a diverse range of topics such as AIDS (Coleman 1993; Lupton 1994; Tulloch and Lupton 1997; Joffe 1999; Watney [1988] 2006; Weeks [1989] 2006) and even lynching at the end of the twentieth century (Wasserman and Stack 1994). However, most moral panic studies revolve around *the safety of children*, whether it be obesity (Stephenson and Banet-Weiser 2007), drugs (Chiricos [1996] 2006; Manning 2007; Muncie [1999] 2004: 176–7), bad mothers (Silva 1996), satanic day-care centres (De Young 2004, [1998] 2006), juvenile delinquency (Cohen 1972; 1984; Fornäs and Bolin 1995; Freeman 1997; Muncie 1984; Schissel 1997) or children's use of computer games (Williams and Smith 2007) – to mention a few.

A special case of moral panic is the *media panic*. In a media panic, the fear is specifically sourced in a distinct medium, more often than not a new one. As theorized by Drotner (1999a, 1999b), in media panics the (old) media is both instigator and purveyor of a highly emotional and morally polarized discussion. The new medium or media technology is seen as either 'good' or 'bad', where the latter becomes the visible narrative. Often, one specific media product and/or output will spark the debate. Butsch (2000: 151–2) describes how the introduction of movies in America stirred new concerns among traditional moral reformers of society. Related pre-movie concerns had been about women's respectability when going to the vaudeville theatres (note: concern not regarding the media content, but the behaviour of other audience members). However, after the introduction of the motion picture, the safety and socialization of children became the issue. Redefined (and in contrast to the Calvinist conception of them as evil barbarians in need of discipline), children were at the beginning of the twentieth century seen as innocent and infinitely impressionable, a notion providing fertile ground for the fear of harm when its subjects were exposed to new auditory and visual media. Since then, discussions, concern and fears related to new media technologies in the Western world have primarily had the welfare of children and young people as the focal point of attention, and the participants are usually professionals, for example, teachers, academic scholars, librarians and cultural critics, with a vested interest in how the 'story' should be told (Drotner 1999a: 596).[3] There are numerous examples of confusion, and conclusions based on assumptions, in the public debate about the use of the internet. The concepts of danger and abuse of children in particular are also found in the academic world; for example, 'The issue of pornography on the Internet automatically leads us to the issue of child pornography on the net' (Carlsson 2001: 62). As argued by Drotner (1999a: 596), media panics follow a classic narrative with a beginning, a build-up, a peak and a fadeout phase.

Thus, a new media panic becomes a pincer movement, a *double jeopardy*, as it combines two key fears: that of the moral implications of new technology, and that of the safety of our children. However, as observed by Livingstone (2008), such fears are rarely clarified and vocalized. What are we afraid of? The end of innocence? Abuse? The creation of future victims or offenders? Problems related to children's cognitive development? Psychological harm? The new technology poses an – often unspecified – threat in itself, as well as an – again often unspecified – threat of harm to children. At the same time, questioning the concern for children's safety or the tools to provide it is problematic. As discussed by Meyer (2007: 100), 'Legitimization and moralizing are inextricably linked dimensions of childhood rhetoric; hence childhood rhetoric is always moral rhetoric and *anything* can be justified via children as children make the case necessarily good and right'.

The lack of clarification can also be said to be part of the narratives constructed. Children are innocent, and being seen as siding against what is perceived as the innocence of a child is often impossible for politicians, for policy makers, and for experts.

However, as media panics by their mere definition lead to the demand for intervention 'measures', such measures could be restricting fundamental freedoms, for citizens in general and for children in particular. By studying such debates, we can provide insights into how democratic processes are influenced and even erupted, and established regulations and restrictions are changed. Moral panics are by their nature volatile, hence there is a danger of loosing the democratic principle of transparency when new measures are considered and implemented.

In the following, we will present the case of the moral panic surrounding the video game *Rule of Rose* (ルール オ ブ ロー ズ, *Rūru obu Rōzu*) (Punchline and Shirogumi 2006), a game that caused a great controversy in Europe, involving the classical characteristics and narratives of a moral, and a media, panic. The case is perceived to be particularly interesting, as it challenged and continues to challenge and directly threaten the key concept of media regulation and protection of children from potential media harm as defined and supported by the European Commission, and as supported by most nation states in the European Union/European Economic Area (EEA). In addition to describing the existing regulatory framework in Europe, the public reactions to the game and the still ongoing legislative debate, we will take a look at the game itself, placing it in a cultural context, and point out some of the narrative measures it employs and the possible link to the surrounding panic. We will discuss why this particular game became the object of a panic, with a particular look at the apparently unbearable notion of children as villains.

Regulatory background

While the (now) traditional media of newspapers, movies (in theatres), radio and television have been regulated on a national level, the introduction of the internet elicited demands for pan-European regulatory schemes. Following the Bangemann report (1994) and subsequent green and white papers (see, for instance, European Commission 1997), the European Union considered self-regulation and co-regulation as the prime strategy for the emerging information society. Thus, when the European Commission started working on a unified system for regulating video games, it chose to focus on providing game buyers with information and guidance through self-regulation by industry stakeholders, rather than the pre-screening process traditionally seen in parallel systems for other audiovisual media (European Council 2002). This was in order to balance the protection of minors against issues regarding freedom of information and freedom of speech, as well as ensuring the best possible flow of games as a commodity. The Council resolution of 2002 resulted in the establishing of the Pan-European Game Information (PEGI) system in April 2003 (Pan-European Game Information [PEGI] 2007). PEGI was established and is administered by the Interactive Software Federation of Europe (ISFE). The system is run on the principle of self-regulation, where compliance is encouraged, but not mandatory, and where each game distributor itself submits its games and describes them within the system. The game is then checked by the independent Netherlands Institute for the Classification of Audio-visual Media (NICAM 2008), which results in an age-rating label and a collection of content descriptors that is then printed on the game packaging. PEGI has a factual approach to the labelling of games, using pictograms in addition to the age rating to show what types of potentially harmful content can be found in the game (violence, bad language, fear, sex, drugs and discrimination), allowing for (cultural) differences in parental mediation styles and concerns. This also exemplifies the newer overall European principles of relating media regulation to 'harm' and 'offence', rather than the previous focus on 'decency' and 'taste' (Critcher 2008: 102; Millwood Hargrave and Livingstone 2009). The success of the PEGI system is regularly referred to as the prime example of a well-functioning self-regulatory system (Reding 2007; European Commission 2008).

The case: *Rule of Rose*

Plotline

Rule of Rose is a game for the Sony PlayStation2 system. The game is set in England in 1930, and the player controls the Jennifer character, a 19-year-old woman who unravels a horror mystery at an orphanage. The game is at heart a classic adventure game, where the protagonist slowly explores and investigates while the story is being told in bursts as new information is discovered. It is also firmly rooted in the related 'survival horror' genre, where the central objective is to survive a series of encounters with monsters and/or aggressive humans while escaping the game world. Games such as *Silent Hill* (Toyama 1999) and the *Resident Evil* (Capcom 1996) series exemplify this.[4] The game is held in this core genre traditional third-person view, where one can see the whole of the character that is being controlled.[5]

At the beginning of *Rule of Rose*, Jennifer is on a bus. She is tricked/lured/goaded off the bus, which subsequently leaves her behind. Instead of walking along the road, she (you) decides to explore a nearby pathway, where she discovers a mansion. A group of masked children is seen beating on a bloody sack containing something, whereupon they leave to go inside the house. Jennifer now has to find an entrance herself, to investigate further. After taking a thorough look inside the mansion, Jennifer is taken prisoner, then released, after which she finds herself inside what is revealed to be an airship. There she discovers something called 'The Aristocrat Club', which leads up to the unravelling of the story of an orphanage run by the traditional evil man, where the children escape into their own fantasy world, filled with horrors, love, princes and princesses. Leaning on literary classics *Lord of the Flies* (Golding 1954), *Alice in Wonderland* (Carroll 1865) and most of Charles Dickens' works, *Rule of Rose* tells its story in psychedelic episodes, interspersed with sections of cruelty not far from the fantasy-horror works of Clive Barker (1984).

Rule of Rose borrows heavily from not only literature, but in equal measures from films. From classic horror movies such as *Freaks* (Browning 1932) with its obvious attempts to shock and scare its audience; to British mad science B-movies *Village of the Damned* (Rilla 1960) and *Children of the Damned* (Leader 1964); and, finally, through to modern chillers *The Omen* (Donner 1976) and *The Shining* (Kubrick 1980). The most obvious influence is, however, the Italian and Spanish horror movies of the 1960s and 1970s from directors such as Dario Argento and Jess Franco. These movies blend the baroque with carefully administered doses of gore, and they often add a sexual subtext for those that are able to or want to see it. This can be in the form of something as simple as a hand gesture, or the hem of a skirt resting just a bit higher on the thigh than is strictly necessary. This *suggestive* strategy is employed liberally throughout *Rule of Rose*, where in reality innocent imagery is placed in a context where it is still possible to interpret it in a far darker way. For example, when Jennifer is taken prisoner early in the game, she is tied up. We see her at the foot of a pole, hogtied, while her captor talks to her through a hole in a door. If one, however, wants to interpret this in a sexual way, the setting is ripe for a series of bondage-related sub-stories, especially given Jennifer's moans while she wriggles to get free. This strategy of suggestion and the explicit opening of the text to interpretation echoes the often used methods of Alfred Hitchcock and Bret Easton Ellis. The result is a text where as much of the story is produced by the viewer/player herself as by the original author. In *Rule of Rose*, this is underlined by the fragmented and sometimes psychedelic narrative, where the evolving story has to be pieced together by the reader/player, resulting in a tale containing not only what is shown, but also the bridging story elements that have been added by the player – simply to try to make sense of it all. At the end of the game, it is still unclear what has really been going on at the orphanage: what is fantasy and what has actually taken place? This is clearly a chosen storytelling device, where the game author intentionally leaves most questions unanswered, which in turn emphasizes the general feeling of uneasiness the player experiences throughout the game. Not only are the imagery and characters disturbing, there is not even an absolute, final resolution or explanation.

Though made in Japan, by a Japanese team of writers, designers and musicians, *Rule of Rose* is set in Europe and looks European. The well-known Japanese *manga* graphic style with exaggerated facial features and/or surroundings[6] is not found in the game, and a more subdued and restrained look is used throughout. This is underlined by the choice of music: it is heard only sparingly, and firmly in the vein of early 1900s classical music, partly romantic and partly experimental. Without delving too deeply into a textual analysis of the game, one can state that this type of duality is found throughout. From the use of *the rose* as a central motif, with its beauty and its thorns, to the continuous shape-shifting of the characters (one of them is even revealed as having disguised herself as a boy throughout the tale), the story uses these devices to discourage a linear reading of the text and cloud any definite interpretation of the events. The result is a player left with an eerie feeling of gloom, something which is obviously *Rule of Rose*'s raison d'être, and something it has in common with most if not all horror fiction (be it games, movies or literature).

Rule of Rose's core theme, that of an evil that has to be explored and laid bare through a series of horrific trials and bursts of action, is not unique to the game. On the contrary, it is a common theme in a lot of games, in very different genres. When pared down, this plot skeleton is the same as the ones in games as dissimilar as *Doom* (id Software 1993) and *Super Mario Galaxy* (Koizumi and Miyamoto 2007). The one thing that sets *Rule of Rose* apart from most other games is its use of children as core characters, and then on the opposition's side. This particular plot device is seldom seen in video games.

Age rating

Rule of Rose was first released in Japan, where the Japanese Computer Entertainment Rating Organization (CERO) rated it as a 'C', meaning it was recommended for players from 15 years and above (CERO [Japan] 2006). In the United States, the game was rated 'Mature 17+' by the Entertainment Software Rating Board (ESRB), where it was described as containing blood, intense violence and suggestive themes. Before its intended release on the European market, the game received a rating of 16 in all countries using the PEGI system, except Finland where it was rated 15+. The game is in the PEGI system categorized as an 'Action/Survival horror game', labelled as containing depictions of violence, but with no mention of any sexual content. Generally, a PEGI 16 rating is applied 'once the depiction of violence (or sexual activity) reaches a stage that looks the same as would be expected in real life. More extreme bad language, the concept of the use of tobacco and drugs and the depiction of criminal activities can be content of games that are rated 16' (PEGI 2007). The game was not classified in the adult category of 18, used for games that depict 'gross violence', defined as violence that would make the viewer feel a sense of revulsion (PEGI 2007).

Act I: The setup

On 10 November 2006, the Italian news magazine *Panorama* features a cover story on the soon-to-be released *Rule of Rose* with the headline '*Vince chi seppellisce la bambina*' [He who buries the little girl wins], with the subtitle '*Viaggio tra gli orrori del divertimento elettronico*' [A journey into the horrors of electronic entertainment] (see also Bittanti 2006). The story contains harsh criticisms of not only *Rule of Rose*, but also of the video game medium per se (Bittanti 2006). The *Panorama* feature includes an interview with Italy's president of the Committee for Childhood, Anna Serafini. Serafini, admitting that she does not know how to even switch on a PlayStation, is terrified by the described content of the game and questions how it could have reached the market.

The same reaction comes from Rome's mayor Walter Veltroni, calling for a national ban of the game. The article also sparks interest from leading Italian newspapers (see, for instance, Fulco 2006) and TV stations. The media frenzy results in a parliamentary discussion on video games conducted only four days after the *Panorama* article. In the debate, the Italian minister of justice proposes a committee to evaluate the content of video games (apparently not being aware of the PEGI system and Italy's involvement in it), and calls for censorship in the sense that video games deemed too violent should not be released at all in Italy. The whole debate has the characteristics of a moral panic, as described above:

> During the parliamentary discussion, representatives from both parties agreed that violent games are directly responsible for the moral crisis of the country (e.g. the abundance of videos of students bullying teachers and other peers [*sic*] on You Tube and Google Video). After reading the transcripts of the discussion, one thing is obvious: most of the politicians that took part in the debate are not familiar with videogames at all and they tend to confuse videogames with online videos.[7] (Bittanti 2006)

Shortly after, the European commissioner for justice, fundamental rights and citizenship, Italian Franco Frattini, summons an urgent meeting of *all* EU home affairs ministers after his (according to *The Times*) revulsion after *watching* 'Rule of Rose' (Charter 2006).

Act II: The development

Within a week, UK newspapers *The Times* and the *Daily Mail* adopt the Italian case under headings like 'Torturing this child is a game too far, says appalled EU boss' (*Times* 17 November 2006, front page), and 'Time for parents to take responsibility' (Wapshott 2006). To *The Times*, Frattini describes the content of the game as 'a young girl who is submitted to psychological and physical violence' stating that 'This has shocked me profoundly for its obscene cruelty and brutality' (Charter 2006). *The Times* quotes Frattini arguing that voluntary ratings are no longer enough to stop obscene games falling into younger hands, adding: 'It is first and foremost the responsibility of the parents to protect children from such games, but I nevertheless think that we at member state and European level also have to take responsibility to protect children's rights. These types of games are dreadful examples for our children' (Charter 2006). After meeting with Frattini, UK home secretary John Reid comments on the case by linking it to the issue of child pornography online (*MailOnline* 2006), hence making it an even hotter political issue in the United Kingdom.

A spokeswoman for the Department for Culture, Media and Sport states that Britain, with jail or fines for supplying 18-rated games to minors, 'has got strict measures which we think go far enough at present' (Charter 2006), ignoring that the game is not deemed extreme enough for an adult rating by the Video Standards Council (VSC), but is labelled 16 for the UK market.

By the next day (18 November 2006), news media in Poland address the case. The Polish Ministry of Education files a report to the prosecutor's office, claiming that the game includes content that is dangerous to children and young people. While no legal provision exists in the Polish penal code to ban the game, the ministry suggests the use of legal provisions, such as presenting pornography to minors or the mistreating of animals, as justifications for preventing access to the game (*VaGla.pl* 2006).

With claims that the game contained children buried alive underground, in-game sadomasochism and underage eroticism, the newspapers are accused by the VSC for exaggerating and making up many of the cited examples (Miller 2006). Quoting the VSC secretary general Laurie Hall, several online technology journals state: 'I have no idea where the suggestion of in-game sadomasochism has come from, nor children being buried underground. These are things that have been completely made up. [. . .] There isn't any underage eroticism [. . .] And the most violent scene does indeed see one of the young girls scare Jennifer with a rat on a stick. But the rat's actually quite placid towards her and even licks her face' (Kuchera 2006b), and 'I wouldn't call the game violent. We're not worried about our integrity being called into question, because Mr. Frattini's quotes are nonsense' (Ballard 2006).

Similarly, the secretary general of the Italian Entertainment Software Publishers Association (AESVI), Thalita Malago, addresses the 'misinformed reactions of people who had not played the game' (Ballard 2006): 'The polemic around this game was based on overstatements by the *Panorama* article, which said the purpose of the game was to bury children alive. But it's just a psychological thriller – it may not be suitable to everybody, but it's not based on perversion or homosexuality like people said.'

Act III – The resolution

By the end of November 2006, due to the media frenzy and political uproar, the UK publisher 505 Games decides not to release the title. Shortly after they are followed by their branch offices in Australia and New Zealand (Ramsay 2006). As of Winter 2010, the game is still not classified by Australia's Office of Film and Literature Classification (OFLC) (Australian Office of Film and Literature Classification 2010), and not listed on the 505 Games' list of products (www.505games.co.uk and www.505games.com). In the United States, Sony forewent the publishing rights due to the controversy surrounding the game, leaving the publishing rights to the smaller distributer Atlus (Anderson 2006; see also Atlus 2006; Grant 2006).

However, the industry's own restriction and de facto ban of the game did not prevent political and regulatory implications. First, referring directly to the media reports, a written question was posed by two members of the European Parliament, Cristiana Muscardini and Roberta Angelilli, stating that given the description of the game in the Italian weekly magazine, the 'only useful thing to do is to take legal action against the production of such sadistic games involving children and adults infected by the horror bug', claiming that 'this game could also have criminal implications since it could be seen as incitement to violence against minors. Moreover, who is to draw the line between games and reality, however imaginary?', culminating in the official questions to the European Commission:

1. Is it possible for the Commission to intervene, on the basis of legislation on violence against minors, in particular the Daphne programme, to prevent such commercial undertakings?
2. Is it prepared, as part of its child protection policy, to promote an initiative in order to avoid other idiotic games of this nature being introduced? (Muscardini and Angelilli 2006)

In addition, a motion was put forward to the European Parliament for a resolution on a *specific ban* on the sale and distribution in Europe of the video game *Rule of Rose*, claiming that the aim of the game is 'to bury alive a girl who has undergone psychosexual and physical violence bordering on perversion and sadism' and that the 'perverse, violent and sadistic images are harmful to human dignity' (Hon Angelilli et al. 2007). The motion also called for the creation of a European Observatory on childhood and minors to be set up to preventively monitor video game content and define a single code of conduct for the sale and distribution of children's video games (Motion B6–0023/2007 E_2). As of December 2010, the motion is still pending.

The commotion also caused internal conflict in the European Commission. While Commissioner Frattini had fronted the case and called a meeting inviting all EC member states' interior ministers, demanding that 'something had to be done', the regulation of computer games and the protection of minors from potentially harmful media content was under the jurisdiction of the Commissionaire for the Information Society and Media, Viviane Reding. This prompted Commissionaire Reding to send a letter to Frattini, stating, according to the *Register* which obtained a copy of the letter,[8] that he 'was speaking out of turn about something he knew little about and that he should think before he acted the next time, and perhaps pick up the phone, because her directorate had it all under control' (Ballard 2006). Being a strong supporter of the PEGI system, Commissionaire Reding reminded Frattini of the core policy of the Commission of 'informed adult choice' without censoring content as 'this is in line with the Commission's view that measures taken to protect minors and human dignity must be carefully balanced with the fundamental right to freedom of expression as laid down in the Charter on Fundamental Rights of the European Union' (Ballard 2006). At the time of writing, this is officially as far as the case has gone within the EC. One should, however, note the European Council's conclusions (12–13 VI, 2007), which without mentioning *Rule of Rose* specifically, make it clear that the Council regards the current legislation and system sufficient to handle 'violent video games' (Council of the European Union 2007).

Discussion: The moral panic of *Rule of Rose*

The case of *Rule of Rose* is the last in a long line of public and/or political attacks on video games (Herz 1997; Poole 2000, 2004; Kent 2001). Even so, the *Rule of Rose* case could probably be analyzed and explained just by researching the wider national political motivations and strategies of Italian and British politicians (see, for instance, Kuipers 2006). Well known to anyone wanting to maximize their persuasiveness on any political issue in the public, the use of *fear* is high on the list of techniques. Making the audience aware of an impending and imminent threat to their lives and/or welfare heightens the chances of raising awareness and changing attitudes (Holsti 1992: 168). In addition, introducing the elements of a media panic heightens the public's sense of alienation and gives journalists opportunities to link any type of news to the 'new' media.

However, there are some particulars to this specific panic that makes it worth looking at the game itself, and the cultural narrative it challenges. Turning back to the theoretical definitions, we find that the storyline of the case fits McLuhan's observation that new media is perceived by 'highly literate people' – in this case commissioners and home office secretaries – as a moral threat to established values. It also ticks three of the clusters of social identity Stanley Cohen defines moral panics as belonging to (2002: viii), namely: school violence/bullying, child abuse and sex and/or violence in the media.[9] It also contains the five crucial elements defining a moral panic as theorized by Goode and Ben-Yehuda ([1994] 2006): it is *volatile*, with *heightened concern, hostility, agreement of reality of threat*, resulting in a *disproportionate* reaction. In addition, the panic was instigated by the traditional print media, where the perceived problem of *Rule of Rose* was expanded into a perceived general problem about computer games, thus fitting into the media panic definitions of Drotner (1999a, 1999b).

In the case of *Rule of Rose*, the prime focus of the critique was not on its potential harmfulness to children playing the game, but rather to the perceived moral tastelessness of the game itself. The game *tortured a girl* and was argued as having potential criminal implications since it could be seen as incitement to violence against minors. Given the media frenzy and subsequent ban or non-release of the game (after descriptions of sadomasochism, underage eroticism, the burying of living people, gruesome violence and perverse images), it is rather puzzling to compare the public process of the reaction to the game to the evaluation of the game by those who have actually played it. The reviewer in *Ars Technica* expressed a strong disappointment, stating the game was boring, giving it a 'skip' recommendation:

> Even the creepy little girl aspect is missing, there are a lot of little girls, but they're just not that creepy. How can you mess up the creepy little girl formula? By making the environments and exploration and combat incredibly boring. The chapters seem unconnected to one another, which doesn't allow the story to pick up much steam, and that story would be the only reason to keep going. I would rather play *Fatal Frame* again, or find a real creepy girl, give her a straight razor, and see what happens. Both choices are more fun than playing *Rule of Rose*. (Kuchera 2006a)

Similarly, *Gamespot* considered it 'repetitive, boring gameplay' (Greg 2006). The overall metacritic rating, based on 44 reviews, is at the time of writing 59 (of maximum 100), indicating mixed or average reviews, with a range from 90 (*AceGamez*) to 30 (*Edge Magazine*).

Those politicians authoring the public narrative of the case had not themselves played the unreleased game, but rather read about it or, as stated by Frattini, *watched* it. It is clear, from the industry representatives in Italy, from the regulators in the United Kingdom, from the reviews of the game, and from the game itself,[10] that none of the alleged in-game sadomasochism or children being buried underground is present. The only character (apparently, but given the storytelling's psychedelic leanings by no means surely) being put in a coffin (but not buried underground) is the protagonist, 19-year-old Jennifer. There is a lack of reflection throughout the whole debate on the fact that the principal character in the game possibly being 'submitted to psychological and physical violence' (or rather the digital representation of a young girl in the form of a character in a computer game), is in fact not a girl, but a young woman of 19 years.

Thus, the premise of the regulatory demands does not follow the plotline. Quite the contrary, in the game it is not (the characters intended to represent) children that are being subjected to abuse and violence, but *the children who are the perpetrators of the violence* against the young adult character Jennifer. So, why was this not discussed?

It is interesting to note how the public debate on *Rule of Rose* illustrates the lack of adult recognition of the issue of children not being innocent per se. In the public discourse surrounding *Rule of Rose* the concept of the evil children, young girls tormenting the main character, is not discussed.

Today it seems that the understanding of children as innocent has prevailed in society[11] with such a force that the mere idea of 'the evil child' becomes almost unbearable, and in need of explanation. As argued by Drotner (1999b: 611), children and young people are continuously defined as objects and vulnerable victims in the panics. When we look at the past 70 years, it is striking how the frightening concept of the evil child has produced a lot of well-known fiction, yet almost all of these seem to need a final, soothing explanation at the end, restoring the audiences' faith in the innocence of children – not unlike the villain's comeuppance in classic gangster fiction (e.g. the child in reality being the antichrist in *The Omen*, a ghost inhabiting a computer in *F.E.A.R* [Hubbard 2005], the result of a genetic experiment in *Firestarter* [Lester 1984] and *Anna to the Infinite Power* [Wiemer 1983], or really an adult posing as a child in *Orphan* [Collet-Serra 2009]).

These examples all illustrate how, while the idea of 'evil children' is a traditional and popular fictional genre, the mere idea of the child just being plain evil (or deviant) is not possible. It seems more 'realistic' (in terms of selling the story to an audience) that the child is possessed or the result of fanatical research (genetic or technological) gone wrong.

As described, *Rule of Rose* uses this to enhance its impact. While the story is told in such a way that numerous interpretations are available, the depiction of children actually being evil is quite visible. Some of this is explained or even excused (e.g. by showing the evil caretaker Gregory), but within the game's spongy narrative all is not resolved. It is, however, very interesting to note that the media panic surrounding the game started not with players who had actually experienced the game's unsettling story, images and labyrinthine psychological twists, but with public figures who had been told only of the game's content. So, in effect, *Rule of Rose* is a game with several in-built panic triggers, yet the mere *mention* of its content was enough to spark a pan-European uproar.

Conclusion

How cultural products are perceived in a democratic society, how they are classified in terms of potential harm and likelihood of impact and how the public discourse is staged will have an impact on the political and democratic processes in that society. Seeing cultural products as risks representing an immediate threat to one's children will inevitably generate calls for political action, action that traditionally materializes in some type of regulation aimed to reduce or remove the perceived threat. Regulation within a democratic society will (or at least should) elicit the need for a transparency in the political processes, an involvement of the public through public hearings and debates, media scrutiny and a clarification of the legitimacy of the regulation versus perceived risk – whatever these might be and whatever the accuracy of the perception.

All the regulatory efforts and implementations in the name of child protection have and will inevitably put pressure on other democratic principles such as privacy, freedom of expression and freedom of information, hence the extensive public debates that have trailed each of these laws. Compelling arguments are often put forward showing unpleasant texts, images and attitudes (such as *Rule of Rose*), on the one side, and the innocence of children and their impressionable minds, on the other side, calling for censorship and bans. For *Rule of Rose*, the media and moral panics were enough to make the distributors withdraw the game from the European market, despite the fact that the allegations of the content of the game were false. Perhaps the withdrawal does not represent a substantial loss for potential players, or popular culture development. But the precedent it sets is disturbing.

What is particularly interesting in the case of *Rule of Rose* is that the game is designed to be *suggestive,* meaning that its disturbing imagery is open for interpretations from the reader. In this sense, a moral concern will be based on the reader's own moral map and level of imagination. Thus, the design in itself is an invitation to moral distress for the player. However, this cannot explain the moral panic of *Rule of Rose*, as none of the actors had actually played the game.

Note on the players

Frattini has left the European Commission and is now (2010) the foreign minister of Italy. Viviane Reding has taken over Frattini's old job as the European commissioner for justice, fundamental rights and citizenship.

Notes

Acknowledgements are due as follows: Staksrud's contribution to this chapter is part of the larger *Mediatized Stories* project funded by the Norwegian Research Council and led by Professor Knut Lundby. The conference presentation of the chapter was made possible by a research grant ('Småforsk') from the Department of Media and Communication, University of Oslo.We also thank Professor Þorbjörn Broddason, University of Iceland, for insightful references; Jürgen Bänsch, EU Affairs Manager at PEGI, for assistance; and Agnieszka Wrzesień for translation of Polish texts.The computer game *Rule of Rose* (ルール オブ ローズ, *Rūru obu Rōzu*) (Punchline and Shirogumi 2006) was, as described in this chapter, not published in Europe, and copies already sent from the distributor to sales agents were withdrawn before the game was launched. While it was available for a short while in the United States, the game played for the purpose of this research was obtained via an admittedly dubious French online source, and is credited to the original European distributor 505 Games, not the American distributed Atlus. However, as official information can only be found via Atlus (the game is no longer listed as part of the 505 Games historical portfolio), the game is listed under both distributors in the list of references. The game has been played by the authors on the Sony PlayStation2 system.

1　Many researchers attribute the term 'moral panic' to its conceptual developer Stan Cohen (1972), while others have made a point to challenge this by crediting Cohen's colleague Jock Young (1971) for the original use of the term (see, for instance, Critcher 2006: 25; Muncie [1999] 2004: 11), or have credited both (Jewkes 2004: 66).

2   The terms are not used in a technologically stringent way, as both the television and the computer depend on electricity and electronics. Strictly speaking, the shift is closer to being from analogue to digital, or from continuous to discrete technologies.

3   It is not difficult to find empirical examples of media panics embedding the double-jeopardy fears of new technology itself as well as its influences on impressionable young minds. All media have at one point in time been new media, consequentially the historical descriptions of media panic is also very old. One of the first examples of a 'new media panic' can be found in Plato's 'Phaedrus' ([ca. 370 BC] 1961), where Socrates refers to a debate on whether to teach young Egyptians numbers, calculus, geometry, astronomy, draughts and dice, and (above all) writing. While not objecting to any of the former, the King objected to the writing part, worrying that if men learn writing, they will cease to remember, hence not develop wisdom and end up being a burden to their fellows (Plato [ca. 370 BC] 1961: 520).

4   While the adventure genre in its pure form (the *Zork* trilogy [Anderson, Blank, Daniels and Lebling 1979–82] and the *Monkey Island* games [LucasArts and Telltale Games, 1990–2010] are prime examples), originally developed in 1976 (Crowther 1976), has received little attention in the past ten years, its legacy is in just about every game that is released, from first-person shooter *Call of Duty* (Infinity Ward, Treyarch, Sledgehammer Games, Amaze Entertainment, Rebellion Developments and n-Space 2003–current) to online blockbuster *World of Warcraft* (Blizzard Entertainment 2004–current). The Survival Horror genre, on the other hand, has since its inception in 1996 (Capcom 1996) established itself as a strong sub-genre, both in its original form and as an influence on other genres.

5   The other common viewpoint in video games is the first-person view, for example, seen in the first-person shooter genre with games such as *Counter-Strike* (Valve Software 1999) and *Quake* (id Software, Midway Games and Lobotomy Software 1996).

6   These exaggerated and stylized graphical elements are found in a huge proportion of Japanese comics and animated media, even in those made in a realistic style overall, such as the hugely influential *Lone Wolf and Cub* (Kazuo and Goseki 1987).

7   Similar and parallel cases of confusion are abundant, for example, in Greece, where the 3037/2002 law was passed, effectively banning all forms of video games, in an attempt to quell illegal gambling; as well as in the Norwegian public debate on digital addiction, where online gambling ('spilleavhengighet') tends to be confused with and bundled together with online gaming ('spillavhengighet'), due to the very slight semantic difference between the two terms.

8   The authors have not been able to obtain a copy of this communication through official channels at the time of writing.

9   The others being young working-class violent males, wrong drugs used by the wrong people in wrong places, welfare cheats and single mothers, and refugees and asylum seekers.

10 The authors have played the game.
11 For more in-depth studies on the imagery of children and childhood in Western societies, see, for instance, Holland (2004, 2008).

Bibliography

Anderson, N. (2006), 'Citing Its Underage Eroticism, Sony America Pulls Plug on Japanese Video Game', *Ars Technica,* 8 June, http: //arstechnica.com/old/content/2006/06/7018.ars [accessed 8 June 2006].

Atlus (2006), *Rule of Rose* [official website], www.atlus.com/ruleofrose/ [accessed 15 March 2010].

Australian Office of Film and Literature Classification (2010), *Classification Database,* www.oflc.gov.au/www/cob/find.nsf/Search?OpenForm [accessed 18 March 2010].

Ballard, M. (2006), 'Euro Commissioners Swap Slaps in Video Game Row. Italians All in a Lather over "Perversity"', *Register,* 24 November, www.theregister.co.uk/2006/11/24/reding_said_to_frattini/ [accessed 24 March 2011].

Bangemann, M. (1994), *Europe and the Global Information Society: Recommendations to the European Council.* Brussels: European Council.

Barker, C. (1984), *Books of Blood* (Vols 1–6): Sphere Books.

Bittanti, M. (2006), 'Moral Panics, Bad Journalism, Videogames, and Italian Melodrama', *Digital Youth Research,* http://digitalyouth.ischool.berkeley.edu/node/60 [accessed 24 March 2011].

Butsch, R. (2000), *The Making of American Audiences: From Stage to Television, 1750–1990,* Cambridge and New York: Cambridge University Press.

Carlsson, U. (2001), 'Research, Information and Sensitizing the Public', in C. A. Arnaldo (ed.), *Child Abuse on the Internet: Ending the Silence,* Paris: Unesco Berghahn Books, 61–4.

Carroll, L. (1865), *Alice's Adventures in Wonderland,* London: Macmillan.

CERO Computer Entertainment Rating Organization [Japan] (2006), ルール オブ ローズ, www.cero.gr.jp/search/search.cgi?name=%A5%EB%A1%BC %A5%EB%A5%AA%A5%D6%A5%ED%A1%BC%A5%BA&txtCP=> [accessed 23 November 2010].

Charter, D. (2006), 'Torturing This Child Is a Game Too Far, Says Appalled EU Boss', *The Times,* 17 November, http://entertainment.timesonline.co.uk/tol/arts_and_Entertainment/article639508.ece [accessed 24 March 2011].

Chiricos, T. ([1996] 2006), 'Moral Panic as Ideology: Drugs, Violence, Race and Punishment in America', in C. Critcher (ed.), *Critical Readings: Moral Panics and the Media,* Maidenhead, Buckingham: Open University Press, 103–23.

Cohen, S. (1972), *Folk Devils and Moral Panics: The Creation of the Mods and Rockers*, London: MacGibbon and Kee.

Coleman, C.-L. (1993), 'The Influence of Mass Media and Interpersonal Communication on Societal and Personal Risk Judgments', *Communication Research*, 20(4): 611–28.

Council of the European Union (2007), *Press Release, 2807th Council Meeting*, Luxembourg: Council of the European Union.

Critcher, C. (ed.) (2006), *Critical Readings: Moral Panics and the Media*, Maidenhead, Buckingham: Open University Press.

— (2008), 'Making Waves: Historical Aspects of Public Debates about Children and Mass Media', in K. Drotner and S. Livingstone (eds), *The International Handbook of Children, Media and Culture*, London: Sage, 91–104.

de Young, M. ([1998] 2006), 'Another Look at Moral Panics: The Case of Satanic Daycare Centers', in C. Critcher (ed.), *Critical Readings: Moral Panics and the Media*, Maidenhead, Buckingham: Open University Press, 277–90.

— (2004), *The Day Care Ritual Abuse Moral Panic*, Jefferson, NC: McFarland.

Drotner, K. (1999a), 'Dangerous Media? Panic Discourses and Dilemmas of Modernity', *Paedagogica Historica*, 35(3): 593–619.

— (1999b), *Unge, Medier og Modernitet – Pejlinger i et Foranderligt Landskap*, Valby: Borgens forlag.

European Commission (1997), *Commission Communication to the European Parliament, the Council and the Economic and Social Committee on the Follow-Up to the Green Paper on the Protection of Minors and Human Dignity in Audiovisual and Information Services Including a Proposal for a Recommendation*, http://ec.europa.eu/avpolicy/docs/reg/minors/comlv-en.htm [accessed 24 March 2011].

— (2008), *Communication from the Commission to the European Parliament, the Council, the European Economic and Social Committee and the Committee of the Regions on the Protection of Consumers, in Particular Minors, in Respect of the Use of Video Games*, http://eur-lex.europa.eu/LexUriServ/LexUriServ.do?uri=COM:2008:0207:FIN:EN:PDF [accessed 24 March 2011].

European Council (2002), *Council Resolution of 1 March 2002 on the Protection of Consumers, in Particular Young People, through the Labelling of Certain Video Games and Computer Games according to Age Group*, http://eur-lex.europa.eu/LexUriServ/LexUriServ.do?uri=OJ:C:2002:065:0002:0002:EN:PDF [accessed 24 March 2011].

Fornäs, J. and Bolin, G. (1995), *Youth Culture in Late Modernity*, London: Sage.

Freeman, M. (1997), 'The James Bulger Tragedy: Childish Innocence and the Construction of Guilt', in A. McGillivray (ed.), *Governing Childhood*, Aldershot: Dartmouth, 115–34.

Fulco, D. I. (2006), *Rule of Rose: Vince Chi Seppellisce Vivo il Videogioco*, *LaStampa.it*, www.lastampa.it/_web/cmstp/tmplrubriche/giochi/grubrica.

asp?ID_blog=35&ID_articolo=86&ID_sezione=50&sezione=> [accessed 24 March 2011] (site discontinued).

Golding, W. (1954), *Lord of the Flies*, London: Faber and Faber.

Goode, E. and Ben-Yehuda ([1994] 2006), 'Moral Panics: An Introduction', in C. Critcher (ed.), *Critical Readings : Moral Panics and the Media*, Maidenhead, Buckingham: Open University Press, 50–9.

Grant, C. (2006), '"Erotic" Themes Too Much for Sony in America', *Joystiq*, 8 June, www.joystiq.com/2006/06/08/erotic-themes-too-much-for-sony-in-america/ [accessed 24 March 2011].

Greg, K. (2006), '*Rule of Rose* Review', *Gamespot*, 22 September, www.gamespot.com/ps2/action/ruleofrose/review.html?om_act=convert&om_clk=gssummary&tag=summary;read-review [accessed 24 March 2011].

Herz, J. C. (1997), *Joystick Nation: How Videogames Gobbled our Money, Won Our Hearts, and Rewired Our Minds*, London: Abacus.

Holland, P. (2004), *Picturing Childhood: The Myth of the Child in Popular Imagery*, London: I.B. Tauris.

— (2008), 'The Child in the Picture', in K. Drotner and S. Livingstone (eds), *The International Handbook of Children, Media and Culture*, London: Sage, 36–54.

Holsti, K.J. (1992), *International Politics. A Framework for Analysis*, 6th edn, Engelwood Cliffs: Prentice-Hall International.

Hon Angelilli, Muscardini, Mussolini, Napoletano, Sbarbati, Zappalà, Poli Bortone, Locatelli, Toia, Sartori, et al. (2007), *Motion for a European Parliament Resolution on a Ban on the Sale and Distribution in Europe of the Video Game 'Rule of Rose' and the Creation of a European Observatory on Childhood and Minors*, www.europarl.europa.eu/sides/getDoc.do?pubRef=-//EP//TEXT+MOTION+B6–2007–0023+0+DOC+XML+V0//EN [accessed 24 March 2011].

Jewkes, Y. (2004), *Media and Crime*, London: Sage.

Joffe, H. (1999), *Risk and 'the Other'*, Cambridge: Cambridge University Press.

Kazuo, Koike (Author) and Goseki, Kijoma (Artist) (1987), *Lone Wolf and Cub*: First Comics.

Kent, S. L. (2001), *The First Quarter: A 25-Year History of Video Games*, Bothell, WA: BDW Press.

King, S. (1982), *Ildbarnet*, [Oslo]: Hjemmets bokforl.

Kuchera, B. (2006a), 'Game Review: *Rule of Rose*', *Ars Technica*, 15 October, http://arstechnica.com/gaming/news/2006/10/5622.ars [accessed 24 March 2011].

— (2006b), '*Rule of Rose* Hatchet Job Results in Cancellations, Truth Nowhere in Sight', *Ars Technica*, 24 November, http://arstechnica.com/gaming/news/2006/11/8281.ars [accessed 24 March 2011].

Kuipers, G. (2006), 'The Social Construction of Digital Danger', *New Media & Society*, 8(3): 379–400.

Livingstone, S. (2008), 'Children's Media – More Harm Than Good', paper presented at the Miniseminar om barn, nye medier og skadelighet, Oslo.

Lupton, D. (1994), *Moral Threats and Dangerous Desires: AIDS in the News Media*, London: Taylor & Francis.

MailOnline (2006), 'Reid Urges EU Crackdown on Net Child Porn', 4 December, www.dailymail.co.uk/news/article-420370/Reid-urges-EU-crackdown-net-child-porn.html [accessed 24 March 2011].

Manning, P. (2007), *Drugs and Popular Culture: Drugs, Media and Identity in Contemporary Society*, Cullompton, Willan.

Marwick, A. E. (2008), 'To Catch a Predator? The MySpace Moral Panic', *First Monday*, 13(6), http://firstmonday.org/htbin/cgiwrap/bin/ojs/index.php/fm/article/view/2152/1966

McLuhan, M. ([1964] 2001), *Understanding Media: The Extensions of Man*, London: Routledge.

Meyer, A. (2007), 'The Moral Rhetoric of Childhood', *Childhood*, 14(1): 85–104.

Miller, R. (2006), '*Rule of Rose* Ruled out in the UK', *Joystiq*, 27 November, www.joystiq.com/tag/Rule+of+Rose/ [accessed 24 March 2011].

Millwood Hargrave, A. and Livingstone, S. M. (2009), *Harm and Offence in Media Content: A Review of the Evidence*, Bristol Intellect.

Muncie, J. (1984), '*The Trouble with Kids Today*': Youth and Crime in Post-war Britain, London: Hutchinson.

— ([1999] 2004), *Youth and Crime*, 2nd edn, London: Sage.

Muscardini, C. and Angelilli, R. (2006), *WRITTEN QUESTION by Cristiana Muscardini (UEN) and Roberta Angelilli (UEN) to the Commission*, www.europarl.europa.eu/sides/getDoc.do?type=WQ&reference=E-2006–5057&format=XML&language=EN [accessed 24 March 2011].

NICAM (2008), www.kijkwijzer.nl/pagina.php?id=3 [accessed 24 March 2011].

Pan-European Game Information (PEGI) (2007), 'About *PEGI?*, *What Do the Labels Mean?*', www.pegi.info:PEGI [accessed 24 March 2011].

Plato ([ca. 370 BC] 1961), 'Phaedrus', in E. Hamilton and H. Cairns (eds), *The Collected Dialogues of Plato, Including the Letters*, New York: Pantheon Books, 475–525.

Poole, S. (2000), *Trigger Happy: The Inner Life of Videogames*, London: Fourth Estate.

— (2004), *Trigger Happy: Videogames and the Entertainment Revolution*, New York: Arcade.

Ramsay, R. (2006), 'Rule of Rose Canned Down Under', *Gamespot*, 27 November, www.gamespot.com/ps2/action/ruleofrose/news.html?sid=6162312&om_act=convert&om_clk=newsfeatures&tag=newsfeatures;title;1 [accessed 24 March 2011].

Reding, V. (2007), 'Self-Regulation Applied to Interactive Games: Success and Challenges', unpublished manuscript, Brussels.

Schissel, B. (1997), *Blaming Children: Youth Crime, Moral Panic and the Politics of Hate*, Halifax, NS: Fernwood.

Silva, E. B. (1996), *Good Enough Mothering? Feminist Perspectives on Lone Motherhood*, London: Routledge.

Staksrud, E. (2002), 'Ytringsfrihet og Sensur på Internett. Politisk Regulering og Kommersiell Filtrering', in T. Slaatta (ed.), *Digital Makt. Informasjons- og Kommunikasjonsteknologiens Betydning og Muligheter*, Oslo: Gyldendal Akademisk. 64–94.

Stephenson, R. H. and Banet-Weiser, S. (2007), 'Super-Sized Kids: Obesity, Children, Moral Panic, and the Media', in J. A. Bryant (ed.), *The Children's Television Community*, Mahwah, NJ: Lawrence Erlbaum, 277–91.

Sutter, G. (2000), '"Nothing New under the Sun": Old Fears and New Media', *International Journal of Law and Information Technology*, 8(3): 338–78.

Tulloch, J. and Lupton, D. (1997), *Television, AIDS and Risk: A Cultural Studies Approach to Health Communication*, St Leonards, NSW: Allen & Unwin.

VaGla.pl (2006), 'Rządy Róży – Kontrowersyjna gra na Play Station 2', http://prawo. vagla.pl/node/6819 [accessed 24 March 2011].

Wapshott, T. (2006), 'Time for Parents to Take Responsibility', *The Times*, http://www. timesonline.co.uk/tol/news/uk/article639506.ece [accessed 24 March 2011].

Wasserman, I. M. and Stack, S. (1994), 'Communal Violence and the Media: Lynchings and Their News Coverage by *The New York Times* between 1882 and 1930', in G. Barak (ed.), *Media, Process, and the Social Construction of Crime: Studies in Newsmaking Criminology*, New York: Garland.

Watney, S. ([1988] 2006), 'AIDS, "Moral Panic" Theory and Homophobia', in C. Critcher (ed.), *Critical Readings: Moral Panics and the Media*, Maidenhead, Buckingham: Open University Press, 256–65.

Weeks, J. ([1989] 2006), 'AIDS, the Intellectual Agenda', in C. Critcher (ed.), *Critical Readings: Moral Panics and the Media*, Maidenhead, Buckingham: Open University Press, 77–87.

Williams, J. P. and Smith, J. H. (2007), *The Players' Realm: Studies on the Culture of Video Games and Gaming*, Jefferson, NC: McFarland.

Young, J. (1971), 'The Role of the Police as Amplifiers of Deviancy, Negotiators of Reality and Translators of Fantasy: Some Aspects of our Present System of Drug Control as Seen in Notting Hill', in S. Cohen (ed.), *Images of Deviance*, Hammondsworth: Penguin.

Video Games

Anderson, T., Blank, M., Daniels, B. and Lebling, D. (1979–82), *Zork* (Version Apple II, Commodore 64, Commodore Plus/4, Atari 8-bit, TRS-80, CP/M, IBM PC.): Infocom.

Blizzard Entertainment (2004–), *World of Warcraft* (Version Microsoft Windows): Blizzard Entertainment.

Capcom. (1996), *Resident Evil* (Version PlayStation): Capcom.

Crowther, W. (1976), *ADVENT* (Version DOS): CRL.

Hubbard, C. (2005), *F.E.A.R* (Windows Version): Vivendi Universal.

id Software (1993), *Doom* (MS-DOS Version): GT Interactive, Activision, Bethesda Softworks.

id Software, Midway Games and Lobotomy Software (1996), *Quake* (Windows Version): GT Interactive.

Infinity Ward, Treyarch, Sledgehammer Games, Amaze Entertainment, Rebellion Developments and n-Space (2003–), *Call of Duty* (Xbox Version 360): Activision & Aspyr Media.

Koizumi, Y. and Miyamoto, S. (2007). *Super Mario Galaxy* (Version Wii): Nintendo.

LucasArts and Telltale Games (1990–2010), *Monkey Island* (Windows Version): LucasArts.

Punchline and Shirogumi (2006), *Rule of Rose* (Playstation 2 Version): 505 Games (Europe) and Sony Computer Entertainment Inc. & Atlus (United States).

Toyama, K. (1999), *Silent Hill* (Version PlayStation): Konami Digital Entertainment.

Valve Software (1999), *Counter-Strike* (Windows Version): Vivendi Universal and Microsoft Game Studios.

Part Three

Crime and Deviance

8

From Media Hypes to Moral Panics:
Theoretical and Methodological Tools

Marcello Maneri*

A growing body of research has used the moral panic framework in the past years. As is often the case, the popularity of the concept has not helped its analytical precision and has led to its conflation. In addition, social phenomena that seem suitable for the moral panic framework are often labelled in different ways: moral or symbolic crusades, public crises, construction of social problems, scares, crime waves and so on. What is the specific field of application of the moral panic concept? In this chapter I do not pretend to give an exhaustive answer. Instead I focus on moral panic as a process whose volatility and structure make it similar to other phenomena, like media hypes, where a social problem is suddenly and dramatically constructed by the media, on the one hand, but whose labelling and moral dimensions remind us of concepts like symbolic crusade (Gusfield 1963) and moral crusade (Becker [1963] 1991). What moral panics and 'media hypes' (Vasterman 2005), or 'crime waves' (Fishman 1978), have in common can help us to understand how moral panics work (and why they are sometimes confused with other social phenomena); what they do not have in common may help us better appreciate the deeply sociological nature of moral panics, which has something (but not everything) in common with moral/symbolic crusades. Through the analysis of two Italian case studies, I will illustrate what can fruitfully be understood to constitute a moral panic – and what is better labelled a more generic instance of media hype. Finally, I hope to show that more carefully analysing the process of media activation, as well as contrasting moral panics with similar phenomena like media hypes, will give us the tools to overcome some of the shortcomings in current theorizing about such panics. Consensus, disproportionality and concern – the most discussed attributes of a moral panic – can be understood in less controversial fashion if they are considered to be properties of the dynamics of mediated discourse.

Media hypes are an interesting case for comparison, because in the literature on moral panics the role of the media – although defined as 'crucial', 'important', 'growing' – has been insufficiently theorized (Critcher 2003), especially in the work that makes explicit reference to the moral panic model. This insufficient elaboration could be in part a by-product of the original work of Stanley Cohen ([1972] 2002), where the conceptualization of moral panic was developed around a list of stages through which the process took place. Although these stages were not meant to be as rigid or linear as in the disaster studies from which they were adapted, Cohen described a sequence (Warning, Impact, Inventory, Reaction) that appears problematic. In fact, the stages seem to work at disjointed analytical levels. The Inventory, for example, is composed of Exaggeration and Distortion (i.e. modalities of mis-representation), Prediction (a kind of speech act) and Symbolization (a metaphorical, illusive representation). In other words, the Inventory stage has to do with properties of discourse. In contrast, Impact refers to the appearance of a problem and to its particular scale. Consequently, Cohen's stages are more easily interpreted as features of the panic to be dealt with rather than as successive stages that lead from one to the other. It is no surprise then that subsequent studies have not taken up the idea of a stage structure (with the exception of Klocke and Muschert 2010). Without such a framework, however, it is impossible to understand the dynamic process at work in moral panics, which are characterized by feedback loops triggered by the media.

Accordingly, in this chapter I will try to reformulate Cohen's stages in order to rework a processual model that describes the typical sequence of a moral panic, and which can be used for empirical studies. To do this, I will draw on my own research using insights from existing studies on the news media that I believe provide important clues that have generally been ignored in the moral panic literature. In an effort to strengthen the analytic power of the model, I will employ the concepts of news theme (Fishman 1978) and news frame (Gamson and Modigliani 1989) and try to make them more reliable using simple linguistic categories that are borrowed from systemic-functional linguistics (Halliday 2004) and are already used in a variety of works in the field of critical discourse analysis (Fairclough [1989] 2001). Although a more comprehensive discourse analytic approach could provide a deeper and multidimensional analysis, in this chapter I hope to show how a close focus on a few key elements of media discourse can allow for a certain degree of quantification that makes comparative analysis an easier task. Through this contrast it is possible to isolate some of the strategic mechanisms embedded in a moral panic.

It is worth noting that this chapter focuses on media-driven moral panics: that is, processes that take off when one or more key events (Kepplinger and Habermeier 1995) activate the attention of the mass media, which is next backed up by politicians, experts and public officials. When the process is started and carried on mainly by campaigns run by moral entrepreneurs or claim makers, other sequences could be evident. Goode and Ben-Yehuda ([1994] 2009) suggest that these latter should be called moral crusades. However, the fact that both the media and moral entrepreneurs play a role in either case means that moral panics and crusades can be seen as two extremes of the same continuum, rather than discrete entities. Nevertheless, their point is valid since different carriers of social action may imply different logics and different social phenomena. They also maintain that what distinguishes a moral panic from a moral crusade is the existence of widespread public concern. I will argue that the association between moral panics and public concern is difficult to establish, both for empirical and theoretical reasons.

Next I contrast two case studies (for an overall analysis, see Maneri 2001), where I used a sequence adapted and reformulated from Cohen's original stages to explore the following issues:

- What is the typical sequence in a moral panic as initially activated by the media?
- When and how do the media and other social actors give prominence to and thematize events that will become the empirical evidence of a moral panic?
- Which elements in the news texts can be used to operationalize the analysis of a moral panic?
- Which 'turning points' characterize it and determine the success or failure of a moral panic, its direction and its consequences? What does each stage imply for the following one?
- Does this media-centred entry point help address in a more satisfactory way the problems raised by concepts such as 'disproportionality', 'public concern' and 'consensus' used in various studies?
- Is this sequence an exclusive property of moral panics? And if not, what are the differences between moral panics and media hypes?

The two cases studies

My case studies are based on a qualitative and quantitative discourse analysis of the three leading newspapers published in 1997 in two cities in northern Italy, Bologna and Rimini. The articles selected are all those published by *la Repubblica*, *L'Unità* and *il Resto del Carlino* (the last a regional newspaper) between 1 April and 26 July in the Bologna editions (for a total of 343 news items in the Bologna case) and all those published by *il Corriere della sera*, *l'Unità* and *il Resto del Carlino* between 26 July and 31 August in the Rimini editions (for a total of 184 news items in the Rimini case).

Bologna, May–July 1997

Bologna is a small, wealthy city of 380,000 people in the north of Italy that is characterized by a tradition of left-wing administrations, a major university and a relatively well-integrated immigrant population. In 1997 it was a middle-class city where conservative political parties were struggling for political dominance, using crime and decay as weapons in their fight.

Let us summarize the facts. On 7 May the news of a sexual assault on a student perpetrated by a group of youths appears with great emphasis in all the city newspapers. The day after, another rape is brought to public attention by the media; the victim is a student again, the offenders a group of youths in this case as well. A gang of young rapists is feared to operate in the city. For several weeks, local news will cover in depth the investigations and other episodes of committed or attempted sexual attacks. The theme of the violent city seizes the attention of newspapers: on peak days, each newspaper publishes at least six or seven articles on the topic. News about new attacks is accompanied by debates between experts, politicians and local associations. Policies advocated include the creation of a 'protected place' where women can report sexual assaults and the patrolling of city parks by male volunteers. The 'reaction of the city' reaches its climax on 31 May, with a demonstration promoted by feminist groups and a meeting promoted by the mayor to lay plans for an association of males against sexual violence.

On 13 June another episode of group violence catches newspaper attention. After a week of extensive coverage, the attention declines earlier this time. It will return on 22 July with news and a heated debate about the judicial decision to close four of the most widely publicized cases without further investigation. The depositions of several victims were incomplete and contradictory, and one of them had been retracted.

Rimini, August 1997

Rimini is located in Emilia-Romagna, the same region as Bologna. It is the biggest Italian resort town and in summer sees its population grow considerably from its 140,000 permanent residents. In the past few decades Rimini has been continuously administered by left-wing coalitions, which from the early 1990s have been targeted by frequent protests on the part of Italian shopkeepers annoyed by the widespread presence of 'abusive' immigrant beach and street sellers.

On 9 August a sexual assault on two Swiss tourists is reported with great emphasis in the newspapers' local and national pages. The offenders are six men, 'maybe Albanians', who acted at night on the Rimini beach. For a week, the front pages of local and national newspapers report a sort of war bulletin from the *Riviera*. The news flow is very high, reaching at its peak ten articles daily per newspaper. On 11 August an attempted sexual assault by a Moroccan citizen at the seaside nearby is reported. The day after, another attempt is reported from another resort village in the area. On 17 August another person is accused of sexual assault. On this occasion the offender is an Italian life guard who is an acquaintance of the victim.

In the meantime, since 11 August 1,000 policemen have been sent to patrol the *Riviera* beaches. They are followed by the 'City Angels', a volunteer corps. Systematic stop-and-searches target the immigrant groups in the area. A meeting in the *Prefettura* (the local government office in charge of security) is held the day after: the mayor of Rimini suggests that the beaches should be lit at night and that regional residency permits should be issued in order to better monitor non-EU citizens. On 15 August, the prime minister and the minister of the interior meet to discuss the situation. A law decree has been approved: new and stricter rules will govern the expulsion of foreign citizens.

Media coverage: The five stages

We can begin the analysis of these two episodes simply by considering the trend in the media output. In Figure 8.1 the number of news items published on the topic on a daily basis is reported. Looking at not just the trend, but also at the leads and (Figure 8.1) headlines, the changes in news selection criteria, and the primary voice, it is possible to distinguish five stages:

- A *Warning* stage, where (even sensational) events are covered according to routine journalistic norms;

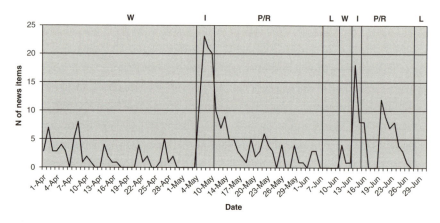

Figure 8.1 Trends in media output. Bologna, Spring 1997

Note: W= Warning I= Impact P/R= Propagation and Reaction L= Latency.

- An *Impact* stage, where coverage is disproportionately high compared to usual journalistic norms;
- A *Propagation* stage, where otherwise minor events gain strong visibility thanks to the newsworthiness of the established news theme, making them appear – to journalists as well as the public – to be new occurrences of the ongoing emergency.

Mostly overlapping with this stage, but distinguished by who is speaking (e.g. politicians, experts, public officials) and by the nature of the news fact (i.e. statements or law enforcement measures rather than new occurrences), come

- A *Reaction* stage, where we find diagnoses and solutions, and where extraordinary law enforcement measures are taken; and
- A *Latency* stage, where coverage returns to the usual level but a prototype of emergency has been established.

The *Warning* stage is noteworthy because it helps address the question of what triggers a moral panic. In the *Warning* (which does not always take place), we often find a particular concentration of minor episodes, or a very particular or weird single episode, that has the effect of alerting the journalists and sensitizing them to similar episodes. They may assume that the episodes that occurred in the *Warning* stage have produced growing public interest and later view these episodes as evidence that an escalating trend is taking place. In this way, favourable conditions for the *Impact* stage are created. In Bologna, for example,

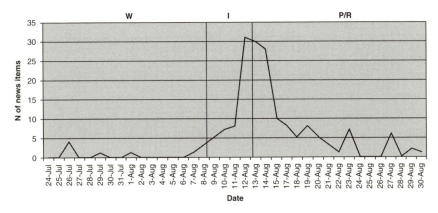

Figure 8.2 Trends in media output. Rimini, Summer 1997.

Note: W= Warning I= Impact P/R= Propagation and Reaction.

a 'shaman' had put his clients to sleep with a special potion in order to sexually abuse them, and a gynaecologist had been condemned for libidinous acts on his patients. In Rimini four rapes had been committed at the beginning of the summer season.

Most important in the activation of a moral panic, however, are contextual factors, also cited in other studies (Thompson 1998; Critcher 2003; Jenkins 2009):

- the accessibility of prototypes (previous similar episodes of moral panic);
- the link with other hot topics;
- a coalition of moral entrepreneurs and/or claim makers willing to exploit that kind of panic;
- the availability of 'useful' and possibly tried and tested folk devils;
- a consensus about the source of outrage; and
- the existence of background anxieties about social change.

As we will see, the Rimini case is characterized by all these features, while in Bologna only one applies.

To return to the object of the news, the emergence of the *Impact* stage is more likely when one or more other enabling circumstances are present. In most studies, we see some of the following circumstances, which have to do with compliance with established news values (Galtung and Ruge 1965):

- several episodes appear in a series;
- the single key event is a very serious occurrence;

- there is scarcity of other important news; and
- symbolic importance is attached to the place of the occurrence(s).

In Rimini, the sexual violence occurred in August and on the beach, the icon of seaside holidays in Italy. In Bologna, several episodes appeared as if they had been committed one after the other (a series which was only apparent, as one episode was made public only one month after it occurred, just the day after the first episode).

With the *Impact* stage, a news theme establishes itself. Following Fishman (1978), by 'news theme' I mean a unifying concept that gives an angle from which to view the story, so that one or more incidents can be seen as instances of something, stripped of their actual context and relocated in a new, more general symbolic context. Other scholars in media studies have used the concept of 'frame', that is, the selection of 'some aspects of a perceived reality [to] make them more salient in a communicating text, in such a way as to promote a particular problem definition, causal interpretation, moral evaluation, and/or treatment recommendation' (Entman 1993: 52; see also Gamson and Modigliani 1989). The two concepts, at least when applied to media studies, are similar enough. What they tell us is that journalists tend to select and give salience to certain aspects of the story in the attempt to find a meaning, so that a particular – and maybe not significant in its own terms – incident can be sold as an instance of something broader and more important.

The problem with the two concepts has always been operationalization (Matthes and Kohring 2008), a task that can be confronted by limiting the scope of the analysis. In fact in order to understand what happens in the *Impact* and then in the *Propagation* stage, it is sufficient to limit the analysis of the news theme/frame to the reports of the incidents. These reports inevitably foreground one or more elements of the news fact. A news fact, the one that is at the core of the story, can be summarized by a clause. Using the framework of systemic-functional linguistics (Halliday 2004), in the representation of reality we can distinguish between Participants, Process and Circumstances.

The foregrounding typically regards one, but often more, of these basic constituents of the clause. In mediated moral panics we have typically some kinds of participants, processes and circumstances:

- Participants: (categories of) Victim, Offender;
- Process: (kind of) Main Event; and
- Circumstances: Place, Time, Episode, Manner, Purpose.

Table 8.1 Constituents of the clause named in the headlines. Bologna and Rimini (percentages; absolute values in brackets)

	Participants		Process	Circumstances		
	Offender	**Victim**	**Sexual assault**	**Place**	**Time**	**Total**
Bologna	26.5	27.1	31.4	13.3	1.7	100
	(167)	(171)	(198)	(84)	(11)	(631)
Rimini	36.7	17.9	21.4	20.8	3.2	100
	(127)	(62)	(74)	(72)	(11)	(346)

Following the insights of critical linguistics (Fowler et al. 1979), it is possible to operationalize the indicators of the establishment of the news theme considering with what frequency and in which position (thematic, in the main clause, in the circumstances, elided) each element appears. A constitutive feature of the news is that the Process (the What, in journalistic terms) occupies in initial reports a central position, and very often it is the theme of the clause. In follow-up stories, however, other elements of the news fact may come to the foreground. In moral panics and more generally in public crises, in the days or in the weeks following the impact more abstract themes emerge, as the work of moral entrepreneurs is to establish a link between the news fact and broader social (moral) problems. For this and other obvious reasons, another important object of analysis is the way in which participants, processes and circumstances are categorized and qualified through successive steps, and also which explanations, diagnoses and solutions appear in the news.

At a basic representational level, however, it is possible to paint a very simple picture of the coverage by counting the constituents of the clause used to describe the incidents at the centre of the moral panic (for a more complete analysis, see Maneri 2001). In Table 8.1., the participants, the process and the circumstances that figure in the complete headlines of the news reports on the relevant incidents are listed. Percentages are calculated out of the total of the references included in the table for each city. Each reference may consist of one or more words (as in 'have been attacked').

A quick look at the table shows that the main difference between the two cases is the focus on the offenders in Rimini (and also a closer focus on the place) and a stronger attention to victims in Bologna.

A look at the grammatical forms (active, passive, nominalization) used to say 'what' has occurred makes clearer what the focus in the two cities is. In

Table 8.2 Grammatical forms used in the headlines to name the process. Bologna and Rimini (percentages; absolute values in brackets)

	Bologna	Rimini
Nouns, nominalizations: 'rape', 'violence', 'assault' ...	58.1	54.1
Active forms: '(they) rape', '(he) does violence to', 'tries to ...'	(115)	(40)
	13.1	25.7
Passive forms: 'raped', 'assaulted', 'attacked' etc.	(26)	(19)
Other (active forms where the victim is the grammatical subject, passive forms where the victim is the grammatical agent)	28.8	12.2
	(57)	(9)
	0	8,1
	0	(6)
Total	100	100
	(198)	(74)

In Table 8.2, the grammatical forms used in the complete headlines to refer to the process in the main event are reported. Percentages are calculated again out of the total of the references included in the table for each city. In Bologna, apart from nominalizations, typical in journalistic headlines' syntax, passive forms prevail over active (28.8% compared with 13.1%). This puts the victim in a thematic position. In Rimini, on the contrary, active forms are twice as frequent as passive forms (25.7% compared with 12.2%). This puts the offenders in the thematic position and makes clear who should be the main target of public attention. In other words, in Rimini the news theme – the broader frame through which facts are narrated and rendered meaningful – becomes that of the 'dangerous immigrants', while in Bologna it focuses on the 'unprotected women'.

To come back to the stages listed before, in the *Propagation* stage new instances of the news theme are more easily selected and actively searched for. The side of the curve at the right of the peak in Figure 8.1 is larger than the side on the left, as the news theme becomes a news value itself and journalists are mobilized to find new instances that can shed new light on the emergency going on. In other words, the threshold for an event to become news changes. The almost unprecedented amount of news on the topic, which results from this change in news values and thresholds (and also as an effect of the *Reaction* stage), gives the public the impression of an escalation of incidents (see also Fishman 1978; Kepplinger and Habermeier 1995).

The news theme(s) established in the previous stage is very important because it regulates the inclusion of new episodes in the current crisis (and their framing according to the theme) or their exclusion if their characteristics don't fit the news theme. It will predetermine, in addition, the range of 'reasonable solutions'. In this process the news theme can distort new incidents in order to fit the scheme. Thus in Rimini attempted rapes were presented as if they had been committed. Alternatively, the news theme can be redefined in order to adapt to slightly different incidents that are appealing to the media. In Rimini, the initial theme passed from 'rapes on the beach' to 'rapes on the *Riviera*' so as to include assaults committed in the villages nearby and outside of the beach. In other words, the news theme is subject to pressures from the incoming incidents, but not exclusively. Declarations from politicians, experts or public officials often play a crucial role in its redefinition.

The *Reaction* stage generally overlaps with *Propagation*. It takes place in the same time span but has a different nature. The 'what' of the news is different: we have statements instead of similar incidents or immediate police operations. The voice changes: there is a prominence of the sources' voices over the journalist's. We find the typical speech acts described in other works (Cohen [1972] 2002; Goode and Ben-Yehuda [1994] 2009; Critcher 2006): diagnoses/interpretations, law enforcement requests and procedures, proposals for long-term solutions. A more complex negotiation of which news theme will prevail takes place. It is often the public statement of an authoritative source or political representative (a 'primary definer' in the words of Hall et al. 1978) that gives a thematic prominence to a particular element of the news fact. Two days after the key event in Rimini, the mayor declared: 'Albanians and Northern Africans are a concrete problem', echoed by others, and the news theme, from the original 'rapes on the beach/*Riviera*', became 'rapes by immigrants'. If this contortion of the original news theme does not meet with strong resistance from other public figures, it will change the selection and framing criteria adopted by the media while they look for and give form to new instances of the emergency going on. In Rimini, rapes committed by Italians were ignored by the media or treated as a different phenomenon.

In this stage, but not generally in the days immediately following the key event (with the exception of serial moral panics about the same topic), politicians and experts give interpretations of the incident(s) that tend to establish a link with a wider 'social problem'. These interpretations are spelt out in explicit terms and need less and less to be translated into common sense wisdom by the media, because the politicians have learnt to do it by themselves. Nonetheless interpretations are also validated by the immediate, extraordinary and often symbolic/demonstrative action of the control apparatus, which targets the folk devils selected by the moral panic, so confirming their deviant nature. It is possible to 'do things with words' (Austin 1975), but it is also possible to 'say things with acts': one thousand policemen on the beach probably will not prevent other sexual assaults but surely will make clear 'who' is the problem and that something 'is being done'.

The *Reaction* stage can precipitate a moral panic or block it. It can silence it in a few days or give it a boost. If authoritative sources say that 'we have no emergency' (bravely, because they run the risk of being accused of denying important social problems), or refuse the interpretation implicit in the news theme, they give a signal that the media usually understand. As different sources may behave in different ways, we have here the possibility of consensual moral panics (where different sources and the media sustain the same framework with minor discrepancies), conflicted ones (where at least one influential source contests some of the defining features of 'the problem', to the point that the use of the concept may become misplaced), or stillborn moral panics (if the emergency is vigorously and successfully denied by a primary definer).

The *Latency* stage leads to the (often provisional) end of a moral panic. The media may feel that the public is saturated, counter-claims may break the consensual nature of the panic and transform it into something else, accusations of fuelling a 'moral panic' may be spelt out, the lack of similar incidents may weaken the possibility of continuing or the passing of a law or a change in the way it is enforced may give a narrative end to the story. Sometimes *Latency* looks more like closure: it happens when counter-facts (the retraction of the accusations by the victims in Bologna, two months after the impact) apparently delegitimize the outpourings of moral entrepreneurs.

Goode and Ben-Yehuda's moral panic attributes reconsidered

In their influential book, Goode and Ben-Yehuda listed five attributes that the public eruption of a social problem should have in order to qualify as a moral panic. They called them Concern, Hostility, Consensus, Disproportionality and Volatility. All of them have been widely discussed in the following years and perhaps only one, hostility, holds up fairly well to close critical scrutiny. As I will argue in the next section, the attribute of hostility (and hence the role of folk devils and morality) remains very useful in order to understand the deep sociological function of moral panics and should be stressed to avoid confusion with public reactions to other threats typical of risk society. Similarly, *volatility* can be used to distinguish moral panics from crusades and campaigns, where planned action on the part of the sources (or the media themselves) plays a much more prominent role. This attribute should not be overemphasized, however: not only has the volatility of moral panics led to their confusion with media hypes, but serial moral panics about tried and tested folk devils are probably much more common than the single, isolated, volatile eruption described in the collection put together by Goode and Ben-Yehuda. The other three attributes listed in that study – namely, disproportionality, concern and consensus – are unfortunately often put to work in ways that are epistemologically problematic and theoretically confusing. They are reconsidered below by better distinguishing the different sources of societal reaction using the entry point of the news media output and considering the dynamics between the five stages of a moral panic that I outlined in the previous section.

Works that allude to the *disproportionality* of moral panic, that attribute to moral panics the ability to exaggerate the importance, amplitude or seriousness of a social threat have been widely criticized (Waddington 1986; Watney 1987; Ungar 2001; Cornwell and Linders 2002). In the last instance, these studies often contain ideas – implicit or explicit – about the 'true proportions' or 'correct representation' of a social phenomenon, about 'reasonable concern' over a particular condition or 'objective threat'. This happens if disproportion is measured using external criteria, like empirical data about the incidence of the social problem and similar ones and raises the problem of finding valid indicators of the 'objective' dimension of the threat and of the risk it poses.

In these cases, conflicts about the 'true interpretation' of statistical data, its constructed nature and its relation with 'real facts' are likely to arise unless there is clear evidence of the non-existence or the downward trend of the problem that triggered the moral panic. The four indicators of disproportionality proposed by Goode and Ben-Yehuda (i.e. the exaggeration and fabrication of figures as well as greater attention compared to that paid to other harmful conditions or to that paid at another point in time ([1994] 2009: 43–4), while seemingly avoiding this risk, have the same problem in that they still make problematic reference to 'real figures' or 'objective harm'. If what is at stake is not the proportion of the problem, but the proportion of the reaction, the likelihood that sociologists will be accused of making value judgements is even higher. In this case they are obliged to make comparisons between perceived and 'real' risk, which require projections into the future or, worse, evaluations of how much a sense of moral outrage is reasonable (Garland 2008). This does not mean that an empirical assessment of the object of concern should be avoided – if such an assessment is possible – nor should a critical analysis of the data used in the debate be foregone. All of this is telling, but can be rather tricky. What should be avoided is the forced alternative between saying that something exists or that it is socially constructed ('just a moral panic'). 'Facts' may be there, but nonetheless the 'problem' is socially constructed and it is precisely the nature of this construction that should be addressed.

If we measure disproportionality by discursive dynamics rather than according to external indicators, the drawback of value judgment is avoided and an analysis of the construction of 'the problem' – of the degree, quality and logics of its amplification – may be carried out. Disproportionality (or better, *amplification*, as the term 'disproportion' conveys the idea of a relation to an objective reality, while 'amplification' refers to dynamics of representation) can be assessed according to at least three criteria, all of them clearly apparent in media output. First, it is the result of journalistic practices whose selection and framing criteria, in the stage of *Propagation*, lead to an apparent wave of incidents and to the perception of a new and threatening social problem. Amplification is also the end product of politicians', experts' and public officials' reaction, which contribute to growing coverage and corroborate, with the measures taken and the statements themselves, the discourse of fear. In both the cases, a correspondence assumption (Kepplinger and Habermeier 1995) – that is, the implicit idea that the greater the coverage, the greater the significance and proportions of a given phenomenon – makes certain that the idea of an incumbent threat is taken for granted by all the actors involved. Finally, amplification is also grounded in language. In moral panics we find an intensive use of figures of speech (hyperbole, metaphor), of big and prominent headlines (the written transcription of oral tone intensity (Fowler[1991]), a striking prevalence of the emotive dimension, a campaigning discourse, ad hoc evidence (statistics, summaries of episodes) and typical tags ('emergency', 'invasion', 'alarm') that convey a sense of exceptionality.

Similarly, the analysis of media production helps better define the notion of *concern*. The concept of public concern is, in Goode and Ben-Yehuda ([1994] 2009) and other studies, an ambiguous one, in that it conflates very different social phenomena. These two authors, for example, in their influential book, say: 'This concern should be manifested or measurable in concrete ways, through, for example, public opinion polls, public commentary in the form of media attention, proposed legislation, social movement activity, and so on' ([1994]

2009: 37). Does concern involve public opinion, organizations (the media), institutions (legislation), activists? Although all these actors may influence each other, they cannot be treated as the same thing.

Besides, the real amount of concern among the public is very difficult to measure, as the polls commissioned during panics (often by the media themselves) tend to reproduce the frame used by the media and to confirm it. And then, what exactly is public concern? The number of people 'concerned'? Is this a durable, deeply felt attitude or just a superficial reproduction of public discourse? How central is concern among other attitudes? Does it shape subsequent behaviour? As a matter of fact, personal concern does not have wide-ranging social effects (Robin 2004) unless it leads to public action or can be constructed as public opinion. Too composite and unevenly distributed between different social groups, concern should not be considered a social phenomenon, an ingredient of moral panics (it can rather be a 'bonus', as Critcher [2003: 137] puts it), but as activity (of concerned claims makers) and as a topic of media discourse. What is necessary to moral panics is the mobilization of a rhetoric of concern that is legitimized by a reference to public opinion. This task is accomplished by or through the media. Whether they speak as champions of 'civil society', quote or promote public opinion polls, publish timely interviews with concerned people, refer to specific complaints, petitions or reactions using generalizations like 'the city', 'the neighbourhood', 'the people', what they do is to construct a simulacrum of public opinion to which politicians and experts promptly react.

Another contested feature of moral panics regards their consensual nature. For the same reasons explored above with respect to concern, the existence of a *consensus* in society is generally questionable, difficult to measure and devoid of effective consequences. However, if we examine social actions and public discourse, the broadness and homogeneity of the panic is crucial. McRobbie and Thornton (1995) have argued that in modern polyphonic societies, the media sphere is more open to the voices of counter-experts who contest alarmist claims, so that 'classic' consensual moral panics are now unusual. In the same vein, Garland (2008) has more recently suggested that the power balance between contending groups is much less asymmetrical today, so that we have something similar to conflictual culture wars.

It is useful to distinguish here between the *representation* of events (largely the task of the media) and the *reaction* to the perceived threat (where sources play a prominent role). As far as representation is concerned, the information system is more integrated than ever. The interdependence between various media platforms and channels, their cutting and pasting of each others' content and their reliance on the same organized sources seems to enhance rather than reduce a consensual representation of the 'important hard facts' that journalists think are the epistemological basis of reality. The *Propagation* stage makes sure that an amplification spiral occurs as a consequence of a consensus about which facts deserve the most attention in a given situation. Neither citizen journalism, nor blogs nor ethnic media can counter a consensual representation of dramatic events, especially in the first crucial few weeks.

As regards reaction, oppositional voices do succeed in gaining media access and may defuse a moral panic when they are organized and when the topic belongs to the field of 'acceptable controversies'. When the 'national interest' (as in the case of September 11) or core values and interests are threatened, or when the action of oppositional voices is difficult to organize (as in the case of illegal immigrants or asylum seekers), contending groups and opinions are hard to find in the mainstream media.

The moral dimension

From the empirical analysis summarized in this chapter, it is clear that the mechanism of media activation is found in many more social phenomena than simply episodes of moral panic. Other concepts, like that of crime wave (Fishman 1978) or media hype (Vasterman 2005), have described analogous 'self-reinforcing news waves'. In these models we see the same wave of coverage, a similar role played by key events and news themes, the same feedback loops, a lowering of the news thresholds, a passage from media-generated to source-generated news, a final decline of the news wave (Fishman 1978; Kepplinger and Habermeier 1995; Kitzinger and Reilly 1997; Vasterman 2005). These kinds of news waves have attracted growing attention. The media-politics system appears to be more and more self-referential, enhancing loops between different media and in media-source relations. The news is also increasingly disseminated using the frame of fear and panic (Altheide 2003) as a consequence of the search for drama and immediate emotions by the media, and as a tactical and rhetorical device used by claims makers to advance the career of their social problem (Hilgartner and Bosk 1988). The alarms evoked by risk discourse (Beck [1986] 1992), such as epidemics, natural disasters, technological failures, have been interpreted as new sites of social anxiety compatible with the moral panic framework (Hier 2003). Other scholars, however, see in such alarms the disconfirmation or the evolution of the moral panic model in the risk society (Ungar 2001), to the point that we should speak of 'amoral panics' (Waiton 2008: 103–4). In this way the 'panic' dimension of the concept has been given probably too much importance. By contrast, the 'moral' dimension is sometimes forgotten. In the process of enlisting a growing array of topics, the moral panic concept loses its analytical clarity to the point that it is increasingly criticized.

If we turn back to our two case studies, from the point of view of the 'panic side' the Bologna and Rimini cases are quite the same thing (another look at the trends drawn in Figure 8.1 can help explain this). We have the same stages (repeated in the Bologna episode), a similar enabling condition of the *Warning* stage, the same synchronous activation of the different newspapers, similar loops between media and sources.

If we take a look to the 'moral side', however, things change a lot. Of the contextual features important in the activation of a moral panic mentioned earlier, only one was common to both episodes: a coalition of claim makers was at work. Feminist groups were very active in Bologna, and helped define the wave of violence as a problem for the victims. Politicians played a major role in Rimini, and were decisive in turning the panic against immigrants. As the problem of machismo selected in Bologna after a long negotiation implied all men as potential rapists (newspapers' readers included), a folk devil could not be targeted (and this was precisely the feminists' intention). Victims remained in the thematic position during the whole panic and the theme of the 'pack' gradually faded away. Folk devils need to be outside the moral consensus, while men as a group are at its very core. By contrast, in Rimini all the contextual features mentioned earlier were present. A folk devil was available and readily targeted. Here, politicians acted not only as claims makers but also as moral entrepreneurs, electing themselves as guardians of the moral community menaced from the outside. A consensus was established about the main cause of public outrage and counter-claims were feeble. The panic also gained national prominence because the offenders in the first attack were defined as 'maybe Albanians', a hot topic in that period, just three months after a national panic about a 'criminal invasion from Albania' had taken place. All the conditions for a successful moral panic were in place. As a result, the consequences of the two episodes have been quite different. In the case of Rimini, illegal (and also legal) immigration has been policed, stigmatized and then legally targeted (more than before). In Bologna, after a long debate, the only apparent consequence has been a rise in participation in self-defence courses.

From a sociological point of view, as we have seen, Bologna and Rimini appear as two quite different cases. What makes the moral panic concept something more than a tool for the analysis of media hypes and of the amplification of threat is the core role played by the folk devil. The folk devil enables the moral confrontation between respectable members of society – the 'we' of the consensual ideology (Hall 1973; Chibnall 1977; Hartley 1982; Fowler 1991) – and social deviants who put themselves outside it – 'them'. Thanks to the folk devil we have a powerful creation of a social relationship, of a community where 'We all stand shoulder to shoulder . . . against a possible invader' (Mead 1918: 591–2), and where we need a Hobbesian State that can protect us, in exchange for a certain dose of freedom. Through its violations, the folk devil reveals the fragile border between Us and Them, legitimizes punishment and gives new power to the political elite and their allies. Self-righteous condemnation and firm measures produce a collective excitement and emotional energy that is rich with opportunities for those willing to ride it (Garland 2008). Risk society is a favourable environment for media hypes of every kind; it cannot be the locus of moral panics if we want to keep the heuristic value of the moral panic concept. Panics are everywhere but they are not always 'moral'.

Conclusions

In recent scholarship the moral panic concept has probably been abused, conflating too wide a range of social phenomena. A focus on its processual dynamics, re-elaborating the idea of a stage sequence, helps delineate its specific terrain where journalistic practices play a more autonomous role than in the parent phenomenon of moral crusade. The similarity of the looping effect due to media activation ensures that all moral panics are media hypes (or crime waves), but the converse is not true: not all media hypes are moral panics (although they can make people panic). To retain the heuristic value of the moral panic concept, it is important to stress that it requires hostility toward a folk devil that is perceived as posing a threat to a moral value or order.

Other scholars think that the model is inadequate to analyse the fears or crises that affect contemporary societies, suggesting that consensual moral panics are increasingly rare, thanks to the ability of counter-claims-makers to make their voices heard. It is possible that the contours of the moral panic debate – which is concentrated mainly in English-speaking and Scandinavian countries – have been shaped by the particular cultural outlooks of those nations. In fact, not all countries have such 'polyphonic' media systems. Formal democracies are not always backed by information pluralism (Hallin and Mancini 2004). As the experience of a Southern European country like Italy shows, and other Eastern European countries would confirm, elite newspapers and network television can be as sensationalist as the tabloid press. In addition, in such countries power elites and news media are more directly intermingled. In the context of the hard impact of social change produced by neo-liberal policies, a (consensual) 'politics of fear' game on the immigration issue has given rise to a powerless category of voiceless folk devils. All of this provides fertile ground for a wide array of new moral panics (Maneri 2001, 2011; Mai 2002; Erjavec 2003; Meylakhs 2006).

The same political and media factors and trends may well work in favour of moral panics elsewhere. Despite the optimistic view of an evolution toward more pluralistic media environments and more balanced access to public discourse by different claim makers, nothing ensures that this trend will continue and is indeed in process, in all countries, in every societal condition. The degree of concentration and homogenization of influential news media outlets is growing. Although the rise in the use of new platforms such as blogs or Twitter in certain situations implies easier media access for the people normally deprived of a public voice, new forms of exclusion from full citizenship counter this trend with the consequence that moral panics are not rare (Husbands 1994; Morgan and Poynting 2012).

If moral panics are alive and well, it is reasonable to take up some of Cohen's ([1972] 2002), Critcher's (2003) and Garland's (2008) considerations about the issues requiring further exploration in order to try to advance the argument. As I have tried to show, other research traditions and disciplines (like journalism studies and critical discourse analysis) can be used to clarify the analytical levels of the moral panic progression and to operationalize its examination. Not enough studies in this field have engaged with the way journalists actually work, and almost none has analyzed the symbolic material produced in the process using the tools provided by the disciplines that deal with its very substance, that is, language.

The comparative case studies summarized in this chapter have provided some hints in this direction. A closer look at language can help to better operationalize the concepts of frame and news theme (and to much more sophisticated a degree than in the analysis performed here). These related concepts can in turn be used to examine the nature of the construction of a social problem, its procedures of inclusion and exclusion of similar instances, the rationales of the various actors to a certain extent, and the negotiations between them. They are also crucial for the clarification of the stage structure of a moral panic, which I deem necessary in order to see which 'turning points' characterize it and determine its success or failure, its direction and consequences. Finally, with this analytical framework in mind, disputed attributes of a moral panic like consensus, disproportion and concern, once qualified, take on new clarity and analytic utility.

Note

1 I wish to thank Fabienne Brion, Chas Critcher and Ann Morning for their precious advice and invaluable help.

Bibliography

Altheide, D. L. (2003), 'Notes towards a Politics of Fear', *Journal for Crime, Conflict and the Media*, 1(1): 37–54.

Austin, J. L. (1975), *How to Do Things with Words*, Cambridge, MA: President and fellows of Howard College.

Beck, U. ([1986] 1992), *Risk Society: Towards a New Modernity*, London: Sage.

Becker, H. ([1963] 1991) *Outsiders: Studies in the Sociology of Deviance*, New York: Free Press.

Chibnall, S. (1977), *Law-and-order News: An Analysis of Crime Reporting in the British Press*, London: Tavistock.

Cohen, S. ([1972] 2002), *Folk Devils and Moral Panics*, 3rd edn, London: Routledge.

Cornwell, B. and Linders, A. (2002), 'The Myth of Moral Panic: An Alternative Account of LSD Prohibition', *Deviant Behavior*, 23(4): 307–30.

Critcher, C. (2003), *Moral Panics and the Media*, Maidenhead, Buckingham: Open University Press.

Critcher, C. (ed.) (2006), *Critical Readings: Moral Panics and the Media*, Maidenhead, Buckingham: Open University Press.

Entman, R. M. (1993), 'Framing: Toward Clarification of a Fractured Paradigm', *Journal of Communication*, 43: 51–58.

Erjavec, K. (2003), 'Media Construction of Identity through Moral Panics: Discourses of Immigration in Slovenia', *Journal of Ethnic and Migration Studies*, 29(1): 83–101.

Fairclough, N. ([1989] 2001), *Language and Power*, 2nd edn, London: Longman.

Fishman, M. (1978), 'Crime Waves as Ideology', *Social Problems*, 25(5): 531–43.

Fowler, R. (1991), *Language in the News: Discourse and Ideology in the Press*, London and New York: Routledge.

Fowler, R., Hodge, B., Kress, G. and Trew, T. (1979), *Language and Control*, London: Routledge and Kegan Paul.

Galtung, J. and Ruge, M. (1965), 'The Structure of Foreign News: the Presentation of the Congo, Cuba and Cyprus Crises in Four Norwegian Newspapers', *Journal of International Peace Research*, 1: 64–91.

Gamson, W. A. and Modigliani, A. (1989), 'Media Discourse and Public Opinion on Nuclear Power: a Constructionist Approach', *American Journal of Sociology*, 95(1): 1–37.

Garland, D. (2008), 'On the Concept of Moral Panic', *Crime Media Culture*, 4(1): 9–30.

Goode, E. and Ben-Yehuda, N. ([1994] 2009) *Moral Panics. The Social Construction of Deviance*, Chichester: Wiley-Blackwell.

Gusfield, J. R. (1963), *Symbolic Crusade: Status Politics and the American Temperance Movement*, Urbana and Chicago, IL: University of Illinois Press.

Hall, S. (1973), 'A World at One with Itself', in S. Cohen and J. Young (eds), *The Manufacture of News: Social Problems, Deviance and the Mass Media*, London: Constable, 85–94.

Hall, S., Critcher, C., Jefferson, T., Clarke, J. and Roberts, B. (1978) *Policing the Crisis: Mugging, the State and Law and Order*, London: Macmillan.

Halliday, M. A. K. (2004), *An Introduction to Functional Grammar*, London: Hodder Arnold.

Hallin, D. and Mancini, P. (2004), *Comparing Media Systems: Three Models of Media and Politics*, Cambridge: Cambridge University Press.

Hartley, J. (1982), *Understanding News*, London: Methuen.

Hier, S. P. (2003), 'Risk and Panic in Late Modernity: Implications of the Converging Sites of Social Anxiety', *British Journal of Sociology*, 54(1): 3–20.

Hilgartner, S. and Bosk, V. L. (1988), 'The Rise and Fall of Social Problems: A Public Arenas Model', *American Journal of Sociology*, 94(1): 53–78.

Husbands, C. (1994), 'Crises of National Identity as the "New Moral Panics": Political Agenda-Setting about Definitions of Nationhood', *Journal of Ethnic and Migration Studies*, 20(2): 191–206.

Jenkins, P. (2009), 'Failure to Launch: Why Do Some Social Issues Fail to Detonate Moral Panics?', *British Journal of Criminology*, 49(1): 35–47.

Kepplinger, H. M. and Habermeier, J. H. (1995), 'The Impact of Key Events upon the Presentation of Reality', *European Journal of Communication*, 10(3): 371–90.

Kitzinger, J. and Reilly, J. (1997), 'The Rise and Fall of Risk Reporting: Media Coverage of Human Genetics Research, "False Memory Syndrome", and "Mad Cow Disease"', *European Journal of Communication*, 12(3): 319–50.

Klocke, B. and Muschert, G. (2010), 'A Hybrid Model of Moral Panics: Synthesizing the Theory and Practice of Moral Panic Research', *Sociology Compass*, 4/5: 295–309.

Mai, N. (2002), 'Myths and Moral Panics: Italian Identity and the Media Representation of Albanian Immigration', in R. Grillo and J. Pratt (eds), *The Politics of Recognising Difference: Multiculturalism Italian Style*, Farnham: Ashgate, 77–94.

Maneri, M. (2001), 'Il Panico Morale Come Dispositivo di Trasformazione Dell'insicurezza', *Rassegna Italiana di Sociologia*, 1: 5–40.

– (2011), 'Media Discourse on Immigration: The Translation of Control Practices into the Language We Live By', in S. Palidda (ed.), *Racial Criminalization of Migrants in the 21st Century*, Farnham: Ashgate, 77–93.

Matthes, J. and Kohring, M. (2008), 'The Content Analysis of Media Frames: Toward Improving Reliability and Validity', *Journal of Communication*, 58: 258–79.

McRobbie, A. and Thornton, S. L. (1995), 'Re-thinking Moral Panics for Multi-mediated Social Worlds', *British Journal of Sociology*, 46(4): 559–74.

Mead, G. H. (1918), 'The Psychology of Punitive Justice', *American Journal of Sociology*, 23(5): 577–602.

Meylakhs, P. (2006), 'The Discourse of the Press and the Press of Discourse: Constructing the Drug Problem in the Russian Media', in C. Critcher (ed.) *Critical Readings: Moral Panics and the Media*, Maidenhead, Buckingham: Open University Press, 175–88.

Morgan, G. and Poynting, S. (2012), *Global Islamophobia: Muslims and Moral Panic in the West*, Farnham: Ashgate.

Robin, C. (2004), *Fear*, Oxford, New York: Oxford University Press.

Thompson, K. (1998), *Moral Panics*, New York: Routledge.

Ungar, S. (2001), 'Moral Panic versus the Risk Society: the Implications of Changing Sites of Social Anxiety', *British Journal of Sociology*, 52(2): 271–91.

Vasterman, P. (2005), 'Media-Hype: Self-Reinforcing News Waves, Journalistic Standards and the Construction of Social Problems', *European Journal of Communication*, 20(4): 508–30.

Waddington, P. J. (1986), 'Mugging as Moral Panic: A Question of Proportion', *British Journal of Sociology*, 37(2): 245–59.

Waiton, S. (2008), *The Politics of Antisocial Behaviour: Amoral Panics*, New York: Routledge.

Watney. S. (1987), *Policing Desire: Pornography, Aids, and the Media*, London: Methuen.

9

Moral Panic and Ritual Abuse: Where's the Risk? Findings of an Ethnographic Research Study

Morena Tartari

Introduction

My doctorate analysed as a possible moral panic allegations about ritual abuse in Italy. My research guide was Mary de Young who in the United States examined 'how the threat of ritual abuse was discursively constructed, by whom and why; how the persuasiveness of this discourse recruited others into the belief that ritual abuse is a real and exigent threat, despite the repeated failure to find evidence to corroborate it; how they acted on that belief and with what consequences' (2004: 4). Starting at the McMartin Preschool in 1983, over the following nine years, more than 100 day-care centres and pre-schools, urban and rural, experienced allegations of what became known as 'satanic ritual abuse'. Other allegations occurred within families, neighbourhoods and communities. Similar claims were made in Canada, Europe, Australia and New Zealand.

Ritual abuse is defined as 'acts of sexual, emotional and physical abuse conducted as part of, or in conjunction with, such ghastly ceremonies and rituals as infant sacrifice, blood-drinking and cannibalism', although 'it seems to be different things in different cases and to different people' (de Young 2004: 3). It is a highly connotative term, evoking images of adults physically, sexually and psychologically abusing children during satanic practices (de Young 2002: 5). The term was later shortened to 'ritual abuse' in order to distance it from satanism but the issue remains controversial. Few of those accused have ever been convicted, though all remain stigmatized.

The social and media construction of satanism and child abuse has been analyzed by American authors such as Jenkins (1992; 1998), Nathan (1991), Nathan and Snedeker (1995), Best (1991) and Victor (1991; 1998) and, in the United Kingdom, by Kitzinger (2004). My interest in such cases arose in the 1990s, when I was working as a psychologist concerned with cases of alleged child abuse. Thereafter, given my background in sociology, I undertook the research to investigate the role of moral panic in the development of such cases and the influence of the mass media on their genesis and evolution. Specific rhetorics related to childhood, and sexual abuse seemed to greatly influence how and by whom the issue was constructed. I was also interested in how such rhetorics were managed and incorporated, constructed and deconstructed by the various professionals involved in these cases – the politicians, the moral entrepreneurs and the parents who were the principal addressees of those rhetorics. The present ethnographic study differs from most of the literature on moral panic, which often pays almost exclusive attention to the mass media and sidelines activities in local communities, quite unlike the classic studies by Cohen (1972) and Morin (1969).

In his recent work, Critcher (2003, 2009a, 2009b) has argued that moral panics should be studied using an approach which supersedes the processual and attributional model, and which analyses along three dimensions: as identifiable processes, as sets of discourses and as expressions of irreducible moral values. This chapter explores such possibilities, as well as the relevance of risk society theory (Beck 1992), as suggested by Thompson (1998).

My main research questions were as follows:

- What were the social and cultural practices (or the rhetorical, symbolic and media mechanisms) on the basis of which different realities were assembled into an 'evident' fact (the child abuse emergency)?
- What were the social tensions behind such differing realities?
- What was the role of the mass media in constructing those social facts?
- What were the roles of different professional and organizational cultures in assembling different realities into an evident fact?
- What discourses on the children and their suspected abusers were conveyed by the mass media?
- What discourses were conveyed by the moral entrepreneurs and the other social actors involved (experts, etc.)?
- Why did these cases develop in certain places and conditions, and at certain times, and not others?

The Flat Village case

Flat Village is a fictitious name for the place where some children involved in the case still live and are legally minors. The village is in a rural area, 40 kilometres from a large city. It has about 8,000 inhabitants.

In the summer of 2006 two groups of parents living in the village reported to the police the sexual abuse of over 20 of their children, alleged to have taken place in the local nursery school and some of the teachers' houses. Some of the children had been diagnosed as having been sexually abused by a Centre for the Assessment of Child Abuse. The children's narratives were typical of ritual abuse narratives: they recounted sexual, emotional and physical abuse with drug injections, rituals involving animal sacrifice and paedo-pornographic photos; all these acts were perpetrated by groups of people, sometimes masked. The public prosecutor opened an inquiry and entrusted an expert psychologist with an examination of the children and families involved. In the autumn of 2006, when the police conducted an investigation inside the school, some local newspapers published a few articles about the case, but nothing else appeared until the spring of 2007. After the investigation, the headmistress, together with all the teachers of the school, adopted some 'precautionary measures' against parental complaints, advocated by a moral entrepreneur involved in the defence of false-abuse cases. These measures increased parental suspicions. A month later parents established an association for defending themselves and their children's rights. This association had, as moral entrepreneurs, two mothers not personally involved in the current allegations. Parents criticized the nursery school policies, demanded the suspension of teachers and requested interventions by local institutions to support abused children and their families. The Ministry of Education was asked to suspend the teachers, which they did some months later. Local authorities did offer support to the children and their families, but they declined to take sides.

At the end of April 2007, after the results of the psychological examination, six people were arrested: three teachers, the caretaker and two other people living in the village but not employed at the school. The charges against them were indecent behaviour, child abuse, unlawful restraint, abduction of minors, aggravated sexual assault, sex acts with minors, corruption of minors, group sexual assault, offences against common decency and obscene language. After 20 days a reassessment court released all the suspects from prison. At the end of April one of the experts who had first assessed the children gave an interview to a national newspaper confirming that the children really had been abused. But the centre where he worked disavowed his claims.

Media attention was immediate and sustained for a month. Parents, suspects, suspects' relatives, lawyers and experts participated in several television current affairs programmes. In July a television station broadcast a clip of one of the children undergoing expert examination. Parents took legal action against a journalist and the editor in chief of the television news; later they were sentenced.

During the autumn of 2007 the public prosecutor asked for DNA examinations of toys and other objects belonging to the teachers but the evidence was negative. In January 2010 the investigation phase was completed and the judge committed for trial four of the six suspects: for an immigrant and the caretaker the charges were dismissed, but they remained for the three teachers and one of their husbands. In May 2012 the four defendants were acquitted of any offence.

Opinions varied about how the allegations had started. Some interviewees and newspapers maintained that those responsible had been psychologists trying to prove the existence of ritual abuse without any scientific evidence. But others identified a 'contagion' among families, starting when one of the accusing parents had made contact via the internet with a moral entrepreneur. His campaign against paedophilia was regarded as polemical, alarmist and exaggerated. Critics alleged he had created several national cases by disseminating on his website erroneous information and overblown rhetoric. The contact between this person and certain parents generated hearsay and rumour.

The controversy also reflected and exacerbated tensions within the local community. Some village inhabitants supported the accusations of ritual abuse. Their children were moved to another school and their families were shunned by the other inhabitants. Parents – housewives, clerks, workers – are still persuaded that the ritual abuse was real and that the teachers are guilty. Local moral entrepreneurs – mothers with children in that nursery school – sustain this belief. Others sided with the teachers against accusations from those regarded as newcomers to the village. The conflict spread nationally but some of its roots were local.

Methods

My data was collected by means of ethnographic observations, in-depth interviews and documentary analysis within the framework of Grounded Theory

(Glaser and Strauss 1967). I studied two cases, though I report only one here . At the local level, I used three different methods: 40 in-depth interviews with social actors involved in the cases; ethnographic study of the two communities where the cases occurred; documentary analysis of (local and national) newspaper articles and television programmes concerning the two cases. At a national level, I carried out 20 in-depth interviews with social actors involved in the national media debate on paedophilia (moral entrepreneurs, policy-makers, politicians, professionals, experts, journalists and so on); an ethnographic study of eight Italian conferences and public events on paedophilia and child abuse; the monitoring of blogs and websites with a role in the cases and/or in the national public debate.

Some moral entrepreneurs invited me to events organized by interest groups concerned with child abuse and paedophilia. I thus came into direct contact with some protagonists of the cases, and I was able to understand the operation of the associations' networks and related interest groups. During my time in the small village, I participated in religious functions, village fairs, festivals, civic and commemorative events and routine activities. I contacted the associations created for and against the suspects and I established relationships with some families involved directly and indirectly in the episode, periodically contacting them and receiving openness and cooperation in exchange. In some situations, I was able to participate in formal and informal meetings among families, associations and practitioners directly and indirectly involved in the case.

Results

I shall focus on the aspects that highlighted the role of the risk society in the emergence of moral panics concerning child abuse, and the applicability of the various models of moral panic.

Interest groups and the emergence of panics

Interest groups performed a crucial role in the genesis and evolution of the cases. They are primarily created by specific professional groups centred on the reporting, evaluation and treatment of child abuse. They, therefore, focus on all types of child abuse, including the ritual kind. The capacity of the discourses of these groups to exert influence has accumulated over time in several domains:

the professional and judicial domains, the social and political ones, those of policy-makers and the media. Some discourses prevail over others, and some of them influence those domains more effectively than others.

The interviewees often began the contacts or interviews by saying: 'I hope you haven't been sent by one of those false-abuse groups', or 'I hope you don't believe in all the abuses like the members of the abusologist lobby do!'. These prevalent representations offered by the interviewees tended to identify and describe two professional spheres opposed to each other and coincident with two interest groups: the 'false-abuses' group and the 'true-abuses' group, also derogatorily referred to as 'abusologists' by the opposite faction. The distinction proposed by the interviewees was, therefore, between a 'false-abuse lobby' and a 'true-abuse lobby'. This bipolar representation simplified the social reality.

The interviewees believed that the power of these lobbies had increased over the past 10–15 years. Obviously, each side accused the other of having business and power interests. Some interviewees belonging to the false-abuse lobby claimed that:

> The abusologists exist because there are lots of unemployed psychologists and it's necessary to find something for them to do. So the abuse business was invented! (Interviewee no. 1)
>
> Causing social alarm about child abuse and paedophilia meets the psychologists' need to make money from trials, from the awareness campaign, and from agreements with the institutions for the formulation of guidelines. (Interviewee no. 15)

Whereas interviewees belonging to the true-abuse lobby argued that:

> There's a paedophile lobby to which all those people belong, also the experts appointed by the court and the lawyers who defend those suspects . . . and then this business expands and spreads as far as the political level . . . and within the Vatican, and so internationally, and then worldwide . . . so, let's get to the point, this lawyer [surname given] is certainly a paedophile. (Interviewee no. 2)
>
> Those on the false-abuse side make a lot of money from defending paedophiles and from expert opinions but in fact they're paedophiles as well, and it's for this reason that they defend paedophiles. (Interviewee no. 17)

Each lobby had its own distinctive views about the interview techniques and assessment procedures used with the children. But each considered itself able to detect cases of both false abuse and true abuse. In the opinion of the false-abuse lobby, the true-abuse lobby often corresponded to the professional culture of psychodynamic psychotherapists, who worked mainly in the public health services but also as private experts. They exaggerated the psychological and emotional experience of the alleged victims, with whom they became too closely involved. By contrast, in the opinion of the true-abuse lobby, the false-abuse lobby consisted of psychologists without experience in the field of psychotherapy, who colluded with legal professionals out of self interest. Each lobby comprised judges, public prosecutors, police officers, journalists and scholars as affiliates or sympathizers. Overall, the representations furnished showed that the sentiments of the two groups were generated by commercial and power interests.

The conflict was often waged by dropping scientific discussion and moving to a personal level. This aspect was amplified by the websites and blogs of members of the two factions, with frequent updates on trials in progress. The two factions did not communicate with each other and came into conflict whenever an institution recognized the guidelines for the evaluation of abuse of one lobby rather than the other. Furthermore, some interviewees reported cases of misconduct in the interviews of minors by psychologists, lawyers and police officers belonging to the true-abuse lobby. This misconduct sometimes consisted of leading questions put to the children and, in extreme cases, in exaggerated and suggestive requests for the children to re-enact alleged sexual acts in the presence of the adults involved in the trials. As opposed to this narrative, in generic terms the true-abuse lobby accused its opponent of 'not believing the children' on the basis of a claim that 'children always tell the truth'.

The true-abuse lobby viewed satanism as an extreme perversion perpetrated by paedophile groups enjoying the protection of politicians and high-ranking members of the church. The discourses of this lobby about the risks posed to children by adults were insistent. Such risks extended across infancy and adolescence, involving all adults in relationships with a child, seen as fragile and defenceless. For the opposing lobby, by contrast, the risks were minimal, and the child was seen as resilient, able to cope with trauma without requiring 'treatment' (psychotherapy). Indeed, 'treatment' was the specific power domain of the true-abuse lobby. It was, therefore, essential for the false-abuse lobby to challenge criminal evidence based on interviews conducted by those with interests in proving the existence of abuse.

Not apparent in the interviews and the events that I attended were reflexivity or self-reflexivity about the influence exerted by such claims and such groups on the emergence of moral panics and on what practices could favour communication, limit the onset of such panics and lead to the development of policies less influenced by them. The panics seemed to stem from the accumulation of alarmist information, on the one hand, and from an ineluctable process on the other. The 'addressees' most easily affected – that is, those most likely to panic – were the parents and practitioners who were constantly urged to ensure that the children in their care were subject to as few risks as possible.

Grassroots model and ritual abuse

Analysis of the social context prior to the case highlights social issues – for instance, three kinds of conflicts – which generated tension between the parents and the people who were subsequently charged with the abuse.

First, some interviewees described conflicts of identity and belonging between parents (who though Italian were 'immigrants' from a large city) and the educators involved (who were native residents of the village). The teachers were viewed as occupying immutable positions in the day-care centre because they had been born in that village and, according to some parents, their status was not attributable to professional merit. Some of the mothers were in contrast seen by the teachers as women who neglected their children as they sought to pursue easy careers in entertainment, show business and journalism – or as indolent television watching housewives.

Second, some interviewees reported differences in child-care practices between young mothers and older nursery school teachers. One interviewee recounted that some of the mothers were often away from their children for the entire day as they pursued their careers in the city, and after school left their children with child-minders or acquaintances. The children often wore soiled diapers for hours without their mothers bothering to change them (an internal rule at the day-care centre forbade the teachers from changing the children's diapers). A frequent cause of dispute between the educators and the parents was compliance with the day-care centre's rules and opening hours: the parents wanted to use the centre whenever they wanted, thus antagonizing the teachers, who felt that their role was being disrespected. Moreover, they openly rejected the teachers' advice and suggestions on how to deal with their children's difficulties, considering them intrusions into their private sphere. A tightening of the day-care centre's rules followed the parents' intransigence and hostility towards the educators.

Third, the interviews showed the presence of religious conflicts between strict Roman Catholic teachers and 'secular', non-observant parents: the teachers were seen as proponents of an obscurantist and extremist Catholic traditionalism disliked by the mothers, who preferred to remain detached from religion.

While these were the social dynamics and the context described by some interviewees, the parents' supporters narrated the matter differently. They emphasized the bad moral behaviour of the accused and their supporters, alluding to paedophile lobbies and their contacts with the political and religious 'establishment'. These interviewees did not resort to scientifically accredited explanations for ritual abuse. Instead, they said that they had been made aware of the 'paedophilia and satanism' phenomenon by moral entrepreneurs and the mass media. They represented society as divided between good and evil, and explained every fact with some sort of conspiracy theory. Such dynamics caused a loss of confidence, a spiral of signification and a contagion among families who thought of the teachers as evil.

A public demonstration: Only a platform for politicians and moral entrepreneurs?

At an initial stage of the trial, a demonstration supporting the parents was held in the village, organized by moral entrepreneurs and right-wing politicians. Participation by the public was massive, and there were also parents with children. Also present were the police and numerous journalists. A video that I made of the demonstration reveals the following elements.

First, there were different kinds of banners and choruses:

Banners	*God, damn and blast paedophiles;*
	Paedophiles, watch out! Lobbies want to protect you, but judgment is by the people;
	Black people don't scare us;
	Protect innocence, condemn violence
	Our kisses are love, your violence is horror.
Choruses	*Get your hands off the children;*
	For the children: let us dream;
	Anyone who doesn't jump is black;
	Don't touch our children
	We are all children.

The choruses were based on popular song motifs derived from Italian underground movements of the Second World War, with a mélange of historical and cultural elements. Both banners and choruses underlined the innocence of children and parental rights to protect them, the alleged existence of a paedophile lobby, and a demand that power be returned to the people. In particular, the banner 'Black people don't scare us', and the chorus 'Anyone who doesn't jump is black', indicates, at the local level, that a black immigrant was involved in the episode and had been investigated; but also, at a general level, that the 'black man' is a symbol of The Other and of difference, racial but also moral. In a sort of Durkheimian ritual, all participants jumped during the chorus to demonstrate their group belonging, their moral integrity, their innocence, and thus confirmed social solidarity.

Second was the noticeable presence of children in the demonstration and the visible social energy expressed during the event. The urging of the children by adults to join in the choruses, and to jump together with the adults during the refrain 'Anyone who doesn't jump is black', can be interpreted – as it was by some interviewees – on the one hand as exploitation of the children by the adults and the moral entrepreneurs, and on the other, as encouragement of the children to participate actively in public action to raise awareness about a social problem. Some interviewees pointed out that the demonstration was deliberately routed past the homes of some of the suspects in order to express the strength of local feeling against them.

Third, moral entrepreneurs and a politician spoke to the public during the demonstration. Here follows some excerpts from the speeches:

> We have to make this journey (toward the truth), by ourselves, all together. (A moral entrepreneur)
>
> [. . .] but those are respectable people! People who have only one colour . . . the colour of Rome, the colour of a city that has given a culture to us all and that cannot accept that children's innocence should be snatched for business interests or other things. It is not a question of one sick person, it is a network! And we must have the courage to denounce it! It is shameful and we must denounce it! (A politician)

These excerpts reflect rhetorical elements already apparent in the banners and choruses: the innocence of children, the power of the lobby against the power of ordinary people, the moral value of respectable people and their fight against institutions that do not guarantee justice but instead protect paedophile lobbies. In short, the demonstration shows the type of social ferment present in the village some months before I directly entered the field. But that ferment was also present months afterwards among the moral entrepreneurs that I interviewed.

The (inexhaustible) energy of the media

The demonstration analyzed in the previous section was organized – with the support of the local association created by the parents of the children involved in the trial – by a journalist-activist on the extreme neo-fascist right. He was not the only journalist to 'transform himself' into a moral entrepreneur during the affair. Other journalists openly took sides in their newspaper articles; yet others took part in television broadcasts to support the parents of the children involved or the adults under investigation.

After the emergence of the case, journalists from the press, radio and television invaded the village, and they behaved in a manner that all the interviewees said was intolerable. The invasion continued for several months, with local reactions ranging from rejection of the journalists to acts of verbal and physical violence against them. Many of the interviewees took pains to describe the strategies used by the journalists to garner confidential information about the social context. They described how small groups of journalists spread through the village, and how they competed with each other. But above all they emphasized the poor quality of the information about the case and the village disseminated by the mass media. In the same period, the daily press frequently published articles which discussed bullying or online paedo-pornography, commented on 'paedophile pride days', investigated the disquieting and obscure aspects of the affair, and claimed that it was no longer possible to 'trust' teachers or neighbours. In other words, they assiduously emphasized the risks for children in contemporary society.

The in-depth interviews with the journalists showed that they rarely engaged in reflexive practices on how they, their behaviour and their discourses were perceived by the residents of the village or by the public at large. Instead, they concentrated on asserting their personal views on the case, often doing so as members of one of the interest groups. Unlike the interviewees from the village, they showed trust in the expertise of one of the two interest groups to the detriment of the other. Their action was driven by consolidated journalistic praxis whose rules, practices and strategies are intended to ensure satisfaction of the commissioner (the senior editor) or the public.

After the case exploded, hundreds of articles were published in national and local newspapers, with peaks of coverage corresponding to developments in the judicial process. Figure 9.1 shows the coverage of two national, quality and left-wing newspapers from the first reports to police (July 2006) until one month after the end of the trial (June 2012).

The first one is the most reputable of Italian daily newspapers, with a circulation of 445,000 copies in July 2012. The other newspaper is second for circulation, with 425,000 copies.

Dozens of telecasts hosted the children's parents, together with journalists, moral entrepreneurs and experts. The demonstration described in the previous section was organized later, around two years after the start of the case. Yet the

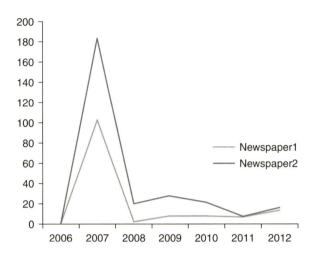

Figure 9.1 Newspaper stories about the Flat village controversy, 2006–12

press release prepared by the journalist who organized the demonstration ran as follows:

> A DEMONSTRATION AGAINST PAEDOPHILIA WILL BE HELD TODAY AT [FLAT VILLAGE]
>
> To be held today [date] at [Flat Village] is a demonstration to express solidarity with the children of [Flat Village] and utterly to oppose paedophilia.
>
> [. . .] The procession is open to everyone and has no political origin or stance. Nor does it want one. The aim of the demonstration is to break through the deafening silence on this issue, and on the case of [Flat Village] in particular.

It is obvious that the 'deafening silence' cited in the press release was not due to the indifference of the media. Nor was it due to the indifference of politicians, considering that both a minister and various members of parliament were involved in the debate on the case and the topic; nor again was it due to institutional and judicial indifference, given that responses by the institutions were invariably prompt because the media spotlight was trained on the case. It was rather a rhetorical device typically used by moral entrepreneurs: the demand that something be done by those responsible for the control or management of the risks to children.

Discussion

Following Critcher (2003), in the analysis presented here, I too asked myself the question: 'How useful is it to apply moral panic analysis to this case?' My intention was not to prove that this was an episode of moral panic or assess the validity of claims and counter claims. Rather, it was to determine whether the sensitizing concepts (in Blumer's 1969 sense) used and current models of moral panic are able to explain what may have happened, using sociological interpretative tools. The analysis that follows, therefore, does not seek to support one side or the other or to criticize the judicial procedure to which the case was subject. Like Mary de Young (2004), I sought to understand by means of what discourses the threat of ritual abuse – which, with its satanic elements, is a mythical threat – was constructed and by which social actors, and how the persuasiveness of these discourses induced numerous people to believe that the threat was real. But the use of the sensitizing concepts made it possible to go beyond interpretations already put forward by other authors. When analyzing the community in which the case arose, I focused *on representation of the malaise and the crisis of roles and cultural order at the moment when the event occurred.*

The findings are also useful for understanding which different moral panic explanatory models work in regard to the case, and how, and to pinpoint the applicability and compatibility of risk society theory to such a moral panic event. Following Critcher (2003), it was first possible to test the characteristics of the processual and attributional models with regard to the case studied. It emerged, in fact, that a strictly mechanistic use of the processual model in stages was not suited to the case that I examined, while the criteria of the attributional model seemed more appropriate.

The centrality or otherwise of the mass media in the construction of moral panics is the element that differentiates between approaches to the problem (Hall et al. 1978; Goode and Ben-Yehuda 1994; Jenkins 1998; Critcher 2003, 2006). The processual model assigns a predominant role to the media in the creation of panics, while the attributional model gives them secondary importance. In the situation studied, the mass media did not play a significant role in the emergence of the panic. But in a period of time prior to the case, from the late 1980s onwards, they prepared the ground for it by disseminating the claims of certain interest groups and professional experts, and, therefore, fomented a climate of anxiety around specific themes concerning childhood. During the onset of the case, the sensationalist tones used by the media and their emphasis on certain aspects of the case did fuel alarm and exacerbate the conflicts among the different parties involved. One cannot say, therefore, that the media were directly at the origin of the emergence of this specific case; rather, they were indirectly responsible for it. They performed a secondary role in that the sedimentation over time of claims concerning violence against children inside and outside the family created fertile terrain for the emergence of that specific panic.

Goode and Ben-Yehuda postulate three theoretical explanations of the origins of moral panics: the 'grassroots' model, the 'elite-engineered' model and the 'interest group' model. A combination of the 'grassroots' and 'interest group' theories was most applicable to my case: 'The grassroots provide fuel or raw material for a moral panic, organizational activists provide focus, intensity and direction . . . issues of morality provide the content of moral panics and interests provide the timing' (1994: 142).

Analysis of the in-depth interviews conducted in the community showed that the emergence of the panic corresponded to the grassroots model, but it did so in the presence of factors both 'local' and 'global'. In the digital age a local community, though geographically circumscribed and identifiable, was not impermeable to influences exerted from the outside, via the internet and the media, by moral entrepreneurs and exponents of interest groups situated hundreds of kilometres from the place where the case emerged. These contacts with the outside galvanized a group of parents and drove the development of the moral panic.

While moral entrepreneurs activated the panic directly and personally at local (micro) level, the media operated at a macro level, supporting a moral crusade and promoting a culture of child abuse risk. The role of the media was to construct social anxiety around childhood issues, reiterating risks to children. They acted as a predisposing factor for emergence of the moral panic. The concept of moral panic, in fact, enables the *macro* aspects of the risk and uncertainty society to be connected with the *micro* aspects of the everyday practices of social actors.

As suggested by Thompson (1998) and Critcher (2003, 2009a), the concept of risk is significant for the analysis of moral panics concerning childhood, and it should be understood in the sense proposed by Beck and Beck-Gernsheim (1995). In the case examined, from a certain point onwards, the risks perceived by the parents were no longer generic and abstract but concerned relationships of trust with the staff of the day-care centre and the everyday experiences of their children there. The risks posed to children by adults, therefore, no longer consisted of the generic threat of paedophilia. Rather, for those parents they acquired concrete form in the unease and tension which they experienced in their quotidian relations with the day-centre staff and specific people in the village. Parents who, as Beck and Beck-Gernsheim (1995) state, must prevent risks and protect their – rare and precious (Zelizer 1994) – children against the 'badness' of the world, therefore, acted consistently in being caught up by the moral panic.

The controversy laid bare conflicts between the intimate space of the family and the public space of the school. They highlight both a crisis of trust in institutions, widespread in contemporary Italy, and large differentials in the construction and accumulation of social and cultural capital (Roniger 1989; Putnam 1993; Mutti 2006; Cartocci 2007). This crisis was two-directional: the parents did not trust the staff; the staff criticized the parents for their behaviour. In fact, women's roles in child care within the family and at work have changed, so no longer matched the staff's expectations of how an ideal or suitable parent should behave.

Also to be considered is the problem of the identity and the affiliations of those parents who had moved from the city to live in the small village. They were unable to understand the trust relations of the small community: they were excluded, treated as 'outsiders' and not accepted into the community; and this fuelled reciprocal mistrust. For those parents, the manner in which the community functioned was incomprehensible, and they stigmatized it as an ancient legacy based on kinship and patronage. Also, the way in which the teachers understood Catholic religious practice was alien and distressing to the parents.

All these differences and tensions were transmuted into suspicions and rumours. The representations of children espoused by the two parties – the parents on the one side, and the care institution on the other – clashed: the view of the innocent and passive child opposed the view of the child as endowed with subjectivity and agency. Thus created were frictions and reciprocal mistrust which contributed to generating mutual suspicion. In the end, pressures applied from outside – by moral entrepreneurs and interest groups – short-circuited relations and defined the issue prior to the onset of the moral panic. The media, interest groups, professional experts and moral entrepreneurs created a spiral of signification. In this process, as we have seen, the risk society performed a crucial role.

In this case, the interest groups acted in different directions and in different ways, addressing different audiences and using different discursive strategies. We can divide the moral crusaders into three categories: the outright moral entrepreneurs, the professional experts and the politicians. Each group reached partly different, partly the same audiences. All of them, through the use of the media and publications, contacted both a broad public and a more specific target, namely the parents. The professional experts, however, were able to reach, in a pervasive manner, various social-health practitioners working in national agencies and schools. The claims, from a simplistic perspective, concerned the evil of paedophiles and the innocence and vulnerability of children. Paedophiles were not distinguished from the alleged ritual abusers; and valid references to psychopathological classifications were not used. Rather, the extent of abuse of any kind, and of paedophilia, was emphasized and exaggerated with respect to statistical data collected according to scientific criteria. The polarization into two interest groups around the issue was strikingly similar to what had happened in the United States (de Young 2002, 2004, 2006).

To understand the nature and diffusion of the claims, it should be borne in mind that the true-abuse lobby enjoys more political support in Italy than does the false-abuse lobby. It, therefore, has greater opportunities to popularize its claims and to turn its demands into ad hoc institutions. Such support is forthcoming from both the political right and left. For the right, the paedophilia claim serves to reinforce perceived insecurity and the fear of crime, thereby restoring or strengthening the bond between citizens and the political sphere (the 'paedophile' is seen largely as an individual extraneous to the family, because the institution of the family must be protected). For the left, some fringes of the feminist movement have mounted sensationalist campaigns on child abuse sometimes outside but mainly inside the family (the 'abuser' located primarily within the family).

Returning to Critcher's (2009a) question as to whether analysis of moral panics is compatible with risk society theory, we may consider the arguments for and against its relevance. Evidence of risk consciousness took four forms. First, the threat that engendered the moral panic can legitimately be considered a risk: the parents perceived the risk that children might suffer at the hands of adults. Second, a moral panic always contains the demand that something must be done by those responsible for controlling or managing risks: in the case considered here, the social workers, the experts, the school and the legislators. Third, the crisis of expertise identified by risk society theory is also very apparent in this moral panic. The views of the experts from the false-abuse lobby, although academics and professionals with national and international reputations, were often ignored or ridiculed. Propounded instead were simplistic or common-sense explanations and solutions: for example, that child abuse is much more common than believed – using statistical data collected or interpreted using inaccurate methods, or simply exaggerated; or that paedophilia and ritual abuse are practiced by numerous professional, political and religious groups, which conflated ritual abuse with the Catholic Church's problem of paedophile priests. Fourth, the extreme reaction which coalesced into the moral panic which erupted in this case can be considered indicative of increased risk consciousness among the parents.

Critcher (2009a) also sets out a series of arguments against the relevance of risk society theory to the analysis of moral panics. He argues that theorists of risk society fail to consider how social problems are constructed in terms of risk. They do not concern themselves with the main protagonists of moral panics: for instance, the press and the media in general, politicians, pressure groups, claims-makers, the judicial system and the police. Moral panics and interest groups are not cited by the theory, notwithstanding their increased strength and presence. Moral panics show scant evidence of the two key concepts of the risk society: individuation and reflexivity.

My research results bear out these arguments and suggest four further implications. First, closer attention should be paid to how social problems are constructed using the key concept of risk. Second, the media, pressure groups, claims-makers, politicians and those responsible for controlling and adjudicating deviants perform a crucial role in emphasizing threats and conveying claims, and in heightening the risk consciousness of parents and professionals. Third, interest groups are of fundamental importance in the creation of moral panics and in evidencing and emphasizing the risks relative to childhood. Fourth, the case of moral panic examined here seems to show scant evidence of reflexivity, while in regard to individuation I believe that, in the public sphere, the collective sentiments are of concern and anger; by contrast, the fear of crime and perceived insecurity concern the intimate sphere, which is personal and pertains to individuals.

In this regard, it is useful to recall Bauman's (1998) concepts of security, certainty and safety, and to determine how they intersect with risk society theory. When the media speak of insecurity, they almost always make explicit reference to the concept of safety, the (dangerous) places in which we live and to those who threaten our safety. But the ways in which this concept is problematized and emphasized also influence the other two senses of the term (security and certainty), creating space for feelings of insecurity tied to the state of precariousness which today characterizes both people's lives and their relationships with the social system of which they are part.

Conclusion

As suggested by Goode and Ben-Yehuda (1994), a moral panic is often the *representation of a malaise* that arises at times when cultural hierarchies enter crisis and the roles of the superior and the inferior, of the man and the woman, of the adult and the child, are no longer well defined. Society reacts to this process of 'indifferentiation' by seeking out scapegoats, the purpose being to re-establish an order, to re-create loosened or destroyed ties of cohesion. Moreover, a moral panic *uses the cultural materials available*, however remote or inappropriate they may appear. A moral panic requires the *mobilization of a group or a movement*; and, in fact, as we have seen, child abuse is of interest for certain moral entrepreneurs, politicians and professionals. The more recent waves of moral panic do not disappear but, with the help of the mass media, tend to produce ad hoc institutions (experts, investigators, therapists, laws and services), and, therefore, become permanent.

In this regard, the past decade in Italy has seen increasing attention to child abuse on the part of politicians, the growth of services and practitioners concerned with the social problem of child abuse and attempts to improve the relevant legislation. The case considered here is the result of a specific and complex interaction among the inhabitants' risk consciousness and reaction, moral entrepreneurs, interest groups and mass media in a society undergoing change in the conception of childhood and its rights. Ritual abuse is not a manifestation of evil; rather, it is an expression and consequence of professional and ideological failings; and parents reproduce the myth, as many authors have shown (de Young 2004, 2006). Goode and Ben-Yehuda (1994) emphasize the need to study more thoroughly how social problems like this are socially constructed. Fieldwork, which is infrequent in the study of moral panics, could be a useful resource for analysis of the contexts and social problems in which they emerge. My ethnographic work, in fact, yielded an abundance of data and information which afforded deeper insight into the social processes in question.

The research that I have presented here highlights the connection between the macro-features of the risk society and the micro-features of social actors' everyday practices which lead to moral panic. Indeed, the parents involved in the origin of the case examined were immersed in the culture of risk. Hence, I agree with Critcher (2009a) when he argues that we need to develop the idea that moral panics are compressed expressions of risk consciousness. In the intimate sphere, Baumanian insecurity and risk consciousness, therefore, create fertile terrain for involvement in collective reactions like moral panics.

If Durkheim ([1883] 1993) speaks of a collective consciousness in a society where the role of the enemy is to consolidate social bonds, producing moral and social solidarity in a time of change and uncertainty, in this specific case the target category consisted not solely of paedophiles/satanists but more generally of those who put the innocence of children *at risk*. This category is constructed socially and by the media as the outcome of social practices that regulate culture and morality. As Foucault (1984) suggests, this concerns the development of new forms of moral regulation in the sexual sphere which are generated by the tension and the conflict due to changes in moral and cultural regulation; and not, therefore, solely to the slackening of customs towards permissiveness.

An Italian scholar (Dal Lago 1999) has replaced the concept of moral panic with that of the 'tautology of fear'. The core of this concept is that of a *perverse mechanism of reality production*, of which the signal is a disproportion between the material reality of 'problems' and the alarm with which they are socially represented. The link or short circuit between local claims and national claims (represented by the media) causes the perverse disproportion between the material reality of facts and their social construction. The facts acquire sense solely in the overall moral dimension of society which, much more today than in the past, is constituted by the media. To cite an old, fascinating but topical concept coined by Thomas and Thomas (1928), when some actors prevail over others to dictate 'the definition of the situation', simplistic discourses, claims and moral crusades on childhood, child abuse and ritual abuse trigger a moral panic circuit.

Bibliography

Bauman, Z. (1998), *Globalization: The Human Consequences*, New York: Columbia University Press.

Beck, U. (1992), *Risk Society: Towards a New Modernity*, London and Thousand Oaks: Sage.

Beck, U. and Beck-Gernsheim, E. (1995), *The Normal Chaos of Love*, Cambridge: Polity Press.

Best, J. (1991), 'Endangered Children and Antisatanist Rhetoric', in J. T. Richardson, J. Best and D. G. Bromley (eds), *The Satanism Scare*, New York: Aldine de Gruyter, 95–106.

Blumer, H. (1969), *Symbolic Interactionism: Perspective and Method*, Englewood Cliffs, NJ: Prentice Hall.

Cartocci, R. (2007), *Mappe del Tesoro. Atlante del Capitale Sociale in Italia*, Bologna: il Mulino.

Cohen, S. (1972), *Folk Devils and Moral Panics*, London: MacGibbon & Kee.

Critcher, C. (2003), *Moral Panics and the Media*, Maidenhead, Buckingham: Open University Press.

Critcher, C. (ed.) (2006), *Critical Readings: Moral Panics and the Media,* Maidenhead, Buckingham: Open University Press.

Critcher, C. (2009a), 'Onto the Highway or Up a Cul-de-sac? *The Future Destination of Moral Panic Analysis*', Seminar paper presented at Brunel University, July 2009.

— (2009b), 'Widening the Focus: Moral Panics as Moral Regulation', *British Journal of Criminology*, 49(1): 17–34.

Dal Lago, A. (1999), 'La Tautologia Della Paura', *Rassegna Italiana di Sociologia*, 1: 5–41.

de Young, M. (2002), *The Ritual Abuse Controversy. An Annotated Bibliography*, Jefferson: McFarland.

— (2004), *The Day Care Ritual Abuse Moral Panic*, Jefferson, NC: McFarland.

— (2006), 'Another Look at Moral Panics: the Case of Satanic Day Care Centres', *Deviant Behavior*, 19(3): 257–78.

Durkheim, E. ([1883] 1993), *The Division of Labour in Society*, New York: Free Press.

Foucault, M. (1984), *The History of Sexuality Volume 3: The Care of the Self*, Harmondsworth: Penguin.

Glaser, B. G. and Strauss, A. L. (1967), *The Discovery of Grounded Theory*, Chicago, IL: Aldine.

Goode, E. and Ben-Yehuda, N. (1994), *Moral Panics: the Social Construction of Deviance*, Oxford: Blackwell.

Hall, S., Critcher, C., Jefferson, T., Clarke, J. and Roberts, B. (1978), *Policing the Crisis: Mugging, the State and Law and Order*, London: Macmillan.

Jenkins, P. (1992), *Intimate Enemies: Moral Panics in Contemporary Great Britain*, Hawthorne, NY: Aldine de Gruyter.

— (1998), *Moral Panic: Changing Concepts of the Child Molester in Modern America*, New Haven, CT: Yale University Press.

Kitzinger, J. (2004), *Framing Abuse: Media Influence and Public Understanding of Sexual Violence Against Children*, London: Pluto Press.

Morin, E. (1969), *La Rumeur d'Orléans*, Paris: Éditions du Seuil.

Mutti, A. (2006), 'Sfiducia', *Rassegna Italiana di Sociologia*, 2: 199–223.

Nathan, D. (1991), 'Satanism and Child Molestation: Constructing the Ritual Abuse Scare', in J. T. Richardson, J. Best and D. G. Bromley (eds), *The Satanism Scare*, New York: Aldine de Gruyter, 75–94.

Nathan, D. and Snedeker, M. (1995), *Satan's Silence: Ritual Abuse and the Making of a Modern American Witch Hunt*, New York: Basic Books.

Putnam, R. D. (1993), *Making Democracy Work: Civic Traditions in Modern Italy*, Princeton, NJ: Princeton University Press.

Roniger, L. (1989), '*Towards a Comparative Sociology of Trust in Modern Societies*', paper presented to the XIX World Congress of Sociology, Madrid.

Thomas, W. and Thomas, D. S. (1928), *The Child in America: Behavior, Problems and Programs*, New York: Knopf.

Thompson, K. (1998), *Moral Panics*, London: Routledge.

Victor, J. S. (1991), 'The Dynamics of Rumor-Panics About Satanic Cults', in J. T. Richardson, J. Best and D. G. Bromley (eds), *The Satanism Scare*, New York: Aldine de Gruyter, 221–36.

— (1998), 'Moral Panics and the Social Construction of Deviant Behaviour: A Theory and Application to the Case of Ritual Child Abuse', *Sociological Perspectives*, 41(3): 541–65.

Zelizer, V. A. (1994), *Pricing the Priceless Child: The Changing Social Value of Children*, Princeton, NJ: Princeton University Press.

10

The 'Chav' as Folk Devil

Elias le Grand

Introduction

Since its sudden emergence in the early twenty-first century, the term 'chav' has been widely diffused and discussed in the British public realm. The term is commonly used to pathologize young, white, British, working-class people adopting specific markers of style and dress – particularly tracksuits, sneakers, baseball caps, designer brands and jewellery – and it is associated with a range of denigratory characteristics. The aim of this chapter is to analyse the public discourse on chavs, particularly in relation to moral panic analysis and the symbolic construction of class boundaries and identities. This is also discussed in the context of processes of moral regulation.

I draw on a multi-dimensional notion of class influenced by Bourdieu ([1979] 1984, 1986, 1987), for whom social classes are the products of unequal conditions of existence. By this he means that classes are relational and hierarchically ordered groupings constituted by collectives of individuals that have differing access to various forms of economic, cultural and social capital or resources. The empirical material used in this chapter consists of British news media, web sites, films and television series (for a discussion of the selection and analysis of data, see le Grand [2010]).

In what follows I first trace the emergence of the chav phenomenon and the etymology of the term. I then explore the moral-aesthetic boundaries through which chavs have been constructed as folk devils. Moreover, I analyse what I argue is the contested character of the discussion on chavs, and how it has been linked to class and whiteness. Finally, I analyse the consequences of the hostile public reactions to chavs: how new and existing forms of policing have targeted chavs, how their alleged consumption of high-end brand Burberry goods has negatively affected the brand, and how they have been used as entertainment to market and sell commodities. In the concluding section I discuss the public discourse on chavs in relation to moral panics, and in the wider contexts of moral regulation and class formation.

Emergence and etymology

Moral panics are usually characterized by the sudden emergence of moral concern among a broad section of people in a particular social context (local, national or transnational) over the behaviour of a person, group or category of people who are seen to threaten deeply held values in 'society'. This spawns a hostile reaction towards the latter who become a 'folk devil' in the eyes of the former (see Cohen [1972] 2002; Garland 2008; Goode and Ben-Yehuda [1994] 2009). Analysed in this way, the chav phenomenon has undeniable features characteristic of a moral panic. The term chav and the meanings currently attached to it emerged very recently in the British public realm, where it quickly became a widely discussed and debated phenomenon in the news media, on web sites and other public sphere institutions. Several commentators suggest that the satiric web site *Chavscum*, which was set up in December 2003 (*Independent* 2004), played a key role in constructing and diffusing the meanings attached to the term. Thanks to modern media such as the internet, the term diffused rapidly, and by the beginning of 2004, chav was all over the place: it was named the buzzword of the year by lithographer Susie Dent in a book published by Oxford University Press (Dent 2004), and was included in the *Oxford English Dictionary* and the *Collins English Dictionary* together with the adjectives chavish, chavtastic, and the closely related terms 'ned' and 'ASBO' (Anti-Social Behaviour Orders). The rapid diffusion of the term in the British public realm is illustrated in Table 10.1, which displays the number of articles mentioning the term in eight major British newspapers. As we can see, chav is not mentioned until 2004, and after 2004, suddenly all the newspapers start to write about the term. The numbers reach a peak in 2005, then decline in 2006, and generally continue to decline each year until 2011 when, interestingly, there is a slight rise in numbers. The continuous use of the term, more than seven years since its emergence in the public realm, indicates that it has become institutionalized in public and everyday discourse.

Table 10.1 The number of articles in eight major British newspapers mentioning the term chav, 2003–11

Newspaper	2003	2004	2005	2006	2007	2008	2009	2010	2011
Daily Express	0	11	77	48	27	19	19	27	33
Daily Mail	0	36	114	104	100	105	30	31	29
Daily Mirror	0	33	138	96	53	53	74	78	106
Daily Telegraph	0	37	72	51	44	47	20	21	24
Guardian	0	50	169	129	137	107	75	57	99
Independent	0	44	94	37	29	18	13	9	22
Sun	0	63	170	110	55	84	78	100	77
The Times	0	57	202	149	131	86	93	82	83
Total	0	331	1036	724	576	519	402	405	473

Sources: Lexis Nexis Academic, www.guardian.co.uk

Yet, the phenomenon of young people dressed in street wear, associated with minor unlawful behaviour and low social status, has existed throughout Britain since at least the 1990s (Hayward and Yar 2006). These youths have been given local names, such as 'ned' in Glasgow, 'kev' in London and Bristol, 'charver' in Newcastle, 'scally' in Liverpool, 'yarco' in East Anglia and 'skanger' in Ireland. Other names include 'bazza', 'divi', 'janner', 'kappa slappa', 'rarfie', 'ratboy', 'senga', 'spide', 'steek', 'stig' and 'townie'. Chav was a local term used in southern England, such as the Medway towns and the East End of London, but with the wide dissemination and institutionalization of the term chav, it has become an umbrella term applied to white, young, streetwear-clad working-class persons all over Britain.

But despite the current spread of the term, chav has been used for much longer, and there are different folk theories about its origins and uses. One theory is that it stems from chavi or chavo, which is the Romani word for child that emerged in the mid-nineteenth century. It has also been argued that chav is mainly a local term used to refer to people from the Medway towns in Southern England. Others argue that it is an acronym for '[Ch]eltenham [Av]erage', which refers 'to young people in Gloucestershire who lack the requisite qualifications to enter Cheltenham College, one of the foremost private schools in the UK' (Hayward and Yar 2006: 16). Another folk theory is that chav is 'a historical East End of London term for child' (Tyler 2008: 21), while others say that, since chavs are associated with Southern England, the term comes from Chatham. Finally, it has been argued that chav has been used among builders and construction workers in the London area in the same way as 'mate' or 'mush', and thus originally lacked derogatory connotations (Young 2004).

The creation of a folk devil

The meanings typically constructed around chavs can be illustrated by two quotes from the respected conservative broadsheet *the Daily Telegraph*. The source – 'serious' news media – indicates the widespread legitimacy of this kind of discourse.

> Chav . . . [is] a suitably monosyllabic noun or adjective designed to illuminate that which is most appalling in the young, designer-label-obsessed under-class of early 21st century Britain.
>
> When you see a stunted teenager, apparently jobless, hanging around outside McDonald's dressed in a Burberry baseball Cap, Ben Sherman shirt, ultra-white Reebok trainers and dripping in bling (cheap, tasteless and usually gold-coloured jewellery), he will almost certainly be a chav.
>
> If he has difficulty framing the words 'you gotta problem mate?' then he will definitely be a chav. Very short hair and souped-up Vauxhall Novas are chav, as is functional illiteracy, a burgeoning career in petty crime and the wearing of one's mobile telephone around the neck.
>
> Chavs are most at home in run-down, small-town shopping precincts, smoking and shouting at their mates. A teenage single mum chewing gum or drawing on a cigarette as she pushes her baby, Keanu, to McDonald's to meet the chav she believes to be his father is a chavette. (Tweedie 2004)
>
> They are the sullen, pasty-faced youths in hooded tops and spanking-new 'prison white' trainers who loiter listlessly on street corners; the slack-jawed girls with mottled legs, hoop earrings and heavily-gelled hair who squawk at each other in consonant-free estuary English and frighten old ladies on buses. They are the non-respectable working-classes: the dole-scroungers, petty criminals, football hooligans and teenage pram-pushers. (Lewis 2004)

The term chav is first and foremost tied to certain visible attributes: white, young, British people adopting particular stylistic markers. The latter include branded clothing, especially sportswear such as baseball caps, tracksuits and trainers, which are combined with 'bling' or jewellery, usually in fake or low carat gold. Boys typically have short-cropped coiffure, while girls, or 'chavettes', have their hair in ponytails combined with large hoop earrings and large amounts of mascara around the eyes.

A person with these attributes is not only labelled chav but is also 'marked' or 'inscribed' with a range of moral-aesthetic distinctions. A chav is a particular type of person, with certain lifestyles, behaviour, body techniques, speech, values and social background. These characteristics serve to construct symbolic class boundaries where chavs are positioned as lacking cultural and economic capital. Often boundaries are drawn through mockery, though blended with what can be interpreted as contempt, disgust or even hatred. Note the adjectives used to describe chavs in the quotes above. They are 'sullen', 'pasty-faced', 'slack-jawed', 'cheap', 'tasteless', 'stunted', 'appalling', 'designer-label-obsessed' and 'dripping' in jewellery.

The consumption and lifestyles allegedly adopted by chavs is coded as crude, vulgar and excessive. They smoke, binge drink and live on a diet of cheap and unhealthy food, especially fast food. This can be interpreted using Bourdieu's ([1979] 1984) analysis of working-class culture, which embodies what he calls a 'taste of necessity'. It is governed by material constraints and thus characterized by a lack of choice and expressed as a preference for practical, informal modes of consumption oriented to satisfying basic needs. Conversely, Bourdieu argues that the 'taste of freedom' or 'taste of luxury' of the middle classes is formed through strategies of distinction vis-à-vis working-class taste, and constitutes an elaborate, stylized form of taste governed by an 'aesthetic disposition' and characterized by 'manners' and form. It is coded as refined, sophisticated and restrained.

However, *contra* Bourdieu's analysis, the lifestyles and consumption associated with chavs have also highly stylized, conspicuous and aspirational aspects, which in Veblen's ([1899] 2007) terms serve to 'show off', to display status and wealth through consumption, often through connotations of 'glamour'. One is chavs' alleged consumption of designer brands such as Burberry and Prada, as well as streetwear brands such as Adidas and Nike. But perhaps the clearest example is chavs' association with the term 'bling' and its adjective 'blingy'. The term derives from 'bling-bling', which is used by African American hip-hop artists wearing heavy gold chains to display wealth, status, success and a luxurious, glamorous lifestyle. The term and its connotations have diffused and translated into a British context in the form of not only jewellery, but also 'blingy' clothing items and accessories with shiny or glittery materials, such as shoes in silvery or gold-coloured materials and jeans adorned with glittery details. Other 'blingy' features also include the cars chavs are said to drive, mockingly called 'chav chariots', 'chaviots' or 'chavmobiles', often inexpensive cars adorned with add-ons.

The conspicuous aspects of chav taste are downgraded for displaying distance from necessity in an obvious, vulgar way lacking in sophistication. The noticeable ways of 'showing-off' one's status are especially denigrated as crude, vulgar, unsophisticated and, therefore, 'cheap' and 'over-the-top', as opposed to middle-class taste, which values the discreet, 'refined' and subtle. The adjective 'chavy' is frequently used to connote the taste associated with chavs, and it is constructed very much in opposition to the more middle- or upper-class term 'posh'. Not the least is this evident in the context of social mobility and celebrity culture. Some British celebrities, almost always from a working-class background, are labelled chav celebrities. They are in fields usually associated with a lack of highly valued cultural resources such as footballers, glamour models, pop artists, participants in reality-TV programs, soap opera actors and TV-presenters, including Katie Price, Peter Andre, Jade Goody, Victoria and David Beckham and Wayne and Coleen Rooney. Chav celebrities are portrayed as having plentiful economic resources but few cultural resources. Their unsuccessful attempts to appear stylish are often mocked.

The aesthetic boundaries constructed against chavs are often morally loaded. Chavs are seen as interested only in excessive, tasteless, mindless consumption and adopting a hedonistic lifestyle. Moreover, chavs are often categorized as ignorant, uneducated, uncultured and stupid. In the quotes above we read about 'functional illiteracy' and how chavs have problems forming sentences. Chavs are often described as 'dole-scroungers' – people who use the welfare system, paid for by 'us' hard-working ordinary people. This is tied to the recurrent images of chavs as largely outside the labour market and thus economically marginalized.

Moreover, chavs are said to congregate in gangs and behave in a loutish manner. They are loud-mouthed and threaten or harass people. Male chavs are often associated with violence such as football hooliganism and with minor forms of anti-social behaviour such as vandalism, assault and muggings. References to chavs as yobs or constituting a 'yob culture' are frequent. Chavs are also associated with ASBOs, a civil order first introduced by the newly elected Labour government in 1997. Hence chav culture, and particularly chav masculinity, connotes danger and violence.

The moral boundaries drawn against chav femininity are particularly sexualized and related to reproduction. Chavettes are represented as promiscuous and 'slutty', basically sleeping with anyone, and thus the very opposite of the ideal of the respectable woman. This is the gist of many chav jokes, such as the following:

Q: What's the difference between a chavette and a Ferrari?
A: Not many people have been in a Ferrari!

Q: What does a chavette have written on the back of her knickers?
A: NEXT.
Q: What's the difference between a chavette and an ironing board?
A: An ironing board's legs are difficult to get apart! (Jokes Forum 2009)

Chavettes are portrayed as sexually irresponsible, failing to use contraceptives, and, therefore, often associated with teenage pregnancy and motherhood. But conversely, 'sluttiness' and teenage motherhood are also strongly linked with the notion that chavettes have children for their cunning, selfish economic interests, namely to get benefits. Motherhood thus becomes a form of willing welfare dependency paid for by 'us', respectable citizens. This is reflected in the use of the derogatory term 'pram face' to describe single, teenage, chavette mothers (Tyler 2008). The stereotypes constructed around chavs are heavily gendered.

There is also a spatialized aspect. Chavs are said to roam spaces such as shopping centres and McDonald's, or just 'hang out' in the street. They live in deprived neighbourhoods, often council house estates with high rates of crime, unemployment and teenage pregnancy. Chavs are associated with the highly derogatory acronyms '[Ch]eltenham [Av]erage' and '[C]ouncil [H]oused [a]nd [V]iolent' and '[C]ouncil [H]ouse [V]ermin' (Hayward and Yar 2006: 16). The lifestyles adopted by chavs are tied to marginalized, low-status spaces of consumption. For instance, on *Urban Dictionary* (n.d.), one can read: 'Chavs are retards who think that they're rebels and also think that their local McDonalds [*sic*] is a 5-star restraunt [*sic*]' and 'Filth hanging outside McDonalds [*sic*] in large groups attempting to look remotely intimidating'.

Chavs are also ridiculed for illuminating the facades of their houses generously with colourful lights, often in the form of figures such as Santa Claus, reindeers and snowmen. As Edensor and Millington (2009: 106) note, this very expressive, conspicuous practice is very much opposed to the 'modest, chic white and blue lighting [that] illuminates middle-class housing areas'.

The stereotypical images of chav spaces are also present in the representations of particular locations (Gidley and Rooke 2010; le Grand forthcoming). The most prolific source on the internet is the web site *Chavtowns*, which features posts on towns, cities, neighbourhoods and regions allegedly 'infested with chavs'. The spaces and places associated with chavs become stigmatized and generally denote socio-economic marginality and a lack of cultural resources, tied to an imagined geography of class.

Taken together, these categorizations create a stigmatized identity, a folk devil. The chav becomes a stereotype, a denigrated 'other' against whom strong moral and aesthetic boundaries are constructed, often through mockery. Here, humour functions as a device to create distance, so that the content of what is expressed can appear harmless, and thus serve to legitimize the use of a strongly derogatory vocabulary (Raisborough and Adams 2008).

Moreover, the chav as folk devil is constructed primarily around consumption and lifestyles, rather than the sphere of production (Hayward and Yar 2006), and is linked with economic and social marginalization. Chavs are categorized as lacking economic and cultural resources, and thus as occupying a marginal position in social and terrestrial space. This serves to create classed boundaries between a 'respectable' us and a trashy, immoral them, constructing chavs as non-respectable white British working-class people. Here chavs incorporate two 'familiar clusters of social identity' (Cohen 2002: viii), which historically have served the role of folk devil, and appear along gender lines. One is young, violent, working-class masculinity (Hall et al. 1978; Zatz 1987; Boëthius 1995; Hay 1995). The other is working-class welfare cheats, which includes a gendered social type, namely the single, unwed, young, working-class mother (Phoenix 1996; Brush 1997; Naylor 2001; Ajzenstadt 2009).

Finally, the classed nature of the chav phenomenon is also spatialized and intimately bound with whiteness, as only white bodies (or at least those approximating a white appearance) are labelled chavs. Whiteness is typically the unmarked, largely invisible norm against which other racial categories are defined (Frankenberg 1993; Dyer 1997; Webster 2008). It is when marginalized, as in the case of chavs, that it can become a marked, racialized identity – a 'dirty' form of whiteness – in a similar vein to 'white trash' in the United States and 'bogans' in Australia and New Zealand.

A contested public issue

As McRobbie and Thornton (1995) note, characteristic of moral panics in contemporary fragmented and mediated social worlds is that they, *qua* public issues, are contested and debated. The great volume of this stigmatizing discourse, not the least when articulated by journalists representing 'serious' news media, illustrates its widespread legitimacy, and in many contexts, a large measure of consensus. But these representations have been criticized and debated, notably in the left-leaning news media, creating a dividing line between those who embrace the ridicule and moral denigration of chavs, and those who oppose it.

The public debate about chavs has explicitly been about social class, and to some extent, race. Several scholars have noted the silence around issues of class in public discourse (e.g. Savage 2000; Skeggs 2004), including the chav phenomenon (Lawler 2005b: 800; Moran 2006: 19–20). But my point is the opposite, namely that the discourse on chavs has actually brought issues of class to the surface. Chavs are frequently categorized as working-class people. For instance, on a blog chavs are depicted as 'the new working-class infection that's sweeping the nation with epidemic-like speed' (Mitch's Blog 2004). And in *the Daily Telegraph* chavs are described as part of 'the wrong kind of working-class culture: the non-working kind', that is, 'the non-respectable working-classes' (Lewis 2004).

Similarly, many critics have argued that the denigratory discourse on chavs is middle-class snobbery of working-class people – a form of 'classism' or class racism. In 2008 Tom Hampson, of the left-wing think tank the Fabian Society, spawned much debate in British news media, blogs and discussion forums stating that the term chav should be banned, and that its usage 'is deeply offensive to a largely voiceless group and – especially when used in normal middle-class conversation or on national TV – it betrays a deep and revealing level of class hatred' (Hampson and Olchawski 2008). A particularly powerful and articulate statement of this position was recently made by writer and social commentator Owen Jones in *Chav: The Demonization of the Working Class* (Jones 2011). The book received widespread national and international recognition, and further put the chav phenomenon onto the public agenda. Jones traces the chav discourse to the dismantling of the manufacturing sector and the welfare state under Thatcher, which led to a sharp rise in unemployment and poverty among the working class. A further consequence was the fragmentation of the working class, which has largely come to be perceived as a backward remnant of industrial society. Important here to Jones' argument is that the marginalization of the working class is presented as the result of individual moral failings or a 'culture of poverty', rather than structural conditions. Hence the class contempt as expressed through the chav discourse serves the interests of the wealthy and privileged by legitimating increasing inequality and masking the class relations underlying such inequality.

Yet, largely unacknowledged by Jones or in previous academic research (e.g. Lawler 2005b; Tyler 2008) is that many self-identified working-class people also differentiate themselves from chavs. Take, for example, this person's furious reaction to a blog post arguing that chavs are working-class people: 'Chav is an attitude, not a fucking social class! I'm working-class and I'm fucked off to the back teeth of being lumped into the Chav catagory [*sic*] because of my working-class roots' (Mitch's Blog 2004). Or, take the following blog post: 'The difference between chavs and the working-class are [*sic*] that the working-class actually work for a living, whereas chavs are the underclass, those who live off benefits and can't even be bothered to look for a job. The working-class are hard-working and have their own culture . . . Chav 'culture' is trash, and its [*sic*] insulting to even compare the two' (Hollyzone 2006).

Such accounts reflect the long-standing moral distinction in Britain between respectable and non-respectable or 'rough' working-class people (Stacey 1960; Bott 1964; Watt 2006). But some commentators argue that chavs are a 'youth tribe', a lifestyle choice comparable to Goths or indie kids, and thus unrelated to social class or socio-economic status.

In some instances, the racialized nature of the chav label has also been brought to the surface. Chavs have been associated with white trash, as in the following quote from *the Daily Mail*: 'Chavs are Britain's answer to America's trailer trash. They're white, they're dumb, they're vulgar. And they don't care who knows it' (Thomas 2004). Such representations have been critiqued by several commentators, such as in newspaper articles, entitled 'Everyone Hates the White Working-Class Male' (Liddle 2004) and 'White Trash, the Only People Left to Insult' (Collins 2004). Indeed, I would argue that the fact that chavs denote marginalized, marked whiteness is an important factor in explaining the widespread legitimacy of the strong derogatory vocabulary articulated against them. If such discourse were applied to, for instance, gays or people of non-white ethnicity, it would most likely be strongly condemned for being sexist or racist. Chavs, on the other hand, as part of the non-respectable, *lumpen*, white working class, are basically morally bad people and thus 'rightfully' deserve to be denigrated. This can be related to Chris Haylett's (2001) argument that political discourse envisioning a multicultural, modern Britain has simultaneously cast white poor working-class people as an unmodern, racist and backward 'other'. I would argue that this group has come to be further demonized and pathologized under the label chav.

Contemporary, contested moral panics are often characterized by the public involvement of the folk devils themselves or people who claim to represent them (McRobbie and Thornton 1995; for a recent example, see Ajzenstadt

2009). What is striking here is the *absence* of self-identified chavs or people representing them. This makes chavs 'a largely voiceless group' in the public discussion (Hampson and Olchawski 2008). One exception is the well-known journalist Julie Burchill (e.g. 2005), who is from a working-class background. Identifying as a chav and championing it as a positive identity, she celebrates what she sees as chavs' hedonistic, glamorous and unpretentious approach to life. Similarly, she thinks the middle class who denigrate chav values are actually envious of them.

One possible explanation for the lack of public representation by self-identified chavs is the stigmatization of the term. As Skeggs (1997) argues, the pathologization of working-class femininity means that it cannot serve as a positive form of identification or the basis for any form of identity politics. And with chav used as a word of abuse for allegedly non-respectable white working-class people, the same logic is even more apparent. Of course, it may also be that people who are labelled chavs lack the economic, social and cultural resources to access public sphere institutions or, if they do, lack the cultural resources to verbally defend themselves and argue their cause.

Consequences

During and after a period of moral panic, the hostile social reaction against folk devils can lead to profound cultural and institutional changes, such as the introduction of new laws and changes in norms, or a strengthening of existing norms (Goode and Ben-Yehuda [1994] 2009). In this section, I will explore the consequences of the social reaction over chavs by looking at three different contexts or cases: first, new and existing forms of policing explicitly targeting chavs; second, the consequences of high-end brand Burberry being associated with chavs; third, the usage of the image of the chav to market and sell commodities.

Policing the chav

In the wake of the chav phenomenon, new and existing forms of policing have come to target chavs. One such form of policing deals with regulating access to public space. Shopping malls, pubs, night clubs and other public establishments (e.g. internet cafes) have started banning people in clothing that is associated with chavs, including baseball caps, 'hoodies' and clothing brands such as Burberry and Prada. This is clearly a way of excluding an unwanted, potentially troublesome and low-status segment of the population. And when the Bluewater Shopping Centre in Kent started to ban hoodies and baseball caps in 2005, this was endorsed by both Prime Minister Tony Blair and Deputy Prime Minister John Prescott (Hier et al. 2011).

Moreover, in 2008 a campaign by the Department of Work and Pensions targeted working-class people in general and chavs in particular. The campaign was advertised widely on radio, television and on posters. One poster depicts a very large-sized woman – an extremely uncommon image on an advertisement in public space – with scraped back hair tied in a knot, large hoop earrings, and a telescopic sight zooming in on her. The caption above in huge red letters reads: 'We're closing in'. The woman, who is allegedly an actual or potential benefit thief, very much looks like a chavette and it is difficult not to think that this is deliberate.

Chavs have also been associated with ASBOs. ASBOs were issued by the Labour government in 1997, and subsequently strengthened and broadened throughout the United Kingdom during 2003–4. An ASBO is a civil order, issued 'to restrict the movement and behaviour of people deemed to be anti-social' (Millie 2008: 379), but it may be transformed into a criminal offence if breached. In common parlance, ASBO does not only refer to a particular civil order, but also to the kind of people against whom such civil orders are issued. One can therefore *be* an ASBO. Moreover, as chavs are associated with delinquency, they are also often portrayed as ASBOs, as in the following two definitions of ASBO on *Urban Dictionary* (n.d.):

> an essential qualification for all chavs and general idiots who think that beating the shit out of random people walking down the street/throwing bricks through people's windows/generally displaying how few brain cells they have, makes them look 'hard'.
> New British Government scheme to crack down on chavs and their behaviour. Acronym for Anti-Social Behaviour Order. Stops offenders from doing certain things, going to certain places and meeting certain people.

Chavs are often conceived as glorifying anti-social behaviour; for them, getting an ASBO is a status marker. A more critical view is expressed in the *Observer* stating that 'Asbos are just the word chav made concrete, a vehicle for old-school class hatred made over to look all pretty' (Callwalladr 2005).

Chavs in me Burberry

The chav phenomenon has also had consequences for the brand Burberry. Founded in 1856, it has the status of a classic, luxury brand famous for its gabardine trench coats and its trademark beige-white-black-red check pattern. But by the 1990s Burberry was seen as old-fashioned and passé, and its main consumer segment were 'middle-aged, fashion-conservative men' (Tungate 2005: 414). The company responded by setting in place a new business model which included a rebranding process. Key here was increasing the visibility of Burberry's trademark check pattern on its products, and 'opening up' the brand to younger and less affluent consumer segments, through producing more affordable items, such as Burberry checked baseball caps. As a consequence, Burberry successfully changed its image to a youthful, cool, luxury brand in touch with contemporary fashion (Moore and Birtwistle 2004; Tungate 2005). But it also made the check pattern popular among chavs, and in the media stories started appearing of chav celebrities wearing Burberry checked clothing. One defining moment was in April 2004 when soap opera actress Danniella Westbrook was pictured with her daughter and their pram in full-on Burberry check. This has been described as disastrous for Burberry's image, as its check pattern became part of the public ridicule and sneering which targeted chavs and chav celebrities such as Westbrook (Kobayashi-Hillary 2008).

In 2004 the Burberry check became tainted by its association with chavs. In the summer of 2004, various media reported pubs banning clothes with the Burberry check due to its popularity among chav football hooligans (Bothwell 2005). In 2005 Burberry experienced a slump in sales in the United Kingdom but not elsewhere. Indeed, in a British context, the check pattern has come to signify chavs. The company responded by cutting down its visibility. From featuring it on 20 per cent of its items, the check was slashed to 5 per cent. Among other things, the company stopped producing its Burberry checked caps, said to be a chav favourite (Bothwell 2005). Since then, Burberry has managed another rebranding, successfully distanced from its trademark check pattern, and thus from 'chavy clothes'.

The commodification of chavness

The role of mockery in constructing moral-aesthetic boundaries against chavs has created avenues for the production of commodities that cater to the alleged non-chav. As Paul Johnson (2008) shows, chav-related commodities and services marketed as 'chav chic' have become commonplace in British gay space. Here, chav masculinity takes on particularly sexual connotations that in other contexts are usually reserved for chav femininity. Masculine sexuality is combined with danger and violence in the form of magazines, telephone sex lines and pornography marketed as chav and scally. Johnson's argument is that the denigrated cultural symbols and practices associated with chavs are appropriated in middle-class-dominated gay spaces where they are converted into valuable cultural resources, which, in turn, generate economic resources in the form of commodities and services.

British gay clubs have also arranged 'chav parties' or 'chav nites' where people dress up as chavs. This practice has been found in many British university student unions. But while sexualized danger is the selling point in gay spaces, irony and humour is the general selling point in more hetero-normative contexts. Drawing on some of the stereotypical representations of chavs circulating in the public realm, middle-class people can perform 'slutty' chavette femininity or 'hard' chav masculinity through a reflexive stance of ironic distance.

Representations of chavs have also featured in popular culture. Raisborough and Adams (2008) analyse the mockery of 'neds', a local term used for chavs in Scotland, in the comic strip *The Neds* – a recent addition to *The Beano* children's comic published by DC Thomson and Co Ltd. It is about the family of the same name, its members being Ned, Nedette and their children Asbo and Chavette. They and other neds are seen dressed in tracksuits and Burberry, are often obese, and frequently portrayed as idle, lazy, feckless, unemployed and dependent on welfare. Thus, we can see how moral-aesthetic boundaries are drawn against neds depicted as a work-shy underclass. When first published in 2006, the comic strip was originally intended as a one-off, but due to its popularity it has come to feature as an 'occasional guest' in the comic *BeanoMAX*. The comic strip was critiqued for its way of labelling and portraying neds, including Scottish politicians. The publishers responded by stating that it was conceived as 'harmless fun' and not intended to offend anyone (Home 2006).

Representations of the chavette have been diffused in popular culture via *The Catherine Tate Show* in the United Kingdom and through the internationally popular British TV-series *Little Britain*, in the form of the character Vicky Pollard, played by Matt Lucas. Vicky Pollard is a girl in her late teens who is overweight, wears a pink tracksuit and gold jewellery, has her hair in a ponytail and uses plenty of eyeliner. She lives on a council estate, goes on welfare, chain-smokes, shoplifts, has about a dozen children, gets pregnant regularly, is fickle, aggressive, extremely foulmouthed and speaks very fast and incoherently. One example of her morally and sexually irresponsible behaviour is shown in an episode where she exchanges one of her children for a Westlife CD. Vicky Pollard has become one of the 'public faces' of the chav phenomenon. The character has frequently been used in tabloids as a reference point in order to illustrate and explain what a chav is. For instance, a *Daily Mail* (2006) article is entitled 'Woman Mugged by Vicky Pollard Look-a-like', and features a picture of the TV character. Another case is 19-year-old Kerry McLaughlin living in North Tyneside, who was dubbed 'the real life Vicky Pollard' by the press. After 111 complaints by neighbours and 25 visits by the police she was issued a particularly powerful form of ASBO banning her from entering her flat, and sentencing her to jail if she did (Metro 2005).

Finally, there was also a plethora of commodities, of chav merchandise, including several satiric books on chavs, such as Chav's Books series published by Crombie Jardine Publishing Limited, including, *The Chav Guide to Life*, *The Little Book of Chav Jokes* and *The Little Book of Chav Speak*. Other products include skateboard stickers, mouse pads, baby clothing and 'become a chav' giftpacks.

In sum, although chav culture is devalued and very much conceived as lacking taste and morals, it has been appropriated in (largely) middle-class contexts through humour or sexuality and turned into entertainment, being used to market and sell commodities and services. The denigrated, 'worthless' culture of the chavs becomes a valuable resource when appropriated by others. This can be related to Beverley Skeggs' (2004) argument that working-class culture is frequently exploited by the middle class in order to generate economic value in capitalist markets. Conversely, but according to the same logic, when chavs appropriate high-status items, these become tainted and devalued. When Burberry items became popular among chavs, the cultural value of the brand decreased, which in turn led to a slump in sales in the United Kingdom.

Conclusion

In this chapter, I have interpreted the chav phenomenon by means of the analytical tools of moral panic analysis. I will now draw out the wider implications of the study, and in particular, situate it in the frameworks of moral regulation and class formation. We have seen that the chav phenomenon displays several elements of a moral panic: a broad section of the British population suddenly reacting with hostility – mixed with moral indignation, mockery and aesthetic denigration – towards people with certain visual characteristics whom they label chavs; the latter thus becoming a folk devil – a symbol of class contempt – to which are attached a range of moral-aesthetic distinctions, typically constructed around consumption and lifestyles. Chavs are portrayed as crude, vulgar, tacky and excessive, and associated with petty crime, welfare dependency and deprived spaces, as well as loutish and anti-social behaviour. Moreover, there is a gendered dimension, reflecting two folk devils familiar from the past: the young, violent, working-class male and the 'dole-scrounging' young working-class mother. Female chavs are also depicted as 'slutty' and particularly sexualized compared with male chavs. Thus, there are notions, characteristic of moral panics, that chavs threaten the moral order of society.

There is also evidence of social control measures targeting chavs, which include regulating access to public space and a government campaign against 'benefit thieves'. Yet, in general, the direct consequences for these folk devils have primarily been symbolic, taking the form of mockery and sneering. This created avenues for commodities and services where chav culture was appropriated as entertainment.

Another piece largely missing from the moral panic model is that there has been no distinct group of moral entrepreneurs organizing campaigns against chavs. Consequently, the chav phenomenon is not a fully fledged moral panic. Rather, I would argue that although the chav phenomenon displays elements of a moral panic, it should be situated within the wider context of moral regulation, of which moral panics are a volatile and extreme type (Hier 2002, 2008, 2011; Critcher 2009; Hier et al. 2011). Moral regulation entails long-standing routine processes, which shape subjectivity in a relational and dialectical fashion by affecting the selves and identities of not only the regulated, but also of the regulators. In this sense, 'projects of moral regulation reveal as much about the identity of those who seek to regulate as they do about those who come to serve as the object of regulation' (Hier 2002: 328, cited in Critcher 2009: 23).

In the context of the present study, this is tied to the construction of class distinctions and identities. As Webster puts it, 'Class contempt . . . serves to project all that is bad and immoral onto the other, while reciprocally enhancing and confirming the goodness, self-regard and status of one's own class' (2008: 294). Chavs constitute a *lumpen*, non-respectable, fraction of the white British working class, against which middle-class and respectable working-class people distinguish themselves and construct their identities. As Jones (2011) shows, this demonization of the marginalized serves to legitimize social inequalities since those on the bottom of the rung are conceived to fully deserve their position.

In this sense, I suggest that the chav discourse is a recent expression of what could be called the moral-aesthetic regulation of white working-class people in Britain, which has a long-standing history. Moral distinctions are here often fused with those of aesthetics (Lawler 2005a; Watt 2009). Chavs are simultaneously lacking in taste and morality. Here, 'aesthetics has been translated into morality . . . so that those positioned as lacking "taste" can also be positioned as morally lacking . . . This is precisely why working-class people are so readily judged by their appearance' (Lawler 2005a: 441, cited in Watt 2009: 2876–7).

Finally, I have argued that the widespread legitimacy of this discourse of class contempt is due to it being connected with racialized whiteness. Such discourse would be considered politically incorrect if levelled against, for example, gays or people who are disabled or of non-white ethnicity. But rather than constituting a potentially oppressed minority, the marginalized fraction of the white British working class of which chavs are a part is conceived as an immoral and backwards and unmodern 'other'. This makes them a particularly suitable object for hostile forms of moral regulation.

Bibliography

Ajzenstadt, M. (2009), 'Moral Panic and Neo-liberalism: The Case of Single Mothers on Welfare in Israel', *British Journal of Criminology*, 49(1): 68–87.

Boëthius, U. (1995), 'Youth, the Media and Moral Panics', in J. Fornäs and G. Bolin (eds), *Youth Culture in Late Modernity*, London: Sage, 39–57.

Bothwell, C. (2005), 'Burberry versus the Chavs', *BBC News*, 28 October, news.bbc.co.uk/2/hi/business/4381140.stm [accessed 30 July 2010].

Bott, E. (1964), *Family and Social Network: Roles Norms and External Relationships in Ordinary Urban Families*, London: Tavistock.

Bourdieu, P. ([1979] 1984), *Distinction: A Social Critique of the Judgement of Taste*, Cambridge, MA: Harvard University Press.

— (1986), 'The Forms of Capital', in J. G. Richardson (ed.), *Handbook of Theory and Research for the Sociology of Education*, Westport, CT: Greenwood Press, 241–58.

— (1987), 'What Makes a Social Class? On the Theoretical and Practical Existence of Groups', *Berkley Journal of Sociology*, 22: 1–17.

Brush, L. D. (1997), 'Worthy Widows, Welfare Cheats: Proper Womanhood in Expert Needs Talk about Single Mothers in the US 1900–1988', *Gender and Society,* 11(6): 720–46.

Burchill, J. (2005), 'Yeah But, No But, Why I'm Proud to Be Chav', *The Times*, 18 February.

Callwalladr, C. (2005), 'Get an Asbo, Get Ahead', *Observer,* 12 June.

Cohen, S. ([1972] 2002), *Folk Devils and Moral Panics: The Creation of the Mods and Rockers*, 3rd edn, London: Routledge.

Collins, M. (2004), 'White Trash, the Only People Left to Insult', *Sunday Times,* 17 July.

Critcher, C. (2009), 'Widening the Focus: Moral Panics as Moral Regulation', *British Journal of Criminology*, 49(1): 17–34.

Daily Mail (2006), 'Woman Mugged by Vicky Pollard Look-a-Like', 24 August.

Dent, S. (2004), *Larpers and Shroomers: The Language Report*, Oxford: Oxford University Press.

Dyer, R. (1997), *White*, London: Routledge.

Edensor, T. and Millington, S. (2009), 'Illuminations, Class Identities and the Contested Landscapes of Christmas', *Sociology,* 43(1): 103–21.

Frankenberg, R. (1993), *White Women, Race Matters: The Social Construction of Whiteness*, Minneapolis: University of Minnesota Press.

Garland, D. (2008), 'On the Concept of Moral Panic', *Crime Media Culture,* 4(1): 9–30.

Gidley, B. and Rooke, A. (2010), 'Asdatown: The Intersections of Classed Places and Identities', in Y. Taylor (ed.), *Classed Intersections: Spaces, Selves, Knowledges*, Farnham: Ashgate, 95–116.

Goode, E. and Ben-Yehuda, N. ([1994] 2009), *Moral Panics: The Social Construction of Deviance*, 2nd edn, Chichester: Wiley-Blackwell.

Hall, S., Critcher, C., Jefferson, T., Clarke, J. and Roberts, B. (1978), *Policing the Crisis: Mugging, the State, and Law and Order*, London: Macmillan.

Hampson, T. and Olchawski, J. (2008), 'Ban the Word "Chav"', *Guardian,* 15 July.

Hay, C. (1995), 'Mobilization through Interpellation: James Bulger, Juvenile Crime and the Construction of Moral Panic', *Social and Legal Studies*, 4(2): 197–224.

Haylett, C. (2001), 'Illegitimate Subjects? Abject Whites, Neoliberal Modernisation, and Middle-Class Multiculturalism', *Environment and Planning D: Society and Space,* 19(3): 351–70.

Hayward, K. and Yar, M. (2006), 'The "Chav" Phenomenon: Consumption, Media and the Construction of a New Underclass', *Crime Media Culture,* 2(1): 9–28.

Hier, S. P. (2002), 'Conceptualizing Moral Panic through a Moral Economy of Harm', *Critical Sociology,* 28(3): 311–34.

— (2008), 'Thinking Beyond Moral Panic: Risk, Responsibility, and the Politics of Moralization', *Theoretical Criminology,* 12(2): 173–90.

— (2011), 'Tightening the Focus: Moral Panic, Moral Regulation and Liberal Government', *British Journal of Sociology,* 62(3): 523–41.

Hier, S. P., Lett, D., Walby, K. and Smith, A. (2011), 'Beyond Folk Devil Resistance: Linking Moral Panic and Moral Regulation', *Criminology and Criminal Justice,* 11(3): 259–76.

Hollyzone (2006), *Chavs and the Working Class,* www.blogs.warwick.ac.uk/hollycruise/entry/chavs_and_the/ [accessed 22 November 2009].

Home, M. (2006), 'Beano Whips Up Storm with Neds Cartoon Strip', *Sunday Times,* 5 February.

Independent (2004), 'Sneering Britain', 28 January.

Johnson, P. (2008), '"Rude Boys": The Homosexual Eroticization of Class', *Sociology,* 42(1): 65–82.

Jokes Forum (2009), *Chavette Jokes,* www.jokesforum.com/adult-jokes/11047-chavette-jokes.html [accessed 2 November 2009].

Jones, O. (2011), *Chavs: The Demonization of the Working Class,* London: Verso.

Kobayashi-Hillary, N. (2008), "Brands and Class," unpublished paper presented at the Network for the Studies of Cultural Distinctions and Social Differention (SCUD) Workshop, University of Aalborg, Denmark.

Lawler, S. (2005a), 'Disgusted Subjects: The Making of Middle-Class Identities', *Sociological Review,* 53(3): 429–46.

— (2005b), 'Introduction: Class, Culture and Identity', *Sociology,* 39(5): 797–806.

le Grand, E. (2010), *Class, Place and Identity in a Satellite Town,* Stockholm: Acta Universitatis Stockholmiensis.

— (forthcoming). 'Class, Community and Belonging in a "Chav Town"', in P. Watt and P. Smets (eds), *Neighbourhood Belonging and Mobilities in the City and Suburb,* Basingstoke: Palgrave Macmillan.

Lewis, J. (2004), 'In Defence of Snobbery', *Daily Telegraph,* 31 January.

Liddle, R. (2004), 'Everyone Hates the White Working-Class Male', *Sunday Times,* 14 November.

McRobbie, A. and Thornton, S. L. (1995), 'Rethinking "Moral Panic" for Multi-mediated Social Worlds', *British Journal of Sociology,* 46(4): 559–74.

Metro (2005), 'Chav Teen Gets Asbo', 3 May.

Millie, A. (2008), 'Anti-Social Behaviour, Behavioural Expectations and Urban Aesthetic', *British Journal of Criminology,* 48(1): 379–94.

Mitch's Blog (2004), *Chavs – Is There Really Any Need?,* www.blogs.warwick.ac.uk/mwilson/entry/chavs_is_there/ [accessed 7 September 2009].

Moore, C. M. and Birtwistle, G. (2004), 'The Burberry Business Model: Creating an International Luxury Fashion Brand', *International Journal of Retail and Distribution Management,* 32(8): 412–22.

Moran, J. (2006), 'Milk Bars, Starbucks, and the Uses of Literacy', *Cultural Studies,* 20(6): 552–73.

Naylor, B. (2001), 'The "Bad Mother" in Media and Legal Texts', *Social Semiotics,* 11(2): 155–76.

Phoenix, A. (1996), 'Social Constructions of Lone Motherhood', in E. Bortoloaia Silva (ed.), *Good Enough Mothering? Feminist Perspectives on Lone Mothering*, London: Routledge, 175–90.

Raisborough, J. and Adams, M. (2008), 'Mockery and Morality in Popular Cultural Representations of the White, Working Class', *Sociological Research Online,* 13(6).

Savage, M. (2000), *Class Analysis and Social Transformation*, Maidenhead, Buckingham: Open University Press.

Skeggs, B. (1997), *Formations of Class and Gender*, London: Sage.

— (2004), *Class, Self, Culture*, London: Routledge.

Stacey, M. (1960), *Tradition and Change: A Study of Banbury*, Oxford: Oxford University Press.

Thomas, D. (2004), 'I'm a Chav Get Me out of Here', *Daily Mail,* 12 February.

Tungate, M. (2005), *Fashion Brands: Branding Style from Armani to Zara*, London: Kogan Page.

Tweedie, N. (2004), 'Cheltenham Ladies and the Chavs', *Daily Telegraph,* 13 December.

Tyler, I. (2008), '"Chav Mum Chav Scum"', *Feminist Media Studies,* 8(1): 17–34.

Urban Dictionary, 'asbo', www.urbandictionary.com/define.php?term=asbo [accessed 28 October 2012].

— 'chavs', www.urbandictionary.com/define.php?term=chavs [accessed 28 October 2012].

Veblen, T. ([1899] 2007), *The Theory of the Leisure Class*, Oxford: Oxford University Press.

Watt, P. (2006), 'Respectability, Roughness and "Race": Neighbourhood Place Images and the Making of Working-Class Social Distinctions in London', *International Journal of Urban and Regional Research,* 30(4): 776–97.

— (2009), 'Living in an Oasis: Middle-Class Disaffiliation and Selective Belonging in an English Suburb', *Environment and Planning A,* 41(12): 2874–92.

Webster, C. (2008), 'Marginalized White Ethnicity, Race and Crime', *Theoretical Criminology,* 12(3): 293–312.

Young, G. (2004), 'Good News for Chavs: They May Be Cool People Soon', *The Times,* 19 October.

Zatz, M. (1987), 'Chicano Youth Gangs and Crime: The Creation of a Moral Panic', *Crime, Law and Social Change,* 11(2): 129–58.

Part Four

Immigration, War and Terror

11

Moral Panic around the Burqa in France: An Eliasian Perspective

Aurélie Lacassagne

Introduction

A few years ago, France adopted a controversial law banning all religious signs from public schools. This was mainly a reaction to the increasing number of young Muslim girls wearing a veil (covering just the hair) and refusing to participate in some curricular activities, in contravention of a court ruling of 1989. But 2009 witnessed the emergence of a collective hysteria about Muslim women wearing the burqa (covering the whole body and face). The National Assembly even set up a commission on the topic, subsequently recommending the complete banning of the burqa in the public sphere. With some ease the issues came to cross almost all political party lines. Numerous articles and blogs in newspapers revealed the 'burqa affair' to be a highly contentious topic that, indeed, bears all the hallmarks of a collective moral panic. A range of volatile emotional responses continue to be expressed by French citizens on this matter. However, it appears that few people have seriously sought to rationalize the discourses implicated in this debate. In this way, it constitutes a good case study to employ as part of a more general reflection on the concept of moral panic.

This chapter will analyse this instance of moral panic by using an Eliasian perspective. In particular, it will make the link between this current social process and the long-term social processes of considering Muslims as 'outsiders'. In other words, it is centrally argued that one cannot understand this moral panic without a critical appreciation of the longer-term relationship between Europeans and the 'Turks' since the Crusades. By doing so, the chapter will highlight an enduring dichotomy that has existed throughout the longue durée between a 'civilized European' and a 'barbarian Muslim'. This dichotomy persists, but has more recently become reframed around a contemporary axis of 'civilization': the burqa is being constructed as an 'uncivilized sign', perhaps even a symptom of a more general 'decivilizing process', working counter to the 'civilized values' of France.

The 'burqa affair' in France as an example of a moral panic

Issue of concern

The burqa affair dates back to a decision of the French Highest Administrative Court (Conseil d'État) on 27 June 2008 (Conseil d'État 2008). In its ruling, the court confirmed a decision taken by the Ministry of Labour and Social Cohesion (16 May 2005) refusing the acquisition of French citizenship by a Moroccan woman. The rationale for the ruling advanced by the judges involved was as follows: 'if Ms A has a good master of the French language, she nevertheless has adopted a radical practice of her religion, which is incompatible with the essential values of the French community, and notably the principle of gender equality; therefore, she does not fulfil the condition of assimilation posited by article 21–4 of the civil code' (Conseil d'État 2008: 2). This was the first time the court denied citizenship using the practice of religion as a sign of non-assimilation. Until then, only radical Muslims who had pronounced fundamentalist public discourses were denied citizenship. So what was 'wrong' with Ms Faiza M. and the practice of her religion? Well, the government commissioner – Emmanuelle Prada-Bordenave – (in charge of giving legal advice to the government) found out in her investigation that Faiza M. was wearing the niqab. Le Bars (2008: 9) offers an account of the commissioner's inquiry:

> Faiza M. affirmed she was not veiled when she was living in Morocco and stated that 'she adopted this custom once in France on the demand of her husband and that she wears it more by habit than by conviction'. According to her own declarations, highlighted the commissioner, she does not go out often and lives outside the French society. She has no idea about secularism and voting rights. She lives under total submission to the family's men, husband, father and father-in-law. Faiza M. seems 'to find that normal, and the very idea of contesting this submission does not even cross her mind'.[1]

This court ruling was reported in news media. Experts – professors of law, anthropologists and sociologists – were called upon to explain why women

Table 11.1 Annual number of documents in *Le Monde* and *Libération* containing the word 'burqa'

Year	1999	2000	2001	2002	2003	2004	2005	2006	2007	2008
Number of documents	0	4	61	29	33	26	10	18	36	33

Table 11.2 2009 monthly breakdown of documents in *Le Monde* and *Libération* containing the word 'burqa'

January	February	March	April	May	June	July	August	September	October	November	December
1	1	6	2	0	34	51	18	6	18	23	65

Table 11.3 2010 monthly breakdown of documents in *Le Monde* and *Libération* containing the word 'burqa'

January	February	March	April	May	June	July
90	41	41	63	52	19	27

would wear the burqa and why it could be considered so incompatible with French republican values. A rudimentary analysis – literally, a frequency count of the word burqa in prominent articles – of the archives of two French daily newspapers, *Le Monde* and *Libération*, revealed a range of intriguing aspects to this phenomenon. In particular, the preliminary research revealed that even if this 'affair' is a French one, one cannot properly understand it independently of the wider international context and, more specifically, the war in Afghanistan. Tables 11.1 and 11.2 summarize the results (no results were omitted; they include all occurrences of the word burqa in all archived documents of both newspapers) (see also Table 11.3).

From the years 1999 to 2008, one might begin to discern the impact of international events simply by looking at the numerical fluctuations presented in the tables. In 1999 and 2000 there was almost no mention of the burqa – then a phenomenon completely unknown to most people in the West (it also shows that the West did not care a great deal about the plight of Afghan women at that time). Then came a surge in 2001. After the 9/11 events and the beginning of the war in Afghanistan, the burqa figures in a number of articles. There is another surge in articles mentioning the topic in the years 2007 and 2008. This corresponds to the development of the conflict: after the installation of Hamid Karzai as president of Afghanistan, and the recrudescence of violence. In the second half of the year

2008, the term burqa becomes increasingly used in the French national context following the June court decision. Perhaps surprisingly, the issue disappears from the media and public radar until the first anniversary of the court decision in June 2009 whereupon a communist MP, André Gerin, followed by 58 other MPs (3 Communists, 7 Socialists, 43 UMP, 2 Centrists, 3 others) co-signed a proposal to create a parliamentary commission of investigation on this matter. Mr Gerin in his role as mayor had shortly before refused to marry a couple because the woman was wearing a burqa. This parliamentary move forced the executive to undertake the initiative. On 22 June, in a speech delivered before the Congress in Versailles, President Sarkozy made a declaration stating 'the problem of the burqa is not a religious one. It is a problem of freedom and women's dignity. It is a sign of enslavement, it is sign of degradation. I want to say it solemnly: the burqa is not welcome in the French republic territory' (Le Bars 2009: 3). This set the tone of the debate which, since June 2009, has agitated French society in a manner and pattern characteristic of a moral panic. The commission was indeed created, and its report was made public in Autumn 2009. On 13 July 2010, the National Assembly passed a law banning the wearing of the burqa in all public places. More precisely – in a manner similar to the 2004 banning of religious signs at school – the burqa itself is not specifically mentioned: what is banned is the 'dissimulation of the face'. The bill was voted for by all right-wing MPs; except one, and some leftist MPs, the rest (most of the Socialists, Communists and the Greens) abstained because they wanted a ban in 'some' public places, not all of them. The Socialist Party underlined the 'juridical risk' of a total ban, arguing that the Constitutional Council may censor the bill. The Senate approved the bill in September 2010, which was promulgated a few days later.

Perhaps the most striking aspect of this affair, and what immediately invokes a key characteristic of a moral panic, is the ostensibly overwhelming consensus on this issue. There was very little public debate, except among jurists – and this argument pivoted centrally on which principle the banning should be based, and not whether or not the ban should come in to force.

Consensus

Chas Critcher identifies five powerful actors in the making of a moral panic, which he calls the 'five powerful Ps: the press and broadcasting; pressure groups and claim makers; politicians and government; police and law enforcement agencies; and public opinion' (2006: 4). In the case of the banning of the burqa in

France, these five actors have indeed worked well together to forge a nation-wide consensus.

The various media outlets immediately devoted considerable attention to the issue by publishing many editorials, news and 'expert' articles on the subject. Less commonly, they published 'real-life' stories of actual women wearing the burqa. The key television networks orchestrated organized debates. Most of the prominent online news articles contained a 'Reader's Response' section, allowing readers to react to the articles. As part of the research undertaken for this chapter, a discourse analysis of some of these web posts was undertaken. Two elements here must be noted: first of all, the number of comments posted was extremely high in many instances, particularly in comparison to posts relating to other highly topical concerns, notably the economic crisis. For example, there were 840 comments posted between 13 and 20 July 2010 on an article that simply announced the vote on the bill. Similarly, on a debate entitled 'Should the burqa be banned?' launched for its web readers by *Libération*, 4281 comments were posted within a few days.[2] Second, a lot of the posts further reinforced the 'consensus' that is believed to exist in the French society about the issue. Here is an archetypical example of a posted comment: 'When I think that we are sending troops to Afghanistan to defend democracy and that we have our "Taleban" at home, and that some are still prevaricating! In all seriousness, it is important that there is a republican consensus to show to the Islamists that the Republic is determined to have its values, law and principles respected.' (Kaoetic 2010).

Bertrand Mathieu (2010), professor of law at La Sorbonne, opened his arguments against the veil as follows: 'If the rejection of the integral veil is the object of a certain consensus in France, it is the juridical basis of the banning itself that is the topic of discussion'. The consensus has existed in the political class while the idea of a commission emerged. MPs from the four main parties (UMP, Socialists, Communists and Centrists) signed the resolution, and, unsurprisingly, the National Front was in favour of the banning of the burqa. Within the political elites, only the extreme-left (the various Trotskyite parties) and the Greens opposed the decision. During the following months, both these political factions were the only ones to voice differing opinions. The fact that it took just one year from the idea of a commission to the voting of a law – an extraordinarily fast 'policy-solving' pace – also reveals the degree of consensus generated among politicians and government.

Among the pressure groups and claim makers, one has to underline the important role played by various 'experts' who worked hand-in-hand with the media to defend the banning of the burqa. Interestingly, none of these experts took a stand against the banning, as if there were nobody against this move. More importantly, the authorities secured the approval of the official Muslim representatives. Trade unions were not heard from regarding the consequences of this banning in terms of access to school and job markets. Only feminist groups supporting the ban were heard in the media. This lack of counter-reaction as well as the consensus (that indeed continues to exist) shows the process of making a collective panic. Opponents were effectively silenced by the media.

Examples of articles of claimed experts include 'To Refuse the Burqa Is to Respect Islam', written by Dounia Bouzar, introduced as 'an anthropologist of religion, former qualified personality of the French Council of Muslim Cult' (Friday 18 July 2008, *Libération*, 22); 'A Way to Adopt the Stigmata by Which One Is Discriminated', Mohamed-Cherif Ferjani, professor of Arab-Muslim civilization in Lyon University (Friday 19 June 2009, *Libération*, 14); 'Burqa: Legal Bases on Dignity and Equality', interview with Pierre-Henri Prélot, Law professor (Saturday 20 June 2009, *Libération*, 16); 'Can We Ban the Integral Veil in the Name of the Principle of Dignity?', Bertrand Mathieu, Law professor at La Sorbonne (*Le Monde*, 30 April 2010); 'Integral Banning, a Danger for the Integrity of Liberties', Jean-Louis Halpérin, Law professor, Normale Sup (*Le Monde*, 13 May 2010).

These various titles set the tone of the discussion. The fundamental values of liberty, equality and dignity are called upon as if they had only one meaning and could not be subject to any interpretation. The use of these very important symbolic words for French people makes it almost impossible to be against the ban: posed in this way, opposition would mark oneself out as anti-democratic and anti-republican. The titles sound very assertive: they do not create any space for discussion and do not reflect the complexity of the question at stake. From a rhetorical perspective, well-known tools are used. For example, asking a question which contains its own answer through the manner of its construction, and the use of prescriptive sentences such as, 'to refuse the burqa is to respect Islam'.

Interestingly, a lot of articles in newspapers by self-professed experts were written by law professors. This reveals the strategy adopted: since the beginning, the question around the burqa has been predicated on legal grounds and construed in a legal fashion. The strategy is very efficient for several reasons: (1) a lack of general knowledge about law and its principles makes it difficult for opponents to argue against the proposals; (2) positivism is still very strong in law circles, law is viewed as objective. In France, the distinction between legality and legitimacy is very sharp; if it is a question of legality, it cannot be contested as if it were a question of legitimacy; (3) a Europeanization of the French society has involved – as for the European construction undertaken by the law – social questions increasingly being decided by legal experts rather than public debates and responsible politicians; (4) law is located at the intersection between politics, law enforcement and 'scientific expertise' which makes it easier to build a coalition between different agencies involved.

A notable absence in these debates is viewpoints from sociologists, for instance, to discuss the consequences of the ban on women's lives; the reason for their wearing the veil; the malaise it reveals about French national identity; the debates around multiculturalism, communitarianism and assimilation. Above all, no claimed experts reflected seriously on the 'unintended effects of the societal reaction' (Cohen [1972] 1980: 173); or 'unintended outcomes', as Elias would have put it, that the ban could have on Muslim women. Indeed, this 'attack' – as it may well be seen – this scapegoating, gossiping and isolation of some Muslim women with particular practices may in fact prompt other Muslim women to adopt the very same practices in a collective gesture of defiance, or in a political/identity-affirmation move. As Cohen ([1972] 1980: 162) wrote, 'the mere reporting of one event has, under certain circumstances, the effect of triggering off events of a similar order'.

Perhaps most significantly, the police and law enforcement agencies did not wait for the bill to be passed in order to take certain measures. The police fined a woman wearing a niqab who was driving in Nantes on 2 April 2010, arguing it was a danger because the niqab limited her field of vision. They used article 412–6 of the driving code concerning 'circulation in non-comfortable conditions' (AFP 2010). Some weeks later, the police reported and fined another woman in the North of France (*Libération* 2010). When these events happened, the bill was not yet passed. The timing for these policemen to use a hitherto unknown article of the driving code to fine these women is no coincidence. According to the first woman, she had been driving for about ten years with her niqab and had never previously been stopped. Notably, thus far, neither the police nor other law enforcement agencies have expressed concerns about the applicability of the ban.

As far as French public opinion is concerned, one also finds a remarkable consensus on the banning of the burqa. The analysis of hundreds of comments posted on the web demonstrates that only a handful of contributors were against the ban. What are the common themes found in such comments?

Many comments were directed towards ostensible concerns for the dignity of Muslim women. People were expressing their discomfort with seeing women totally veiled, typically exclaiming that it was 'humiliating' and disrespectful, and a mark of gender inequality. A lot of those who commented made a point to distinguish this practice and Islam. According to them, the wearing of the burqa had nothing to do with religion, but was 'a declaration of war against French values'. It was seen as undemocratic, uncivilized, from another age (the notion of Middle Ages appeared quite often). Another set of comments called for more efforts to integrate women who wear veils into French society, which meant respecting dress code norms. They noted that if French people had to go to Saudi Arabia, French women would have to be veiled. Paradoxically, a lot of the comments recognized that the issue had been exploited by the government and President Sarkozy.

Numerous surveys were conducted whose results serve to lend further support to the argument that a clear moral consensus had been mobilized. For instance, one survey (Sofres 2010) conducted in April 2010 asked the question: 'In your view, is the question of the burqa':

- 'A priority topic' (10%)
- 'An important topic but not a priority' (43%)
- 'A secondary topic' (30%)
- 'A topic we should not deal with' (15%)?

A majority of the respondents thought it was an important topic. The same survey asked about the ban, with the question 'Concerning the wearing of the burqa in France, would you say':

- 'It must be banned by law everywhere in France' (33%)
- 'It must be banned by law, but only in some public spheres' (31%)
- 'It must not be banned but the concerned population should be sensitized' (22%)
- 'Nothing must be done' (10%)
- 'No opinion' (4%)'?

About 64 per cent of the respondents favoured a legal ban of the burqa. The detailed results from the questionnaire show no significant differences according to the gender, age group or the occupation of the respondents.

A similar survey was conducted in January (Ipsos 2010) revealing comparable results but a slightly less favourable opinion (57%). The question was 'Are you totally in favour, rather in favour, rather opposed, or totally opposed to voting in a law banning the burqa in France':

- 'Totally in favour' (30%)
- 'Rather in favour' (27%)
- 'Rather opposed' (22%)
- 'Totally opposed' (15%)

Hostility

Hostility is a key characteristic of a social panic because as Critcher (2006: 9) points out, 'Defining, labelling and punishing their unacceptable behaviour confirms who we are, what we believe in or stand for and where we draw the boundary around our community. The need for such confirmation increases whenever established moral certainties no longer hold'. And indeed, the burqa as a social panic did not emerge and crystallize in a social vacuum. Rather it developed at a point in time where French people were questioning what constitutes their national identity. This is by no means a new line of questioning. It has been in part facilitated by (1) the problem of integration which French immigrant populations have experienced acutely since the 1980s; (2) European integration and European citizenship developed in the Maastricht treaty in 1992; (3) the different works of memory (on the Shoah, the Algerian War and the colonization) the French State and population started to reflect upon by the 1990s – these are not without consequence for questions of national identity. This concern has also been exploited by the government, who decided to launch an ill-fated 'debate on national identity'. The debate ultimately served only to further polarize arguments, failing to achieve any kind of positive resolution or outcome.

This national identity crisis ran in tandem with a moral crisis, itself deeply rooted in historical developments which include: secularization at the turn on the twentieth century; 1968 and the emergence of new social movements (ecology, feminism); the development of the LGBT (lesbian, gay, bisexual and transgender) movements; the increasingly significant role of money in a society which remains rooted in a catholic habitus (where money is characteristically understood to be a source of evil); and an endemic circle of violence in which the balance between self-control and external constraints has possibly tilted in favour of the latter, to speak in Eliasian terms. Therefore, it is no surprise that women wearing the burqa have frequently been used as scapegoats. As Goode and Ben-Yehuda (1994: 52) underline,

> When a society's moral boundaries are sharp, clear, and secure, and the central norms and values are strongly held by nearly everyone, moral panics rarely grip its members – nor do they need to. However, when the moral boundaries are fuzzy and shifting and often seem to be contested, moral panics are far more likely to seize the members of society.

That the '5P's chose to frame the debates in a legal fashion should not obscure the fact that the debate was and is about *moral* values. Once again, the web commentaries analysed for this chapter are consistent in this respect. Most of them make direct references to values: the comments typically revolve around the dichotomy between an 'Us' and 'Them' (we will see later that this dichotomy aligns to a 'civilized' and 'barbaric' dichotomy) – a dichotomization that is based upon stereotyping (Goode and Ben-Yehuda 2006: 50). Thus, according to the commentators (but also more implicitly in the articles of claimed experts) women who wear the burqa can be divided into two homogenous groups. The first group comprises women of a foreign origin forced to wear the burqa because their fathers, brothers and husbands are 'fanatical' and 'primitive'. Women in this group are characteristically understood to have no agency and no education. Strangely, and probably because of this level of hostility, few commentators express empathy for them but agree that we should help them; that is, we should assimilate them, by force if necessary. The second group is made up of women of French origin who have converted to Islam. They wear the burqa as a mark of identity and as a means of sending a pointed cultural and political message. Women in this second group are generally perceived as educated, more agential, but much more dangerous. They too, it is typically held, are fanatics. They face a much higher level of hostility than the first group. However, the French public's real issue with these women is not so much their radical political commitment, but the fact that they are French ('true French'). They reveal the main problems of the society: the moral and national identity crises. They are mirrors of the failures of the French society. They are the real 'deviants, bad guys, undesirables, outsiders, criminals, the underworld, disreputable folk' (Goode and Ben-Yehuda 2006: 52).

Volatility

The question of volatility is interesting insofar as it relates to the short-term and long-term processes discussed later in this chapter. As Goode and Ben-Yehuda (2006: 55) propose, 'moral panics are volatile; they erupt fairly suddenly (although they may lie dormant or latent for long period of time, and may reappear from time to time) and, nearly as suddenly, subside'. The tables shown above concerning the number of occurrences of the term burqa illustrate the sudden appearance of this question, and in some cases, its equally sudden disappearance. Before June 2008, the term burqa was used in French newspapers to speak mainly about the situation of Afghani women in the context of the war. It started to be used in the French context after the court decision refusing citizenship to the previously discussed Moroccan woman. In the same vein, it is noteworthy that as soon as the bill was passed in July 2010, the media became quiet on this topic. New scapegoats were found in August: the gypsies (unfortunately very old targets of recurrent and very volatile moral panics). The Jew, the Arab and the Romani have long been traditional targets of French moral panics. The Muslim woman is a new actor on the scene. Her arrival dates back to the end of the 1980s when an increasing number of young Muslim girls started to wear headscarves at school. This generated considerable social turmoil at the time, culminating in 1989 in a jurisprudential ruling: the Conseil d'État decided that they could wear the headscarf so long as it was not preventing them from following the nation-wide curriculum. A compromise was made satisfying most parties; Muslim women disappeared from the media circus. Then, in the first decade of the twenty-first century (2000s), they reappeared: the compromise of 1989 was increasingly challenged by young girls who refused to go to music classes or to the swimming pool for their sport classes. Of course, this happened in the international context of the 9/11 events and the scapegoating, stereotyping and 'otherization' of Muslim populations in the 'West'. In turn, this led to the adoption of a law banning all religious signs from French schools in 2004. The major intention behind this law was the banning of the headscarf. But this could be achieved only by banning all religious signs, so as not to give the impression of targeting a specific population. The same process was used in the 2010 law banning the covering of the face in public spaces, not specifically the burqa or the niqab. Once again, Muslim women disappeared from the radar to reappear – completely veiled – in 2008. Muslim women have become 'traditional' targets of moral panics, reappearing and disappearing from the public scene depending on the mood, fear and anxiety of the French population. A feminist reading (which is somewhat beyond the scope of this chapter to develop in full here) of these processes would be helpful to understand these trends. Since the outburst of violence in the 'suburbs' in the 1980s (with the underlying but key factor of the Algerian War), the French population have 'chosen' Muslim men as a principal scapegoat; they have replaced the Jews (who cannot be openly used as a scapegoat because of the collective guilt developed around the Shoah). Whenever it becomes too difficult to deal frankly with Muslim men, it is their wives and daughters – Muslim women – who become the target. Thus, the shifting targets of social concern are indicative of a shifting fulcrum: whenever the balance of power tilts a little towards Muslim men, non-Muslim French people typically counter-attack Muslim women. Cohen ([1972] 1980: 198) is right in affirming that a moral panic is always linked to a conflict of interest:

> More fundamentally, a theory of moral panic, moral enterprise, moral crusades or moral indignation needs to relate such reactions to conflicts of interests – at community and societal levels – and the presence of power differentials which leave some group vulnerable to such attacks. The manipulation of appropriate symbols – the process which sustains moral campaigns, panics and crusades – is made much easier when the object of attack is both highly visible and structurally weak.

Finally, as Cohen ([1972] 1980: 53) puts it, 'It's not only this'. It is not just about the burqa or the niqab, it is about immigration and its perverse association with delinquency in the suburbs, jihad, terrorism and above all national identity crisis, the crisis of the Republican model of integration. Cohen ([1972] 1980: 57) also explains that 'the process of spurious attribution is not, of course, random' and later that '[a]ttitudes and opinions are often bolstered up by legends and myths'. The racial stereotyping, which exists in France concerning Muslim populations, makes these women easy targets. The defiance and hostility towards them also echo the stories of the Algerian War about women transporting weapons in their baskets (Pontecorvo 1966) or under their robes. In the current international political context this defiance and hostility echoes that of Muslim women terrorists in Chechnya, Palestine and Iraq (see Sjoberg and Gentry 2007). Even though there have been only a few instances of such activity, it has been reported by media such that, step by step, a mental construction of 'Muslim women as terrorists hiding weapons under their robes' has emerged and sticks in people's minds. Cohen ([1972] 1980: 77) refers to part of these processes as 'sensitization'.

Disproportionality

If the four above criteria can be said to be active or efficient variables, the criterion of disproportionality can be said to be an enabling or permissive variable.[3] In other words, disproportionality is essential, necessary, for processes to qualify as moral panic. When disproportionality is combined with the four other criteria, one faces a strong case of moral panic.

In the burqa affair, the media hype, the grandiloquent discourse of the President in Versailles, the information mission, the symbolic resolution of the National Assembly, the law focusing on the burqa is disproportional – again a classic hallmark of a moral panic. First, it is disproportional because of the number of women actually wearing the burqa.[4] The first approximation of the number of women in France were regularly wearing the burqa that circulated in the media was 367 (Coroller 2009). This figure came from the Renseignements Généraux (French Central Directorate of General Intelligence, that is, intelligence services of the French Police). The Information Report of the 'Information Mission on the practice of the wearing of the integral veil on the national territory' refers to that figure stating

> A press article came out in July indicating the figure of 367: it was unconvincing . . . More importantly, according to a study made in the summer and fall 2009, whose figures were confirmed by the hearing of the Home Minister, Mr. Brice Hortefeux. If we could conclude to the quasi-inexistence of the phenomenon in the beginning of the years 2000, today one observes a multiplication of the number of integrally-veiled women on the national territory. The above mentioned study evaluates at 1900, the number of women wearing the integral veil, in the case in point the niqab, phenomenon incidentally difficult to quantify but very likely in augmentation. (Mission d'information sur la pratique du port du voile intégral sur le territoire nationale 2010: 28)

This extract exemplifies many of the core issues discussed thus far. First, why should the figure 367 not be convincing? It was approximated by an agency of the Home Ministry, the same institution that, a few weeks later, produced another report with the figure 1900. Second, from a scientific standpoint, how can it be claimed that the practice was quasi-inexistent in the early 2000s considering no study was done at that time? Third, the reporters themselves admit it is difficult to quantify; however, after stating this claim the reporters maintain that the phenomenon is 'in all likelihood' increasing. Making the fourth point. But there

---

Presence of the integral veil on the national territory

1900 might wear the integral veil on the national territory, amongst whom 270 in the overseas: 250 in La Réunion and 20 in Mayotte. The phenomenon of the wearing of the integral veil concerns all metropolitan regions, except maybe Corsica. The main concerned regions are:

- Ile-de-France [Paris region] (50% of the women wearing the niqab on the Mainland);
- Rhônes-Alpes [Lyons region] (160 recorded cases);
- Provence-Alpes-Côte-d' Azur [South East region] (a hundred of recorded cases)

Nevertheless, the wearing of the veil appears circumscibed to urban zones and concertrated in sensitive neighbourhoods of big cities.

(According to the data extracted from a study made beteween August and December 2009 by the Home Ministry)

Figure 11.1 Breakdown of the Information Report of the 'Information Mission on the practice of the wearing of the integral veil on the national territory'
Source: Mission d'information sur la pratique du port du voile intégral sur le territoire nationale (2010: 29).

is more to this. A breakdown of the study is given in the Report under a table format that is reproduced in Figure 11.1.

How is it that MPs – who should have basic education – can both recognize the difficulty in collecting data on this issue and, simultaneously, posit such spuriously precise data? Any first-year undergraduate university student who is taught the very basics of methodology would be prompted to question the table. Surely such precision in the (rounded) numbers is not possible? Moreover, how is it that public servants – above all policemen – agreed to undertake such an investigation? France, we must remember, to this day lives in the shadows of the traumas of the Second World War. Significantly, these include memories of French police cooperation with the Nazi regime in the arrest and deportation of French and foreign Jews. The relative effectiveness of the massive arrests of Jews was possible only because the police had racial and ethnic profiles of the population. Since that time, it is forbidden for French authorities to collect any data making reference to racial, ethnic or religious background. This is – or maybe this was – a sacrosanct principle in France. In his hearing, the Home Minister, Mr Hortefeux, presented demographic data about burqa-wearing women, such that one can learn, for example, that 'half of them are 30 years of age or less, and the vast majority, around 90%, were under the age of 40 . . . two thirds were French-born . . . Roughly a quarter had converted to Islam' (Mission d'information sur la pratique du port du voile intégral sur le territoire nationale 2010: 42). How could the minister know these details? Did the police interview the alleged 1,900 women wearing the burqa? They must already have known these demographic details. Ironically, when one does look at the transcript of the hearing of Hortefeux (Mission 2010: 611–12) in the Report, he says:

> The wearing of the Afghani burqa, which is to be distinguished from other feminine Islamic effects by the complete dissimulation of the body but also eyes, hidden by a mesh screen, is not attested in France. It is different with the niqab, traditional dress worn in some Gulf States, that covers the whole body but is often open around the eyes.

First, if Mr Hortefeux really thinks that there are no women in France wearing the Afghani burqa, it is a confirmation that his services have not set foot in these 'sensitive neighbourhoods' – they do, indeed, exist. Second, Mr Hortefeux shows some ignorance of his subject matter when he uses the adjective 'often' for the niqab: by definition, the niqab is a veil that leaves the area around the eyes clear. Third, the fact that the media, the president, the Mission and other claimed experts have been focusing on the burqa for two years – using that specific word (even if sometimes they were also referring to the niqab) – is all the more surprising when one considers that, according to the home minister himself, it is not attested that women with burqa are in France.

Ultimately, as Mrs Badinter – a famous French feminist philosopher – told the Mission, it is not important how many people are wearing the burqa (Mission d'information sur la pratique du port du voile intégral sur le territoire nationale 2010: 333). It is the supposed transgression of the values and principles of French society that matters most. Even if it were two persons, action would be taken. She has a point. But the reaction is disproportionate compared to the threat. Even if one admits it is an unacceptable threat and challenge to French societal values, the ban is counter-productive. As many have predicted, there is a good chance that this law will be challenged before European courts (both the European Court of Justice and the European Court of Human Rights) who will likely condemn France, because the ban is likely to be considered as disproportional compared to the risk and/or infringement to freedom of religion.

The moral panic around the burqa in France is also disproportionate if one considers that the media hype, discussions, legislative processes set in motion to address this 'problem', are set against the backdrop of an extraordinarily difficult domestic economic period – with a recession, skyrocketing unemployment, housing and poverty issues and the more general Euro crisis, to say nothing of the gloomy and bleak international context.

Finally, the law is disproportionate in its terms. A woman risks a fine of 150 euros and/or a citizenship internship. Moreover, any person obliging a woman to wear an integral veil is liable up to a one-year prison sentence and a fine of 30,000 euros. Why should these women risk having to pay a fine? Why should not the person obliging the wearing of the veil be sent for a citizenship internship? What could be the virtue of sending such people (particularly as they themselves are commonly held to be victims of an oppressive religion) to prison? How might incarceration be said to facilitate their integration into French society?

'Thickening' the moral panic concept in an Eliasian perspective

Short social processes intertwined in long social processes

Elias, in the pure tradition of the school of the *Annales*, enjoined sociologists to look closely at the intersection of long-term and short-term processes. One of the fundamental tenets of Elias' sociology is the idea that there is no absolute 'beginning' to any process; in other words, that the social reality unfolding in front of us is always the outcome of older social processes. There is no beginning, there is no end; as Elias (1991: 27; see also 159–60) puts it, 'There is no zero-point of the social relatedness of the individual, no "beginning" or sharp break when he steps into society as if from outside as a being untouched by the network and then begins to link up with other human beings'. It is at the same time the rejection of teleological explanation and metaphysical – disguised as rational and scientific – discourses of an 'origin'. This is the first Eliasian lesson social scientists engaged with the concept of moral panic could use to thicken their epistemological and theoretical apparatus. Historically, where do instances of moral panic come from? How do they unfold within the longue durée (see Elias 1987: xxii)? Seeking to elucidate and trace the different historical layers and processes within which cases of moral panic are embedded and inscribed can bring a deeper understanding of the social phenomenon at stake.

In terms of the case discussed here, one cannot fully understand how the phenomenon of the moral panic around the burqa developed without a broader historical understanding. In the first part, we have briefly inscribed this process in three generations: the beginning of the 2000s with the battle over religious signs at school; the 1980s with the rise of a malaise in the *banlieues* (the French suburbs), increasing tensions between Muslim populations and other French people; and the 1950s and 1960s with the Algerian war. Such contextualization can, loosely speaking, be said to extend only to a relatively short-term *durée*. Yet, these realities are outcomes of much deeper and longer-lasting social processes: an ancient dichotomy between the 'civilized European' and the 'Barbaric Turk' that has existed at least since the Crusades. For centuries, Europeans – the French among them – have developed an 'other'. This 'other' has variously been constructed around the figure of the Turk, the Arab, the Ottoman and, most recently, the Muslim. As Edward Said (1979: 1–2) pointed out in the opening of his seminal book on the topic, 'The Orient has helped to define Europe (or the West) as its constraining image, idea, personality, experience'. The stereotypical and historical figure of the Turk has acted as a mirror for Europeans to develop an identity of the modern, the rational, the civilized reflection of their self-image. Multiple examples of this otherization are well-known. French literature is a prime example of how a mystified image of the Orient has been diffused. And because most French children at school have to read extracts or full texts of *The Persian Letters* by Montesquieu; of *Zadig* by Voltaire; of *Salammbô* by Flaubert; of *Les Orientales* by Victor Hugo; of *Voyages en Orient* by Nerval; to cite just a few, this Oriental literary imaginary moulds the actual political and personal imagination of generations of French people. In this way, literature can be understood to be simultaneously constitutive of, and constituted by, social reality. Unfortunately, there is not space here to deconstruct these various literary discourses (in the case of Nerval and Flaubert it has been partly undertaken by Said). But it is important to note that these literary discourses create two imaginaries: one about the Turkic man, the Arab man, the Muslim man, the Persian man; another one about the Turkic woman, the Arab woman, the Muslim woman, the Persian woman.

Most importantly, this essentialized Arab woman has been fantasized. She is the object of a multitude of myths, and especially of sexual fantasy. Accordingly, we can see how the veil has long been an object of excitement. Let us first consider one example from Voltaire. Zadig, after a long separation with Astarté, finds her in the garden of Ogun.

His voice and the words he uttered roused the lady. Lifting her veil with a trembling hand, she looked at Zadig, and uttering a tender cry of joy mingled with surprise, she yielded to all the varied emotions which beset her and fell fainting into 'his arms' (Voltaire 1964: 80).

Astarté tells Zadig about her adventure after her flight from the Babylonian court: 'The messengers who were looking for me did not know me by sight. I had scarcely ever unveiled myself, except only to you, in the presence of my husband and at his orders' (Voltaire 1964: 81).

As far as Nerval is concerned, Said (1979: 182) explained: 'He is predisposed to recognize that the Orient is "le pays des rêves et de l'illusion" [the land of dreams and illusions], which, like the veils he sees everywhere in Cairo, conceal a deep, rich fund of female sexuality.' And in relation to Flaubert, Said (1979: 187) points out:

> The Oriental woman is an occasion and an opportunity for Flaubert's musings; he is entranced by her self-sufficiency, by her emotional carelessness, and also by what, lying next to him, she allows him to think. Less a woman than a display of impressive but verbally inexpressive femininity, Kuchuk is the prototype of Flaubert's Salammbô and Salomé, as well as of all the versions of carnal female temptation to which his Saint Anthony is subject. Like the Queen of Sheba (who also danced 'The Bee') she could say – were she able to speak – 'Je ne suis pas une femme, je suis un monde' [I am not a woman, I am a world]. Looked at from another angle Kuchuk is a disturbing symbol of fecundity, peculiarly Oriental in her luxuriant and seemingly unbounded sexuality.

He makes clear that

> In all of his novels Flaubert associates the Orient with the escapism of sexual fantasy. Emma Bovary and Frédéric Moreau pine for what in their drab (or harried) bourgeois lives they do not have, and what they realize they want comes easily to their daydreams packed inside Oriental clichés: harems, princesses, princes, slaves, veils, dancing girls and boys, sherbets, ointments, and so on. (Said 1979: 190)

While Montesquieu wrote the *Persian Letters*, France was discovering the *One Thousand and One Nights* translated and published by Galland in 1711 and a Persian version (*One Thousand and One Days*) translated by Pétis de La Croix in 1712. These stories were an immediate success throughout Europe, contributing immensely to mould a mythical image of the Arab/Persian/Oriental Woman. The fantasy of Scheherazade still resonates in the minds, hearts and bodies of many young European males. This myth of the hypersexualized and essentialized Oriental woman is not only found in literature, but also in many other arts by figures such as Pier Paolo Pasolini (cinema), Fritz Lang (cinema), Rimsky-Korsakov (classical music) and Ravel (again, classical music), to name but a few. Scheherazade has even invaded the virtual world of video games (see Yamanaka and Nishio 2006). She is an atemporal and aspatial icon of popular culture and as such has participated and still participates in the European/French perception of the Muslim woman.

Elias taught us to look at social processes as invariably simultaneously psycho and social processes – both being inherently intertwined:

> The structures of the human psyche, the structures of human society and the structures of human history are indissolubly complementary, and can only be studied in conjunction with each other. They do not exist and move in reality with the degree of isolation assumed by current research. They form, with other structures, the subject matter of the single human science. (Elias 1991: 36)

Now, the fairy tales of the *One Thousand and One Nights* have socialized Europeans in the same manner as European fairy tales like those of Grimm and Andersen. But we also know, thanks to Bruno Bettelheim (1976), that fairy tales have an important psychological function. From this long-term process of picturing the Muslim woman as a Scheherazade, there has emerged an imprint of the 'other' Muslim woman forged deep within a shared internalized habitus. Perhaps this helps explain why French men become so annoyed at the sight of Muslim women hidden behind their burqas? Is it that they want to see their eyes, guess the forms of their bodies? In a manner redolent of Said's notion of the 'Freudian Orient', their fantasy is beyond reach: hidden behind the bars of the burqa. This socio-psychological and historical perspective gives us a better understanding of why such a collective hysteria emerged concerning a few thousand women wearing the burqa. Ultimately, they do not disturb anybody, but they disrupt something deeply internalized: a centuries-old fantasy of the Muslim woman. This is not to say that on a short-term basis, the feminist narrative used by bloggers in their verbal attacks against the burqa has to be dismissed. But there exist several layers of habitus that explain such a powerful reaction as a moral panic. 'In the present structure of human society, by contrast, the expression "we", and so, too, the social habitus of individuals in a wider sense, has many layers' (Elias 1991: 202; see also 183).

If moral panics are intense emotional moments, figurational sociology is certainly well-equipped to deal with these as it takes into consideration the 'experiential':

> Hence, problems of drives, and drive-control, of emotions and emotional control, of knowledge and reflection as controllers or, alternatively, as dependents of emotions and drives – in short, the experiential aspects of people – play in figurational sociology no less a part than the visible movements of people's skeletal muscles that are singled out by behaviourists and action theorists. (Elias 1987: 116)

Civilizing and decivilizing processes

The civilizing process experienced by French people over the course of history means that they restrain their use of physical violence in their society. French people can no longer express through physical violence their anger at women hiding their bodies behind the burqa. Therefore, they have recourse to two forms of violence: verbal violence and legal violence with the use of legal bureaucracy to ban the burqa. So paradoxically, this instance of moral panic is in many ways a highly 'civilized' response. As Elias (1987: 111) pointed out, 'The differences in the levels of civilized conduct correspond to differences in the level of danger and danger-control in different spheres of life. The difficulty is, as has been shown, that the interdependence between danger-control and self-control is circular'. This instance of moral panic is an indicator of a tilting of the balance between the self-control and the external constraints within the French figuration because, as explained earlier, French people feel an increased danger and insecurity about their own national habitus and identity. Habitus involves a continuous moulding of the personality structure of the individuals. It refers to 'ways of feeling, thinking and speaking, to aspirations and moral precepts as well as ways of being, acting and behaving' (Delzescaux 2002: 55). In this respect, the outburst of a moral panic case can equally be perceived as a form of 'decivilizing' processes. It is a symbolical form of violence that displays not only the French national identity crisis but also the French state crisis. For Elias, the development of the modern state is intrinsically linked to civilizing processes. The failure of the republican model of integration in the French nation of Muslim populations; the emergence and development of a European identity; the rise of individualism; liquid modernity; the loss of prestige; the historical shame of the role played by France in the Holocaust; and the brutish decolonization processes (especially in Algeria) represent a series of factors that contributes to the identity crisis experienced by the French, to a questioning of their national habitus. These represent external constraints that increasingly challenge the self-control of individuals. This malaise is dealt with in a characteristically symbolical fashion: the banning of the burqa.

Moreover, an important aspect of the civilizing process as described by Elias refers to norms and habits as well as changes in attitude towards relations between sexes. In particular, sexuality has become associated with embarrassment and shame ([1939] 2000: 142–160). The civilizing process centrally involves a shift towards increasing self-control through the development of shame, repulsion and embarrassment – particularly concerning animal aspects of human conduct, principally sexuality. Sexual fantasy is a way of dealing with sexual drives and impulses; it is an expression of the sexual self-control and self-restraint. We have noted the importance played by the myth of the Oriental woman in the European sexual fantasy. Even without resorting fully to psychoanalysis, it is easy to understand how the complete veiling of these women conflicts with the expression of sexual fantasy. One way of dealing with these urges and increasing self-control has been the establishment of norms and places where instincts could be expressed but controlled. Elias and Dunning (1986), for example, have provided a detailed discussion of sport as a case in point. If one looks closely at the case of France, the dominant patterning of self-control is characteristically one involving high degrees of restraint. This is particularly the case when one considers the practices and codes on French beaches. France is most likely the country most conducive to showing your naked body on a beach – which again reveals a high degree of 'accomplishment' in the maintenance of 'civilized' restraints, predicated as such norms are on a very high degree of mutually assured self-control. But this extremely high degree of self-control is not without its contradictions. Always having to refrain and restrain: tensions, drives, urges, desires and emotions can become in and of themselves the sources of stress and pain. My hypothesis would be that the moral panic around the burqa thus represents an expression of this pain and stress. The burqa prevents the possibility of psychologically fantasizing about women's bodies by hiding them. The wearing of the burqa is like taking away the last sexual toy that French men have at their disposal.

Established and outsiders

In their study of Winston Parva, Elias and Scotson ([1965] 1994: xviii) highlighted how 'exclusion and stigmatisation of the outsiders by the established group were thus powerful weapons used by the latter to maintain their identity, to assert their superiority, keeping others firmly in their place'. The same points can be made about moral panics. Therefore, we can certainly learn from this seminal study and integrate it in our discussion. In particular, the established/ outsiders framework can be useful to better understand cases of moral panics as it brings a figurational perspective based on the dynamics of interdependence. The focal point of an established/outsider figuration is the 'uneven balance of power and the tensions inherent in it' ([1965] 1994: xx). Therefore, theoretically, ontologically and epistemologically, moral panics studies would be improved by working within a figurational framework that rejects both individualist and holist approaches. As Elias and Scotson ([1965] 1994: 170) pointed out,

> Individuals always come in configurations and configurations of individuals are irreducible . . . To say that individuals come in configurations means that the starting point for every sociological enquiry is a plurality of individuals who in one or the other way are interdependent. To say that configurations are irreducible means they can neither be explained in terms which imply that they exist in some ways independently of individuals, nor in terms which imply that individuals exist in some ways independently of them.

Implicitly more than explicitly, the study of Winston Parva also appears to be very much informative about time and duration discussions. If it is true that a case of moral panic emerges and disappears within a short period of time, it is also true that it cannot happen without underlying reasons inscribed in duration and that their disappearance may also be (always?) latency (or a latent period). In other words, moral panics may be an unintended outcome of a gap between a deeply internalized 'we-image' that no longer matches with the historical conditions in which the group lives. The group does not yet know how to handle change of 'we-identity' and accordingly develops fear and discomfort, finding scapegoats to blame.

> A striking example of this in our time is that of the we-image and we-ideal of once-powerful nations whose superiority in relation to others has declined. Their members may suffer for centuries because the group charismatic we-ideal, modelled on an idealized image of themselves in the days of their greatness, lingers on for many generations as a model they feel they ought to live up to them. They may *know* of the change as a fact, while their belief in their special group charisma and the attitudes, their behavioural strategy which goes with it, persists unchanged as fantasy shield, which prevents them from *feeling* the change and, therefore, from being able to adjust to the changed conditions of their group image and their group strategy. (Elias and Scotson [1965] 1994: xliii)

This applies perfectly to our case: the French do not know how to manage the change, the fact that France has lost its glory; that the French identity no longer can be defined as a civilized and superior identity. It is, of course, no longer the nineteenth century, but the comparison remains pertinent. For example, the same kind of relational pivot also applies to mods and rockers: their appearance and behaviours were seen to stand in total contradistinction from the we-image of the established group – well-dressed British men and women, naturally conscious of their superiority and lead in the world.

Often enough, phenomena of moral panics as figurations of established/ outsiders engender forms of 'structural violence' to use Galtung's terminology (1971). In other words, the stigmatization, otherization, exclusion of a group becomes internalized by this group which, on the one hand, reinforces the perceived superiority of the established group, and on the other, makes more difficult a change in the balance of power between the two groups.

Conclusion

I have demonstrated that the burqa affair in France constitutes a classic example of a moral panic. I have also advanced some elements of the Eliasian approach that could be of use theoretically to 'thicken' the concept of moral panic. First, moral panics have to be approached as historical processes on the longue durée. Second, moral panics have be approached as simultaneously social and psychological processes. These two approaches require the introduction of a discussion on the several layers of social and national habitus in order to obtain a better understanding of the underlying reasons for the panic. Third, moral panics have to be approached as decivilizing processes (despite their advancement often in the name of 'civilization') as they represent a tilting of the balance between self-control and external constraints in favour of the latter. Fourth, moral panics have to be approached as figurations, *id est* as processes between two interdependent groups of people engaged in relations of power.

Notes

1 The two quotes within this quote are excerpts of the commissioner's report of 2005.
2 As a point of comparison, an article by Kostas Vergopoulos, an economics professor, on the risk of a continental deflation following the Greek and Euro crisis published in *Libération* on 27 May 2010, received just one comment.
3 I have borrowed this distinction from Alexander Wendt (1999: 343) in his discussion of the causes of collective identity.
4 I have adopted the terminology burqa, and I have focused on this case, but it must be noted that the debates also extend in many important respects to women wearing the niqab. As I show, the authorities seem to have somewhat contradictory discourses on these two forms of veiling, often conflating or confusing the two.

Bibliography

AFP (2010), 'La Conductrice Verbalisée Pour Niqab au Volant se Défend au Tribunal', *Libération*, 28 June, www.liberation.fr/societe/0101643948-la-conductrice-verbalisee-pour-niqab-au-volant-se-defend-au-tribunal [accessed 18 August 2010].

Bettelheim, B. (1976), *The Uses of Enchantment: The Meaning and Importance of Fairy Tales*, New York: Knopf.

Cohen, S. ([1972] 1980), *Folk Devils and Moral Panics*, New York: St Martin's Press.

Conseil d'État (2008), Judgement no.286798, reading of Friday 27 June, http://arianeinternet.conseil-etat.fr/arianeinternet/ViewRoot.asp?View=Html&DMode=Html&PushDirectUrl=1&Item=1&fond=DCE&Page=1&querytype=advanced&NbEltPerPages=4&Pluriels=True&dec_id_t=286798 [accessed 18 August 2010].

Coroller, C. (2009), 'Niqab 'Une loi Serait Contre-Productive', *Libération*, 14 November, www.liberation.fr/societe/0101602872-niqab-une-loi-serait-contre-productive [accessed 18 August 2010].

Critcher, C. (2006), 'Introduction: More Questions Than Answers', in C. Critcher (ed.), *Critical Readings: Moral Panics and the Media*, Maidenhead, Buckingham: Open University Press.

Delzescaux, S. (2002), *Norbert Elias: Civilisation et Décivilisation*, Paris: L'Harmattan.

Elias, N. (1987), *Involvement and Detachment*, Oxford: Blackwell.

— (1991), *The Society of Individuals*, London: Blackwell.

— ([1939] 2000), *The Civilizing Process*, London: Blackwell.

Elias, N. and Dunning E. (1986), *Quest for Excitement: Sport and Leisure in the Civilizing Process*, London: Blackwell.

Elias, N. and Scotson, J. ([1965] 1994), *The Established and the Outsiders*, London: Sage.

Galtung, J. (1971), 'A Structural Theory of Imperialism', *Journal of Peace Research*, 8(2): 81–117.

Goode, E. and Ben-Yehuda, N. (1994), *Moral Panics: The Social Construction of Deviance*, Oxford: Blackwell.

— (2006), 'Moral Panics: An Introduction', in C. Critcher (ed.), *Critical Readings: Moral Panics and the Media*, Maidenhead, Buckingham: Open University Press.

Ipsos (2010), 'Près de Six Français sur dix Favorables au Vote d'une loi Interdisant le Port de la Burqa', 18 January, www.ipsos.fr/CanalIpsos/articles/2969.asp [accessed 18 August 2010].

Kaoetic (2010), 'Liberté Contre l'Obscurantisme!', *Libération* blog following the publication of the article 'Voile Intégral: Ayrault Dégaine sa Proposition de Loi', Friday 30 April.

Le Bars, S. (2008), 'Une Marocaine en Burqa se Voit Refuser la Nationalité Française', *Le Monde*, Saturday 12 July, 9.

— (2009), 'Pour M. Sarkozy, "Ce N'est Pas un Problème Religieux"', *Le Monde*, Wednesday 24 June, 3.

Libération (2010), 'En Bref', Friday 4 June, www.liberation.fr/societe/0101639373-en-bref [accessed 18 August 2010].

Mathieu, B. (2010), 'Peut-on Interdire le Voile Intégral au Nom du Principe de Dignité?', *Le Monde*, Friday 30 April, www.lemonde.fr/idees/article/2010/04/30/peut-on-interdire-le-voile-integral-au-nom-du-principe-de-dignite-par-bertrand mathieu_1345094_3232.html?xtmc=peut_on_interdire_le_voile_integral&xtcr=1 [accessed 18 August 2010].

Mission d'information sur la pratique du port du voile intégral sur le territoire nationale (2010), *Rapport D'Information*, deposed to the Presidency of the National Assembly on 26 January, report no. 2262, www.assemblee-nationale.fr/13/pdf/rap-info/i2262.pdf [accessed 18 August 2010].

Pontecorvo, G. (Director) (1966), *The Battle of Algiers* [motion picture], Criterion.

Said, E. (1979), *Orientalism*, New York: Vintage Books.

Sjoberg, L. and Gentry, C. (2007), *Mothers, Monsters, Whores: Women's Violence in Global Politics*, London: Zed.

Sofres (2010), 'Les Français et la burqa', detailed results of the survey made on 22 and 23 April, www.tns-sofres.com/_assets/files/2010.04.24-burqua.pdf [accessed 18 August 2010].

Vergopoulos, K. (2010), 'La Menace d'une Déflation Continentale', *Libération*, 27 May.

Voltaire (1964), *Zadig / L'Ingénu*, London: Penguin [Translated by John Butt].

Wendt, A. (1999), *Social Theory of International Politics*, Cambridge: Cambridge University Press.

Yamanaka, Y. and Nishio, T. (eds) (2006), *The Arabian Nights and Orientalism: Perspectives from East and West*, London: Tauris.

12

Elite Power and the Manufacture of a Moral Panic: The Case of the Dirty War in Argentina

Jon Oplinger, Richard Talbot and Yasin Aktay

Well over a generation ago Murray Edelman (1971: 1) wrote that 'political history is largely an account of mass violence and the expenditure of vast resources to cope with mythical fears and hopes'. The purpose of this chapter is to argue that (1) the concept of a moral panic is central to explicating this general social process; (2) the Dirty War in Argentina (the Guerra Sucia – or as it is often called now in Argentina, The Process), which lasted from roughly 1976 to 1982, may be taken as an exemplar of how the various social processes associated with the genesis of a moral panic are manipulated by a ruthless elite; and (3) the concept of a moral panic, *as part of a broader focus of the sociology of deviance*, has the ability to explain major historical events of the sort that Edelman has argued are all too common or, indeed, typical of the nation-state.

Admittedly, these goals overlap but let us begin by noting that Joel Best (2004) has characterized the sociology of deviance to be cycling down, fragmented and suffering from the inroads of more lively areas of discourse such as the study of social problems or criminology. All the same, we would like to take a broader view: namely that the sociology of deviance is an overarching area of study, and that the social construction of a moral panic is central to this encompassing subdiscipline. The scholarly work of explaining – if only in part – a major moral panic, or more hopefully to anticipate and perhaps forestall a moral panic, draws upon a variety of fields and schools both inside and outside the sociology of deviance.

The question comes down to this: how does the state manufacture a threatening conspiracy? There are times when the manufactured conspiracy is wholly chimerical. And there are times when it serves the state to dramatically exaggerate the dangers of a genuine, but weak, internal conspiracy. The Dirty War, or The Process, represents an instance of the latter case.

Before we address the particular process of the Dirty War, we would like to briefly remark upon the various schools of thought and concepts that are often marshalled in the explanation of a moral panic. Much of this might be put under the general rubric of 'boundary work', which we define as the activities pursued by an interest group, and most especially the state, that serve to advertise and enforce a moral boundary as defined by Kai Erikson in *Wayward Puritans* (1966). Erikson's analysis of deviance in seventeenth-century Puritan society is a classic, but we do not agree with his unalloyed functionalism. Indeed, except at rarified levels of abstraction, we do not see the establishment of a moral boundary as a function of the social system at all. Stated otherwise, we do not see power in society as a systemic process that functions to reinforce the moral order and foster social solidarity. Rather we see it as something that is manufactured by powerful interests. On the ground, at the level of symbolic interactionism, a moral boundary is marked by repeated acts of public punishment (or notoriously rumored acts of brutality and murder) inflicted upon those who have, or are said to have, transgressed the moral boundary. Moral boundaries are put in place by powerful interests and, more specifically, by agents of social control, whether official and legal or unofficial and illegal. Moral boundaries are a fundamental means by which political elites maintain dominance. Nothing is more critical to the construction of a moral boundary than the climate of fear that surrounds the marginalization of certain acts (or even thoughts of such acts); or – across the boundary, so to speak – nothing is more reinforcing to that boundary than the chorus of approval from right-minded citizens when miscreants are punished. We are not talking of mere regulations here. This is not about the rules governing board games or the flow of pedestrian traffic. What is at issue is power, control and the enforced public definition of morality and righteousness.

Moral panics may be seen as a central part of this process. More limited in time and more acutely focused on a particular category of transgression, moral panics are, wholly or in part, creatures of dominant interests. The relation of a moral panic to a moral boundary may be seen as loosely analogous to the relationship of a local witch panic to the overall European witch craze of the sixteenth and seventeenth centuries.

The European witch craze was in many respects a creature of the printing press. Pre-eminent among the fifteenth-century treatises on witchcraft was the

Malleus Maleficarum (Kramer and Sprenger 1487), which included a preface written by Pope Innocent VIII establishing the heresy of witchcraft. Couched in formal Latin, the *Malleus Maleficarum* presented the educated reader with hair-raising tales of the witch as servant of the devil. The following century witnessed an unprecedented number of books aimed at the popular audience. These metaphysical potboilers depicted to an agitated public the powers of magicians, the devil and his servants. The number of copies printed of these 'devil-books', as Midelfort (1972: 70) styles them, runs into tens of thousands. But such books were surpassed in popularity by vast numbers of broadsheets and pamphlets. In sum, witchcraft, as presented in the media of the sixteenth and seventeenth centuries, was universally terrifying and universally accepted. Europe was hag-ridden by the fear of witchcraft. It was a threat that lay profoundly beyond the margins of Christian morality and was thus deeply unsettling to all.

This is not to argue that the Great Witch Craze was purely a crass tactic of the elite (Harris 1989). But, at the same time, to argue that witch panics were fostered purely by local stresses and hardships is not supported. The geography and timing of witch panics strongly suggest that the fears of powerful interests were in play. Variations in the legal system were very important (e.g. some Continental legal systems placed few restrictions on the use of torture). Nevertheless witch panics were everywhere strongly connected with elite fears and threats to elite dominance. England, as is well known, killed relatively few witches during the sixteenth and seventeenth centuries (except during the latter years of the Civil War). During this brief span, perhaps as much as 20 per cent of all English executions for witchcraft came about at the hands of England's self-styled Witchfinder General, Matthew Hopkins, a remarkably lethal moral entrepreneur who made full use of a climate of elite fear (L'Estrange Ewen 1929).

Colonial New England's celebrated Salem Witch Hunt is unusual for two reasons: it was quite late, 1692 by the modern calendar, and it was well documented in comparison to the hundreds of local witch panics that comprise the European witch craze as a whole. In *Wayward Puritans*, Erikson has argued that this outbreak, which killed half of all the supposed witches executed in the American colonies, was the result of systemic forces. A closer look at the evidence does not support this. The immediate catalyst is to be found in accusations inspired by local animosities arising from land disputes and suspected magical practices, but the panic swiftly escaped the boundaries of Salem Village, entering into a larger arena of conflict. The Massachusetts Bay Colony was split between the old guard Puritan clerics, who had held power since the founding of the colony, and the newly influential commercial faction. Pursuing witches to their death (19 were hanged and 1 pressed to death) was an exemplary way of advertising the moral boundary that protected the worldview and the social position of the Puritan divines. This threat and the true and diabolical nature of the witches (the internal other) within the colony were publicized by, among others, the indefatigable Cotton Mather ([1692] 1862) in *Wonders of the Invisible World*. The opposing faction was defended (somewhat after the fact, since open opposition was potentially lethal), most notably, by Robert Calef ([~1700] 1914) in his bitingly satirical and, probably by modern standards, libelous *More Wonders of the Invisible World*. There were others. So sharply are these factions divided that they wrote in starkly different literary genres: Mather and others in classic Puritan jeremiads; and Calef in mordantly reasoned arguments, the style of the commercial elite.

We have dwelt a bit longer than might be expected on the rather esoteric topic of the witch craze because it was very much a creation of the media, however primitive that media might seem at this remove. During the European witch craze, the horrific menace of the devil and his servants was established by numerous books (James the First, an undoubted defender of privilege, was among the authors of such learned treatises) and many hundreds of broadsheets. This perilous worldview, which marked the moral boundary of the Christian world and the elite that surmounted it, was fiercely and graphically defended in both the ecclesiastical and secular courts. Under the Code Caroline the penalty for witchcraft was death by fire, and many thousands died that way for the crime of witchcraft. Under the Spanish Inquisition an Auto-da-Fé was theatre on a vast scale – thousands attended to witness these deadly pageants.

If one examines local outbreaks, the witch panics that are the constituent parts of the witch craze, the role of the media is likewise apparent. In New England that ardent defender of the Puritan belief in a diabolically menaced world, Cotton Mather, quite literally galloped off to the printer as each of his chapters of *Wonders of the Invisible World* was completed. 'The Devil was never more let loose than in our days', was the urgent message (Mather [1692] 1862: 70). The broadsheets, appearing during the Civil War at the time of Matthew Hopkins' entrepreneurial witch hunt, which may have had over a hundred victims, provide another instance of the media's role in the genesis of a moral panic during the early modern period.

To drive home the impact of the sixteenth- and seventeenth-century print media in the genesis of a moral panic might seem an odd thing to do in a book on Moral Panics in the Contemporary World, but we think it is fundamental. This is when and how the process takes form. Indeed, as Eric Midelfort (1972: 21) has argued, the state has been more effective in this role than any other it has undertaken.

In the contemporary world the task of understanding the creation of a moral panic is a more complex process. And in the contemporary world this task is not only important, it is imperative. We live, after all, in a world where street gangs recruit membership over the internet. The great array of media, in combination with the interconnectedness of the world's population, renders the potential of the state to foster a moral panic – in order to bring about particular political, religious and social ends – unparalleled. Nowadays, 'stigma contests', to use Schur's (1980) felicitous phrase, are multimedia events and take place on an international scale.

Before we embark on our discussion of the social processes at work during the Dirty War in Argentina, it is only reasonable that we should at least provide a rough description of our image of historical/social process.

History? We do not agree that history is entirely ideographic. It is not just 'one damn thing after another'. We take history to be somewhat patterned and thus somewhat predictable. In addition, we take the role of comparative sociology as foremost in the hard work of explaining that pattern.

Society? We do not see society as systemic, except at very high levels of abstraction. Instead, at lower levels and on the ground level, we see society as structured by interaction and the application of power. We see power as residing within coalitions of people acting in their self-interest (Dahrendorf 1979; Schattschneider 1975). Power is never completely centralized – a realization savagely expressed by Stalin – and in most political systems power accrues to coalitions of interest groups. This was surely so in Argentina when the church, state and military formed an intimate alliance. From such a perspective the landscape of public morality, the moral landscape, if you will, is a matter of bitter wrangling over the construction of social reality and the very nature of good and evil. This conflict, often violent, is never wholly resolved.

Culture? In 1987 the bones of Prince Lazar, who died fighting the Turks in the Battle of Kosovo (1389), were taken in accordance to Serbian Orthodox custom for an outing. Prince Lazar's bones travelled from monastery to monastery in Bosnia, Croatia and Kosovo – the principle being that 'Serbian land is where

Serbian bones are' (Verdery 1999: 18). We mention this event not because it is unusual, but because it is so common (Zbarsky and Hutchinson 1998; Audoin-Rouzeau and Becker 2002). In truth, the modern state, which is said to epitomize rational action, rests on reasoning and feelings that are tribal and mystical. It is the manipulation of these sentiments and symbols that greatly enable the genesis of a moral panic. Our view is that language and symbols, and the ability to manipulate them, are fundamental to the genesis of a moral panic. Thereby the deep sentiments of nationalism and moral order are marshalled.

We intend to bring anthropology into this analysis, particularly as anthropology explicates the boundary between the sacred and the profane and the potent sentiments (the root metaphors) that attach to ritual pollution. This view overlaps significantly with the perspective of cultural criminology (Ferrell et al. 2008), but draws more directly upon aspects of structural anthropology. The consistent cultural conception of ritual cleanliness and the opposing state of pollution is a fundamental consideration (Douglas 1966). Conspirators, real or imaginary, fall naturally into the realm of being evil, polluting and possessing preternatural powers (befitting a folk devil) to do insidious harm from within.

We would also like to note that often the enforcers and benefactors of the moral boundary, as well as ordinary citizens, were equally gulled by the symbolism of this frankly demonic reality. 'The Bolshevik mind', writes Adam Ulam (1973: 412), 'was unable to distinguish between theoretical and factual reality, between the world of ideologically inspired dreams and the world of hard fact'. Much the same could be said of the perpetrators of the Dirty War in Argentina.

The process: Argentina's Dirty War

Early in 1976, at the very beginning of the military takeover, General Luciano Menendez stated, 'We are going to have to kill 50,000 people: 25,000 subversives, 20,000 sympathizers, and we will make 5,000 mistakes' (Lewis 2002: 147). In the event, the number of killings has been estimated as high as 30,000. The National Commission of the Disappearance of Persons, in its 1986 report *Nunca Más*, documents 8,961 individuals who are known to have been disappeared. The actual number is unquestionably far higher. Alberto Romero puts the true number of killings as closer to 30,000 (Romero 2002: 218). But General Menendez was entirely wrong in two respects: he vastly, perhaps knowingly, overestimated the number of committed subversives and he vastly underestimated the number of 'mistakes'.

And the mistakes were not really mistakes. The Argentine military targeted a wide variety of people by category: union members and supporters, educators and scholars (evidently they killed all the anthropologists in the country), liberals, members of the press, rural activists, students, the carelessly spoken and so forth – the list goes on and on. In short, 'The Process' (*El Proceso*), short for the Junta's official plan, The Process of National Reorganization, was a highly organized campaign of murder and intimidation carried out by the country's military government. (Argentines prefer the term The Process, since to call it a war of any kind is to dignify what was, in fact, state terrorism.) Because of court cases and other sources of information, the work of the National Commission, and the testimony of survivors and perpetrators, the social forces at play during the Dirty War are well documented. It has been the subject of intense scrutiny by Argentine scholars and others upon which this analysis entirely depends.

Isolation

The traditions and worldview of the Argentine officer corps may be seen as conducive to the use of the most extreme measures. Argentine military academies, closely modelled on the Prussian *Kriegs Akademie*, held cadets to the strictest discipline. Cadets were also steeped in a conservative and intensely nationalistic Catholicism and thus readily accepted the view that the military, and especially the officer corps, was the protector of the honour of the nation – its soul – from the forces of evil. Communism was regarded as a manifestation of the Antichrist. This conviction was all the more tightly embraced because of the caste-like isolation of the officer corps from the mainstream of Argentine society. Officers lived in special neighborhoods and were members of exclusive clubs. High-ranking officers were members of secret societies. This commitment to hermetic isolation was such that military buildings were equipped with segregated elevators – officers only (Mignone 1987; Graziano 1992).

Thus distanced from any real understanding of (or sympathy for) the social issues besetting Argentine society, the worldview of the officer corps became filled with menace: the Antichrist had already begun to take over Argentine society. By the early 1970s there were, in fact, two ruthless Marxist organizations – the Montoneros and the Ejército Revolucionario del Pueblo (ERP) – in a state of open, if ineffectual, rebellion (Anderson 1993; Lewis 2002; Romero 2002). The influence and military potential of these revolutionary groups was greatly magnified by the military elite.

Argentine Military intelligence was prone to exaggerate the impact of Marxist doctrine among liberal elements of Argentine society. Students and those on the margins of student life discussed Marxist doctrines, the need for social change and the perceived successes of Cuba. Che Guevara was idolized, and behaviour that might have been regarded more objectively as superficial political chic was taken by the military to be a dire threat to the values of Argentine society. This view was reinforced by the cachet attached to claiming some tenuous connection with this or that revolutionary group. All this proved deadly when the military – belatedly in the opinion of many Argentines – removed the surreally disastrous government of Isabel Peron in March in 1976. The Dirty War began apace.

It is important not to lose track of the timing of the Dirty War. At its beginning, the ERP had already been crushingly defeated in the province of Tucumán during a brutal campaign which treated the local population as though they were hostile peasantry. It would be the ERP's 'Stalingrad' crowed General Menendez in an absurdist comparison. Anderson (1993: 141) takes note of the future tense; it was much too valuable a little 'war' to be abandoned because of a premature announcement of victory. The ERP's numbers in the field were at most in the hundreds. An army intelligence report puts the total figure – including combatants, couriers, suppliers and sympathizers – at only 226 (Marchak 1999: 121). Committed to the doctrine (and mythology) of Che Guevara, the ERP combatants were nevertheless poorly equipped and woefully incompetent. An army report notes 'great organizational and operational deficiencies that reveal little military capacity' (Marchak 1999: 122). Similarly the Montoneros, whose leadership was probably infiltrated by intelligence operatives, had been greatly weakened by the end of 1976, and by 1980 it had been dissolved (Lewis 2002: 161). Marchak (1999: 122) neatly encapsulates the military situation at the inception of the Dirty War: 'The army prepared for an all out war against the enemy that it had now completely vanquished.'

It is noteworthy that on the first page of *Nunca Más* (National Commission on the Disappeared 1986) there is the following quote by the Italian General Della Chiesa. Upon receiving a request that one of the suspects involved in the kidnapping of Aldo Moro be tortured, General Chiesa responded by saying, 'Italy can survive the loss of Aldo Moro. It would not survive the introduction of torture.' The clear implication is that measures within the bounds of the constitution would have kept the country secure. It would be idle to suggest that the internal threat to the Argentine Republic was chimerical. Both the

Montoneros and the ERP were made up of fanatically dedicated guerrillas who were often murderous. The military did not create them. But they did conjure them in vastly greater numbers and in wholly diabolical form. And much more to the point, it was at the moment of victory that the Dirty War began. The Dirty War did not bring about the defeat of the revolutionaries. What it was intended to do was something different: it was to create a moral panic which served to defend and make plain the Junta's perception of Western morality.

The saviors of Western Christendom

The forces of militant Christianity moved against the pagan minions of the Antichrist. In the minds of the ranking members of the officer corps, nothing in the preceding statement can be regarded as the least bit exaggerated or metaphorical (Graziano 1992). The nature of this supposed diabolical menace justified savage tactics. In a manner that can best be described as theatrically clandestine, squads of men drawn from all branches of military service kidnapped individuals who were identified, with indifferent accuracy, as members of guerrilla groups. The victims were then taken to special camps to be tortured, dehumanized and then murdered. That is the long and the short of it.

Torture: one passes too easily over the word. Drawing upon essays written by French officers who had fought in Algeria and Vietnam, the Argentine military had for many years embraced an essentially colonial doctrine of torture (Lewis 2002: 143). As attested to countless times in *Nunca Más,* the use of the electric cattle prod was combined with the practice of holding the prisoner's head underwater to the point of near suffocation. Excruciatingly painful and terrifying, these procedures were standard. There were, of course, other tortures (Feitlowitz 1998). Family members were tortured in front of one another. Prisoners were kept in hideously foul conditions, fed little, denied medical attention and subjected to mock executions preliminary to the real execution (Feitlowitz 1998). Typically, prisoners were not killed until the degradation was complete. Women, including pregnant women, were routinely raped. This too furthered the process of degradation.

These crimes took place in hundreds of centres located on military bases or in federal police stations (Robben 2000). Pits, they were called. Women gave birth under these conditions, after which they were murdered and their babies sold to be raised by 'better sorts of people'. Bodies were disposed of in a variety of ways. Most of the dead were secretly buried in mass graves. Some were incinerated. Drugged prisoners were tossed out of naval aircraft over the River Plate estuary. Bodies showing signs of torture were often found along the banks of the river during this period.

Throughout, the military junta described Argentine society in metaphorical terms that are chillingly reminiscent of terms used by the Third Reich. Argentine society was sick, cancerous. The tumor must be removed; hence the brutal remedy that the military was forced to employ. Radical surgery was needed to protect the life of the nation (Graziano 1992).

This 'surgery' was controlled at the highest levels. As soon as an individual was ensnared by the military dragnet, they were assigned a number and a file and their case scrutinized until senior officers made the decision to have them murdered (Romero 2002). People were arrested on the street and within factories; most often they were arrested at night in front of their families. Houses were ransacked and valuables confiscated as 'war booty'. If the assigned victim was not at home, the abduction gangs were quite as happy to seize another family member. It didn't matter since the purpose was to terrorize.

Family members searching for their relatives found that the trail grew immediately cold. The victim had disappeared, had become a *desaparecido,* a new status in Argentine society. One had ceased to exist, had been sucked up, *chupado,* to vanish forever. Some family members still wait and hope (Gonzales 2004).

In the words of Luis Alberto Romero, the abductions were carried out with a strange blend of 'anonymity and ostentation' (Romero 2002: 217). The institutional green Ford Falcon with tinted windows from which the abduction squads sallied forth became a terrifying sight. At first the targets were members of the Montoneros or the ERP. Most of the victims were young – between 15 and 35 – middle or upper class and idealistic. Within a few months the ERP was entirely destroyed. In the province of Tucumán, which was under military control before the coup, the ERP had already been defeated by the end of 1975. The Montoneros likewise swiftly crumbled and were thereafter capable of little more than simple banditry. But, if anything, the pace of the Dirty War increased (Romero 2002).

Abductions came to include social scientists, journalists, union leaders, priests, intellectuals. Names jumped from people's lips under torture; relatives were arrested. In a concerted attack, agrarian leagues, which sought to change the near-feudal practices found in some provinces, were systematically destroyed (Feitlowitz 1998). Factory owners fingered troublemakers. In short, many thousands who had no connection with subversion were 'disappeared'.

Argentine officers (including chaplains) and non-commissioned officers were drawn into this cycle of abduction, torture, rape and murder in very large numbers (Mignone 1987). It was, by design, a blood pact from which more hideous crimes could be extracted. There was nothing new in this tactic; it had already been pioneered and refined by the SS. The German word for this is *blutkitt*, literally 'blood cement'. The ritual of *blutkitt* creates a bond and commits the perpetrators to a common task of torture and murder (Alexander 1949).

A cruelly arch Aesopian language emerged among the torturers. Torture was 'therapy' or 'work' or 'treatment' or 'interrogation'. Kidnap victims were 'packages'. The torture chamber was the 'operating theatre'. *La parrilla*, a grill for cooking meat, referred to the metal table upon which people were tortured. *Vuelo* (flight) denoted the death flights by which people were tossed into the Plate River from aircraft. Nearly all Argentine naval officers were called upon to perform this task at one time or another.

A culture of fear gripped Argentine society (Corradi 1985). Some fled. The majority tried to become apolitical faceless citizens. A member of the Permanent Assembly of Human Rights (*La Asemblea Permanente de los Derechos Humanos*), which collected information on the Junta's terrorism, recalls sharing a very dangerous confidence with a friend, telling of the detention centres, the tortures, the killings. Her friend laughed, 'This is not Germany; there are no concentration camps' (Ubeira 2010). There were variations to encountering this unwanted information. 'How come you know and we don't?' 'We would know. You are exaggerating.' People routinely took refuge in self-delusion and denial. The victims 'must have done something'. Argentines became circumspect and hooded in their social interactions, for they knew that people spied and informed.

But the regime's control was far from total. The courageous protests of the mothers and grandmothers of the disappeared would not be denied; nor could they be ignored. Stalin would have murdered them all (witness his confusion over the fact that Churchill did not have Gandhi killed). The protests of *Las Madres de Plaza de Mayo*[1] together with the Falklands debacle brought the regime crashing down. Within months the National Commission on the Disappearance of Persons was convened under Ernesto Sabato to reveal in excruciating testimony to the Argentine public the true nature and dimension of the terror. Public trials followed. The documentation runs to 50,000 pages. The nature of the Dirty War was not unusual; it was merely better documented. Its social effects are manifest: people want to believe; people want to conform. It is a matter of survival.

How to manufacture a moral panic

However chilling, the above is no more than a synopsis of the comprehensive course of terror that was the Dirty War. We now set out to highlight those tactics and manipulations that served to impose a moral panic upon Argentine society. To isolate these factors one by one, while heuristically useful, is to perhaps render their impact less forceful, more sterile. One must remember that in combination, all of the factors discussed below fell crushingly upon the social fabric of Argentina.

The media

A cornerstone of The Process was the artful and brutal use of the media. Censorship and control of public opinion were not new to Argentina, but the Junta's control was comprehensive. Where the various media outlets were not compliant – and some such as *La Nación* were already organs of the Conservative landed establishment – they were swiftly co-opted or cowed. Members of the press were brutalized and often killed. According to Graham-Yooll (1984: 153), by early 1978, 40 journalists had been disappeared, 29 killed outright and many others were imprisoned.

It is unsurprising that the military's 'Principles and Procedures to Be Followed by Mass Communication Media' were adhered to. Graham-Yooll (1984: 118) provides the complete list of admonitions and prohibitions. Certain subjects were 'not for public debate'. The Junta's view of the media was clear. Its purpose, confides the 'Principles and Procedures', was to 'foster the restitution of fundamental values which contribute to the integrity of society . . . within the context of Christian morals'. At the same time that public reference to the military's activities such as arrests, discovered bodies, reports of torture and so forth vanished from the news, the media were filled with reports of military successes with inflated body counts, captured arms caches that fostered the image of a country at war against an insidious internal threat that imperiled the nation and Western civilization. Intelligence officers reviewed page proofs, issued information kits to informants, and ran a news service on their own. Criticism of the military was punishable by imprisonment. No avenue was unexplored, including a bumper sticker campaign. Particular use was made of popular magazines such as *Para Ti* and *Somos,* which presented the stories and photos provided by the intelligence services (Anderson 1993: 215–17).

The church

The activist editor, Emilio Mignone, who lost a daughter during the Dirty War, has led the fight to expose the activities of the church hierarchy and right-wing priests. The link between the conservative and highly religious military and the church was traditionally very strong. Marchak (1999) defines the Roman Catholic Church in Argentina as a state church. Members of the clergy actively supported the military's holy war; indeed they enthusiastically defined it as such. The Process was a crusade in all respects. It was preached from the pulpit and, as Mignone (1988) and others have written, army chaplains participated in raids and torture sessions and, in a scene startlingly reminiscent of the Inquisition, implored the supposed guerrilla to confess. The lack of any resistance to the course of the Dirty War by the church hierarchy dramatically reinforced the embattled worldview of the Junta members and convinced them of the righteousness of their defence of Christian society and the need for a war to defend Western civilization. Many of the laity, devout in their religious beliefs, were also convinced.

State terror

During the Dirty War a culture of fear permeated all aspects of Argentine society. Whole categories of people were at risk. The available statistics reveal the relative liabilities – 81 per cent were between the ages of 16 and 31; 70 per cent were male; 30 per cent were classified as blue collar; 37 per cent white collar; 21 per cent students. Housewives, self employed, military conscripts, security forces and members of religious orders make up the remainder (Marchak 1999: 154). But everyone was at risk, or given the randomness of the attacks, would feel endangered. Even members of the military, especially if they refused to engage in torture, were at risk.

If the torture and murder centres, and there were evidently hundreds, were clandestine, the intimidation tactics of the military were open for all to see, by design. Neighborhoods were blanketed by an aggressive soldiery armed with automatic weapons. All were stopped, questioned, searched and perhaps an exemplary few were arrested. Squad-sized or larger units broke into apartments or suburban houses to make arrests, leaving the remaining family members and the neighbors terrorized. All efforts to locate missing family members met with an impenetrable wall of silence or willful ignorance. The local authorities did not know the location of the abducted family member nor did they wish to know. There was nothing but an official silence reinforced by indifference. Relatives inquiring from outside the country through the Organization of American States might, after some time, receive a mimeographed form right out of *Catch 22* indicating that the Argentine authorities had no knowledge of the father, husband, son, mother, daughter, wife (correct category of relationship circled) in question.

Gangs of abductors who made little secret of their status or their mission roamed the cities in standard and notorious vehicles. Bodies appeared on the streets, outside the cities and along the shore of the Plate River. Some abductees were released and told fearful tales. Midway through the Dirty War, mass graves began to be discovered. To an unknown but substantial degree, the nature of the Dirty War began to circulate by word of mouth, the 'Buenos Aires grapevine' (Graham-Yooll 1984: 126). Parents were consumed by fear for their children: did they have the wrong friends, did they talk too openly, did they read the wrong books, was their son's hair too long?

The great fear was to be anonymously accused. In *Naples 44* Norman Lewis (1978), who served as a linguist in the British Army's Field Security Service, marvelled at what the records of the local fascist office revealed: it was lumbered with anonymous accusations. In fact this is a general social phenomenon and one that has been given little attention. Moral panics feed on and at the same time generate informants. Such was the case during the Dirty War. Arising from all sorts of motivations, accusations of deviant talk, actions, associations, provided grist for the military abductors. To accuse meant to embrace The Process and its worldview. It also meant that one participated in the process of destruction. Argentines withdrew from outside associations and were circumspect and hooded in their friendships. The circle of trust was small. It was indeed a 'culture of fear'.

The Manichaean world

As is so often the case, those who manufacture a moral panic live in a Manichaean world (Oplinger 1990). There is no middle ground. Anyone not in open support of the military regime, notes Robben (2004: 203), was regarded as supporting evil. A leading architect of The Process, Admiral Massera, was quoted in *La Nación* (12 December 1976) as stating that 'The enemy are not only terrorists, but enemies of the Republic are also the impatient, those who place sectarian interests above the country, the frightened and the *indifferent*' (emphasis added). Killing the indifferent is often mentioned. During the French Revolution, Saint-Just expressed exactly the same opinion. The indifferent cannot be allowed to blur the moral boundary; indeed, in a Manichaean world they cannot exist except as evil.

Metaphor and miasma

George Lakoff, a cognitive linguist, has written about the metaphors we live by, those deep-seated, ancient metaphors that are often accepted as literal descriptors (Lakoff and Johnson 1980). Games become 'battles', competition between political parties a 'battle ground', argument is 'war'. And so the public discourse is framed. What was presented to the Argentine public (and brutally reinforced by the thuggery and intimidation of the Argentine military) was a valiant and titanic struggle with the 'Antichrist' of communism for the 'salvation' of Western civilization.

The military at all levels embraced this holy image. References to the number of ERP guerrillas in the field in Tucumán range well into the thousands (6,000 by one account, which would have required a logistical tail the size of the Ho Chi Minh Trail). Contrast this image of a valiant 'crusading' military engaged upon a great battlefield with the image presented at the trial of the Junta members by the state prosecutor, Julia Cesar Strassera. It was, sniffed Strassera, 'simply a rabbit hunt' – *cacería de conejos* (Lewis 2002: 241). On no such piddling activity – a rabbit hunt – could the destruction of dissident and liberal elements be waged. No! The Process had to be waged against unholy elements in the context of a manufactured moral panic. The threatening, the undesirable, the annoying and the indifferent had to be demonized. As such these evils were set in contrast, almost as a structural inversion, to the root metaphors that are sacred to Western society. These evil people, like worms, bore from within (as during the Great Purge under Stalin, *vredital* denoted an insect-like destroyer that 'bored from within' [Southard 2003]). With variations on the theme – 'ox ghosts and snake spirits' during China's Cultural Revolution – the internal other is characterized in this metaphorical language of deeply held sentiments of fear.

The compelling nature of a dangerous internal conspiracy does not derive solely from the fact that fictitious or real conspirators are accepted as genuine and are thus logically a threat. It is not enough to merely gull the public. The moral panic taps into the miasma-like quality that attaches to internal conspiracy. This evil, which demands special expiation, undermines the godly order of society and brings pollution and destruction (Parker 1983). These ancient sentiments run deep. Those in industrialized states, and most especially the elite, are as likely to ascribe preternatural origins to this pollution, as were the ancient Greeks. Pollution is discordant and impure; it is 'matter out of place' which must be bounded and controlled if society and the interests of the powerful are to be protected. The alien source of pollution must be made visible and destroyed (Deliege 2004; Douglas 1966). Moral panics in this view run their course only when the social reality of panic and destruction and its metaphors are exposed and contrasted with another social reality, one that is courageous and virtuous. This the *Madres de Plaza de Mayo* did.

Note

1   *Las Madres de Plaza de Mayo* refers to the Mothers of the Plaza de Mayo, mothers whose children were 'disappeared' during the Dirty War in Argentina.

Bibliography

Alexander, L. (1949), 'Medical Science under Dictatorship', *New England Journal of Medicine*, 241(2): 39–47.

Anderson, M. E. (1993), *Dossier Secreto: Argentina's Desaparacidos and the Myth of the Dirty War*, Oxford: Westview Press.

Audoin-Rouzeau, S. and Becker, A. (2002), *14–18 Understanding the Great War*, New York: Hill and Wang.

Best, J. (2004), *Deviance: The Career of a Concept*, Bellmont, CA: Thomson-Wadsworth.

Calef, R. ([~1700] 1914), 'More Wonders of the Invisible World', in G. L. Burr (ed.), *Narratives of the Witchcraft Cases*, New York: Charles Scribner and Sons, 293–97.

Corradi, J. (1985), *The Fitful Republic*, Boulder, CO: Westview Press.

Dahrendorf, R. (1979), *Life Chances: Approaches to Social and Political Theory*, Chicago: University of Chicago Press.

Deliege, R. (2004), *Lévi-Strauss Today*, New York: Berg.

Douglas, M. (1966), *Purity and Danger: An Analysis of the Concepts of Pollution and Taboo*, London: Harmondsworth.

Edelman, M. (1971), *Politics as Symbolic Interactionism*, Chicago: Markham.

Erikson, K. (1966), *Wayward Puritans*, New York: Wiley.

Feitlowitz, M. (1998), *A Lexicon of Terror: Argentina and the Legacies of Torture,* New York: Oxford University Press.

Ferrell, J., Haywood, K. and Young, J. (2008), *Cultural Criminology: An Invitation,* Los Angeles: Sage.

Gonzales, E. (2004), Personal communication.

Graham-Yooll, A. (1984), *The Press in Argentina, 1973–1978,* London: Writers and Scholars Educational Trust.

Graziano, F. (1992), *Divine Violence: Spectacle, Psychosexuality and Radical Christianity in the Argentine Dirty War,* Oxford: Westview Press.

Harris, M. (1989), *Cows, Pigs, Wars and Witches,* New York: Vintage Books.

Kramer, H. and Sprenger, J. (1487), *Malleus Maleficarum,* Germany: Cologne.

Lakoff, G. and Johnson, M. (1980), *Metaphors We Live By,* Chicago: University of Chicago Press.

L'Estrange Ewen, C. (1929), *Witch Hunting and Witch Trials,* London: Kegan Paul.

Lewis, N. (1978), *Naples 44,* New York: Pantheon Books.

Lewis, P. H. (2002), *Guerrillas and Generals: The 'Dirty War' in Argentina,* Westport, CT: Praeger.

Marchak, P. (1999), *God's Assassins: State Terrorism in Argentina in the 1970s,* London: McGill-Queen's University Press.

Mather, C. ([1692] 1862), *Wonders of the Invisible World: Being an Account of the Tryals of Several Witches Lately Executed in New England,* London: John Russell Smith.

Midelfort, H. C. E. (1972), *Witch Hunting in Southwestern Germany: 1562–1684,* Stanford, CA: Stanford University Press.

Mignone, E. F. (1987), 'The Military: What Is to Be Done?', *Report on the Americas,* 11(4): 15–24.

— (1988), *Witness to the Truth: The Complicity of Church and Dictatorship in Argentina,* Marynoll, NY: Orbis Books.

National Commission on the Disappeared (1986), *Nunca Más,* New York: Farrar, Strauss Giroux.

Oplinger, J. (1990), *The Politics of Demonology: The European Witchcraze and the Mass Production of Deviance,* Toronto: Associated University Presses.

Parker, R. (1983), *Miasma: Pollution and Purification in Early Greek Religion,* Oxford: Oxford University Press.

Robben, A. (2000), 'State Terror in the Netherworld: Disappearance and Reburial in Argentina', in J. A. Sluka (ed.), *Death Squad: The Anthropology of State Terror,* Philadelphia: University of Pennsylvanian Press, 91–113.

— (2004), 'The Fear of Indifference: Combatants' Anxieties about the Political Identity of Civilians during Argentina's Dirty War', in N. Scheper-Hughes and P. Bourgois (eds), *Violence and Peace,* Malden, MA: Blackwell, 200–06.

Romero, L. A. (2002), *A History of Argentina in the Twentieth Century,* University Park, PA: University of Pennsylvania Press.

Schattschneider, E. E. (1975), *The Semisovereign People,* Hillsdale, IL: Dryden.

Schur, E. M. (1980), *The Politics of Deviance: Stigma Contests and the Uses of Power,* Englewood Cliffs, NJ: Prentice-Hall.

Southard, A. (2003), Personal communication.

Ubeira, A. (2010), Personal communication.

Ulam, A. (1973), *Stalin: The Man and His Era,* New York: Praeger.

Verdery, K. (1999), *The Political Lives of Dead Bodies,* New York: Columbia University Press.

Zbasrsky, I. and Hutchinson, S. (1998), *Lenin's Embalmers,* London: Harvill Press.

Author Index

Entries in italics indicate whole chapters by the author.

Subject Index

Entries in italics indicate whole chapters on the subject.